many of us.

But say, Bill—if we can write our ticket anywhere we like, why not write Denmark—and Germany—and Italy—Norway —Croatia—Bohemia—the ... or just THE ... CK in OLD COUNTRY ... or T ... great big letters so there'll be no mis ...

This may be an idea. Let's think about it. Maybe "Defense" isn't only defense. It may be something else—even bigger than it looked a minute ago.

And why wait till '43, Bill Knudsen? Can't we get at this whole thing sooner? Why can't we finish Hitler and this crazy war, say by summer 1942?

Let's think about it, Bill. Don't be just a mechanic all your life. This is the idea, Bill: write the ticket—THE PASSAGE BACK.

Let's go!

(See inside back cover)

Price
$2.50

TWO-WAY PASSAGE

By

LOUIS ADAMIC

That Western civilization, of which the United States is the greatest power, finds itself in the depths of its most critical period is clear enough. The question is: *What can America do about it?* That we will have to do something is obvious.

Must the American process toward general welfare and a decent life for the individual continue to be hamstrung by Europe's periodic crises? Why should America be forced, every generation or so, to sidetrack her progress toward deeper and wider democracy; go on food and fuel rations, give up her aluminum pots and pans, send her sons into the armed forces, and bleed herself white with taxes every time Europe has a convulsion? It is not a question of "keeping America out of Europe's wars," but a question of *keeping Europe's wars out of America!*

What can America do?

Mr. Adamic has a suggestion which, he explains, exists in pieces all over the country and just happens to have con-

verged in his head. It is not another League of Nations, not a union of peoples of common speech, not another "class war," not the messianic indocrination of the world with another abstract political religion. What he proposes, in outline, is the *full utilization* of the most famous and successful practical experience in history—the American Experience.

With documented fact, highlighted by drama and wit, he presents here one of the most original and provocative ideas to appear in our time: an idea that will appeal alike to sincere "isolationists" and "interventionists" who, as Mr. Adamic shows, are but two sides of the same coin; an idea, in short, that will appeal to everyone in the United States except Hitler's agents—to old-stock American and latest refugee, to Jew and Gentile, and to those descended from all the national stocks of Europe.

The suggestion this volume presents is a challenge to America, to her present, and above all to her *potential* spiritual, economic and industrial resourcefulness, whose realization looks toward the preservation and unchecked growth of the American Experience, and outlines a passage to freedom for mankind.

TWO-WAY PASSAGE

by

Louis Adamic

HARPER & BROTHERS PUBLISHERS

New York and London

To

ROSS B. WILLS

CONTENTS

Author's Note

In view of the nature of the suggestion offered in these pages, I want to say that it is wholly and solely my own. There is no one else "behind" it.

The idea began to roll around in my mind early in July. As I tell in some detail, it evolved from the work in which I have been engaged since 1938. Before deciding to write the book, I discussed what I meant to say with a few personal friends, none of whom has any kind of official Government standing or organizational connections in the United States or elsewhere.

LOUIS ADAMIC

Mountain View Farm
Milford, New Jersey
Midsummer, 1941

THINKING BACK

The "Next War" As It Seemed to Me
in 1938

In the closing chapter of a book called *My America*, published in May 1938, I said that the "next war"—as it was being referred to—would break out "before 1940." It seemed to me inevitable: Old Europe was heading furiously for a crack-up. And I suggested that the United States "immediately"—that is in 1938—appropriate forty billion dollars to prepare itself against the event.

I am no prophet nor prophet's kin. Nor was I in possession of any special information. In 1932–'33 I had spent ten months in Yugoslavia and three or four days in Italy; since then I had talked occasionally with people lately returned from abroad. I read fairly regularly three New York newspapers and about a dozen weekly and monthly magazines. Off and on I read or leafed through a book by some American foreign correspondent or analyst of international affairs. . . . And, to my way of looking at it, the situation in the Old World during the winter of 1937–'38 was such that it had to explode—and soon.

What would that mean?

My first and paramount concern was for the United States. Not only because I am an American citizen, or because I was writing a book about the country. I think I am no nationalist in any usual sense. It was something else that chiefly determined the focus of my perturbation. Some time before, I had begun to believe that—in spite of depressions, unemployment, and current spiritual chaos—the United States was the human world's best long-range hope, the main passage, or certainly the principal way station, to any sort of desirable future; and we Americans should, I thought, explore all possible means and exert every possible effort right away—for our own sake, Europe's and the rest of the world's—to get this country on an even keel before the next cataclysm over there.

The United States was then in many respects on anything but an even keel. It was wrenched by a complexity of dislocations which no one quite understood. There was little perspective. Economically things were askew. There was a vague, widespread confusion about nearly everything. The preponderance of people saw no reason why they should bother their heads about the "next war." Certainly not to do anything concrete about it. . . .

And I imagined that after the "next war" started the confusion would grow worse. Tensions would tauten. Alien-baiting, anti-Semitism, and many other lunacies would increase. Demagogy of all varieties would get going full blast.

Could anything be done to forestall or alleviate this?

The best and the speediest conceivable effort that had any precedent in the national experience would probably not be good or quick enough, and I had no reason to expect anything substantial and unorthodox would be attempted in the near future. There was no imaginative recognition of what was coming even in Washington, to all appearances. And if the Administration and some members of Congress did suspect what might lie ahead, the formulation of their policies was dependent upon public opinion which could evolve only out of aroused interest.

What aroused interest there was, expressed itself for the most part in mere pacifism and in the traditional grim, do-nothing isolationism.

Newspapers editorialized about the "next war," but mainly in the abstract, as something too removed in space and time to be the immediate practical concern of the people of the United States. There was a great lack of foresight about the repercussions that an outbreak of big-scale hostilities in Europe would force upon America along with the rest of the world.

One day early in '38 I saw a friend of mine who had lately returned from a four years' term of service as an American diplomatic official in Europe. Off and on during that period he had visited or lived in England, Holland, Germany, France, Scandinavia, Russia, Poland, Czechoslovakia, Austria and Italy. He is an acute observer and a consistently realistic, intelligent man. He gave me a gloomy report. ·

The so-called Spanish civil war was "not a civil war at all but a rehearsal for the next world war" and "a scheme of the Fates to kill off a great number of Europe's most idealistic young men."

Meantime, England was "scared stiff beneath its seeming smugness, stupidly scheming, and weak."

France was "rotten at the head."

Russia was a "puzzle."

The smaller countries didn't count.

Germany, however, was "developing terrific power," and there was no doubt that Hitler would make war.

"He's got to. His racket is such that he can't stop. He has to keep moving, and faster and faster all the time. . . ."

But my friend had no idea what the United States could, should or would do about it. We parted agreeing there were extremely dangerous—and significant— times ahead.

Awhile later I had lunch with the editor of a national magazine. For an hour or so we discussed The Whole Situation. Perhaps I did most of the talking; I was trying to induce him to publish an article I wanted to write. But he thought Hitler and the Nazis were over-rated. His attitude was: to hell with them! Eventually they and the Reds of Russia might tangle and that would be the end of one or the other, or both.

"Or possibly," he said, "it may not come to a war at all. I think even Hitler is afraid of it; he is a lunatic, but no dope. Maybe somebody will assassinate him one of these days; then the rest of the big-shot Nazis will fight it out among themselves and in the process very likely ruin their movement. Or if this doesn't happen, there are other possibilities. Things may just go on the way they are for a long time, with

Hitler and Mussolini bluffing, with local wars like Spain and China. Stalin will keep on bumping off his old pals, while Hitler will continue taking it out on the Jews—the boys have to have a little fun. Then by and by the whole farce over there will resolve itself—I don't know how, but some way or other. Maybe there will be a general economic collapse, which will reduce the current men on horseback to impotence. Then some new leader will pop up and take hold. . . . Anyhow, it's none of our business right now."

I wished I could have agreed. I couldn't. What he was saying and his bland complacency annoyed me. Also I suspected he thought me overconscious of the "old country," worried about Europe because I was born there.

"I'm thinking primarily of the United States," I said, then added an idea which had been forming in my mind. "You know, one of these days this country may actually need saving."

There was concern for my sanity in the long look my friend the editor gave me; then he changed the subject.

You can't always be sure of your own sanity. You can think only what you think and feel only what you feel: that is how you are. You can do only what you can; not very much if you are only a free-lance writer.

I felt, though, that I had to say something about the "next war" in *My America*; so in the concluding chapter—after assuming it would break out before 1940—I offered the already-mentioned suggestion, which I

called "crazy" in the same breath: that the United
States appropriate without delay forty billion dollars
and that those responsible for national leadership get
busy at once and prepare the country economically,
militarily and spiritually against the coming international conflagration.

I was a conditional isolationist then. The condition
was that we prepare ourselves against the "next war"
—or the chances were we would be unable to stay
out of it, no matter how much we might want to.

Reviewing my book in one of the liberal weeklies
late in that idyllic, far-off spring, a New York critic,
who as a Communist fellow-traveler believed in Maxim
Litvinoff's "collective security" idea, called my isolationism "fantastic" and "queer"—partly, I think, because I advocated the huge defense appropriation before
the European cataclysm had got going so obviously
that no one could miss noticing it.

My suggestion *was* fantastic. I made it as a kind of
grim joke. I did not expect anybody to pay any attention
to it. The country is a political democracy (one of the
things I like about it), and I knew that democracies as
now constituted act only after events compel them to
act—when it is a little too late.

The book was published also in England, where some
reviewers resented the pot shots I took at the Britain
which reached its logical and awful climax in Munich
the ensuing autumn, and which—along with France—
had seemed untrustworthy to me long before. A London
critic said sharply I could keep "my America" and one

of the few English readers of the book sent me a sizzling letter which ended: "I burned it!"—while, no doubt for very different reasons, the Gestapo banned it in Germany.

My conditional isolationism in '38 was compounded of a number of elements.

If at all possible, I wanted America to stay out of the "next war"—any war. I had been in the one which was supposed to have ended all wars, and I had not found it too attractive. I was not indifferent to Europe, to the peoples of Europe and their civilization and diverse cultures—how could I be? But I had absolutely no use for any of the leaders in power or soon likely to come into power in Britain or on the continent. There was in Europe no one anywhere near the top whom we in America could trust, and there was nothing we could do about it at this late date. The League of Nations was a tragic joke. . . . But more than anything else, I did not want the United States to be sucked helplessly into the oncoming disaster.

I wished Uncle Sam could get a move on and work up sufficient wisdom to see the imperative need of action against a dark international future, so that—in 1939 or '40 or '41 or later, however long the "next war" might last—we would be prepared materially and psychologically to stay out or go into it, whichever might eventuate as the less undesirable thing to do.

I had a sporadic feeling, too, that if America could confront the growingly critical situation in Europe with a strong internal economy as well as with a powerful war arm, Europe's sick men and madmen might think twice before flaming into war; Hitler, in particular, might well reconsider his aggressive plans against the then existing world order—although I had no attachment to many of its phases.

But most of the time I thought the "next war" would come very suddenly and might be awful beyond imagining. It might easily result in complete economic and spiritual exhaustion, and consequent profound disruption of the Old World. And I thought it would be well for the one great country which was not interested in grabbing anything to keep itself intact, so that at the end it might serve as the leader—as the source of sanity, moral strength and material supplies—in some possible reconstruction.

The "Plymouth Rock and Ellis Island" Project

In *My America* I touched on some of the ways in which old-stock Americans and new-immigrant groups affect each other. I discussed the "Plymouth Rock and Ellis Island" situation, a shorthand label for the interplay of relations among people of different backgrounds. It seemed to me replete simultaneously with great long-range advantages and serious immediate dangers. The diversity of the American people was an asset, I thought, in the enhancement of a New World civilization and culture, while the dangers, if not intelligently dealt with, might easily become factors in the decline of that civilization and culture.

In relatively normal times this would have been a strictly internal American fact. But the intricate and negatory European crisis, as it rose to its climax and reverberated in America, was certain to strengthen both advantages and dangers—perhaps especially the latter.

At times, under the press of my belief that the "next war" was close, I thought mostly of the dangers. I believed we might soon witness an upsurge of antagonisms among the different groups; a spread of misconceptions about one another, of prejudices and discriminations which would constitute a sort of American psychological civil war—what Hitler's nihilistic propa-

ganda genius, Josef Goebbels, doubtless had in mind
when he said to Hermann Rauschning: "Nothing will be
easier than to produce a bloody revolution in the United
States. No other country has so many social and racial
tensions. We shall be able to play on many strings
there."

In fact highly competent, purposeful, well-heeled
Nazi and Fascist agents were already here, focusing
their propaganda on immigrants from Germany and
Italy and their native-American children. They were en-
couraging anti-alien, anti-Semitic, Know-Nothing and
K.K.K. tendencies in the population at large. Their aim
was to create and augment as many cleavages as possible among Americans. And they had plenty to work
on. American cultural and political leaders had never
paid any intelligent, consistent attention to the obscure
and subtle "Plymouth Rock and Ellis Island" problems.

But I thought too that the dangers could best be met
indirectly by revealing and strengthening the advantages. Negative forces cannot be fought successfully
with "against" programs; the momentum and volume
of positive forces must be increased to supplant them.

So in the spring of 1938 I decided to make the "Plymouth Rock and Ellis Island" situation my special concern during the next few years—at least until 1942.

I determined, though, not to go into my project in an
emergency mood. I would not concentrate on the problems and dangers linked to the growing world crisis
which was bound to engulf the United States in one way
or another; I would aim instead toward something that
might be useful not only as soon as I could produce re-

sults, but also when—or if—the world returned to
sanity. The dislocations present in the country's life
would probably become extreme; I anticipated new ones;
and they might endure for a long time. But they would
not destroy all of the best things traditionally incorpo-
rated in America as a state and as an idea.

I needed to work out a method, and then start digging
into the "Plymouth Rock and Ellis Island" saga, into its
exterior and interior—its historical and psychological—
phases. I had had glimpses of it, and it began to emerge
as one of the greatest stories under the sun: the arrival
and meeting and blending on the American continent of
people representing nearly sixty different racial, national and religious backgrounds. I would fill my head,
files and notebooks with it. Then I would write a series
of independent books whose connecting theme would be
the traits and trends in American life generated by the
following facts:

That the dominant element in the Colonies and in the
early United States was of Anglo-Saxon-Protestant
stock, which still retains a gradually weakening sway.

That in the last hundred years nearly forty million
new immigrants, most of them non-Anglo-Saxons and
non-Protestants, came over and then reproduced themselves numerously, till today well over one-third of the
population is of non-Anglo-Saxon, non-Protestant derivation—Slavic, Teuton, Latin, Levantine, Finnish,
Oriental; Catholic, Jewish, and Greek-Orthodox.

And that there are also some hundreds of thousands
of Indians and about thirteen million "colored" people

descended, for the most part, from Negro slaves and from Negro women and Anglo-Saxon American men.

If vividly presented, the picture should prompt this conception of the United States:

That, considering the composition of our population, Ellis Island is rapidly becoming as important historically as Plymouth Rock and Jamestown.

That today the country is—racially, socially, culturally, religiously, spiritually—a human extension not alone of the British Isles, The Netherlands, France, Germany, Ireland and Africa, as it was in the late 1700s, but of all Europe, of the West Indies and Mexico, of parts of Asia.

And that the present-day United States, with its industries, skyscrapers, railroads, highways and power lines, is as much the result of the labor and genius of comparatively recent comers as of old-stock Americans —themselves but earlier immigrants.

This conception, in turn, should gradually lead to a less restricted Americanism; to one which expands, taking in all Americans, whether native or naturalized, regardless of accent or exotic names. It should lead to a firmer disposition in the United States toward becoming a nation—"a people who have done great things together and want to continue," as Renan put it.

In twelve weeks that summer and early autumn—
while Hitler was forcing the "Czech crisis"—I drove
thirteen thousand miles between the Atlantic and Pacific
coasts, zigzagging about, stopping in scores of cities and
towns, and talking with hundreds of people of different
origins about the "Plymouth Rock and Ellis Island"
project. I was looking for a way of getting at the whole
story as quickly and thoroughly as possible.

But I did not find it. Not on that trip. Although I had
told myself I would not be distracted by European
events since there was nothing I could do about them, I
was nevertheless unable to concentrate on what I was
doing. It is hard to keep on building a new cupboard inside your house while smoke is curling out of the windows of the place next door.

Czechoslovakia, Czechoslovakia ——

Suddenly the whole United States was athrob with
excitement over dispatches from Prague, Berlin, London
and Paris. Papers and radio the country over were full
of the news. There were headlines about it clear across
the page not only in Chicago but in Bemidji, Minnesota;
Fargo, North Dakota; Billings and Butte, Montana;
Tacoma, Washington; and Eureka, California. Hardly
anyone was willing to talk about anything else.

The news deeply affected me personally. It was diffi-

cult for me continually to bear in mind my belief that
this was but an episode in the European process to be
followed by others. Czechoslovakia might fight, but she
would go down, for her allies, France and England, obviously would not—possibly because they could not—
help her. I hoped she might fight alone; then I thought
of the beautiful spires and roofs of Prague which Hitler's
bombers might destroy, and I didn't know if unsup-
ported she should stand up against the Third Reich or
not. ——

During August and September, while Hitler waged
his cunning war of nerves against the world over
Czechoslovakia, I visited a number of homes across the
country where Czech immigrants and their American-
born sons and daughters sat around radios, with tears
streaming down their faces. A year before some of the
older folk had seldom thought of their native Bohemia,
while to most of their children Czechoslovakia had been
almost as remote as Syria or Latvia. But now all of a
sudden they were very "Czech," very conscious of
Bohemia.

In Santa Barbara I spent a few days with a friend who
at four had been brought to America from Ruthenia,
then in Austria-Hungary, now a part of Czechoslovakia.
An American soldier in 1917–'18, he had been disabled
in France; and had married an old-stock American
woman. But now he was beside himself over the plight
of Prague and what Benes ought to do, and over Neville
Chamberlain and his umbrella. For years he had hardly

thought of Czechoslovakia; he had been simply an "American"; now he could not sleep or eat for days.

One evening right after Munich I found myself in Pasadena—in the home of another disabled veteran of the First World War, Humphrey Cobb, author of the powerful war novel *Paths of Glory*. He was in a white rage over Chamberlain and Daladier. He had served in the Canadian and British forces prior to our entry into the war; now he sent a cable to No. 10 Downing Street expressing his sharp sense of outrage over Munich and his regret at having served under the British flag.

Driving East in mid-October, I was told in a Nebraska town that the local string orchestra, famous for a hundred miles around, had broken up after Munich because the musicians of Czech descent had refused to play again with those who were of German origin, although they had practiced and performed together for years.

In St. Louis I met a manufacturer, an immigrant from Germany whose son had died as an American officer in France. He told me in anger that he had lost a great deal of business since the beginning of the Czech crisis. Only the last two weeks, he went on, five firms had failed to renew their orders. Four were Jewish; the fifth was a Chicago concern run by a Czech immigrant he had done business with for eighteen years. He attributed it all to Munich. "But, goddam 'em," he said, "if they do this to me, how can they expect me to like Czechs or Jews? They *make* me 'German.' I don't agree with Hitler, but now ——"

In Chicago there was a sudden cleavage between

Czechs and Poles and Czech and Polish Americans. A few Czech immigrants I knew were bitterly incensed because the Polish government had collaborated with Hitler in the dismemberment of Czechoslovakia, "grabbing" the valuable Silesia mining district, and their resentment carried over to Polish Americans. On the other hand, two or three of the latter with whom I talked maintained that that mining district had by rights always belonged to Poland, and expressed disapproval of everything Czech, including Czech Americans.

An old immigrant from Bohemian Moravia told me that since about 1925, when Czechoslovakia had begun to get on her feet, he had paid very little attention to the "old country." He had American-born children and he would be an American. His attitude was: "I'm here to stay. Good-by Europe." For twelve or thirteen years he had concerned himself almost exclusively with American affairs. In 1932 his daughter married a young American of German parentage, of whom he approved; now he was strongly Czech and anti-German. He bemoaned his "German" son-in-law, although the young man, whom I met, seemed quite "American."

I didn't know if the reactions of these Czech and Polish immigrants to Munich were typical of their respective groups; but—along with the string orchestra in Nebraska and the St. Louis manufacturer's state of mind—they were disconcerting symptoms.

In Cleveland I had a long session with a levelheaded friend of mine, a German immigrant, an American citizen, an anti-Nazi, who was keeping a cool if worried eye

on the "German element" there. He told me there were
Nazi agents in Cleveland; he knew a few personally.
Working apparently under the direction of someone in
the German Consulate, they were aggressively active
among the "German element"—meaning German immigrants, alien and naturalized, and their American-born
children who still lived at home or otherwise remained
close to their group. But the agents' chief effort at the
moment was to bring about a Nazi-controlled amalga-
mation of German American organizations. My friend
thought this was probably going on in most towns
which included any considerable number of Germans
and German Americans.

"So far as I can see," he said, "the Nazis are not getting very far in Cleveland; at least not with the organizations, not with anything concrete. I think many German
Americans here are more or less anti-Nazi, although the
great majority, particularly those born abroad, are
afraid to say so. But these agents have for some time
now been subtly creating an atmosphere of terror. There
are rumors which probably can't be clearly traced but
which obviously were started by Hitler's propagandists
—rumors to this effect: the Nazis in Germany have a
sure-fire plan for world domination which takes in the
United States; they have the name, address and family
history of nearly every 'German in America' and also
every 'American-born German' unto the third generation; the Fuehrer personally expects all Germans in this
country to do their duty; and they'd better realize which
side their bread will be buttered on five or ten years
hence. ——

"So far," my Cleveland friend continued, "this terror-ization has had no very definite result except to put most of the 'German element' on the fence, which is damned uncomfortable and a source of inner confusion. It may be all the Nazis want for the present.

"The inner confusion is great. Most people I know are either anti-Nazi by nature or conviction, or afraid to be pro-Hitler because the United States in general is against him, especially since Munich. On the other hand, they don't dare to be suspected of being anti-Nazi. Who knows what is likely to happen in the near future? Hitler really may have a feasible plan for world domination. He may succeed where Bismarck and Kaiser Wilhelm failed. Then what? It might be advantageous to be of German blood. Then one could get even with the 'Americans' for what they did to the 'Germans' in this country during the war in 1917–'18. Who knows? Who knows—per-haps the Nazi agents *do* have a pretty complete roster of 'Germans' in America. It is something to worry about. For the rumor goes that if any 'American German's' attitude toward the Third Reich doesn't suit the Nazi agents here, his relatives in Germany will suffer. In fact," added my friend, "I may be so bold—I may not care who knows what I think about Hitler because I have no relatives over there! ——"

He went on: "Every once in a while I hear things. There is a German-owned baking company in Cleveland which employs Nazi agents as delivery-truck drivers. They circulate among a good many Germans and Ger-man Americans, and can thus supervise their ideological development. . . . A couple of weeks ago one of these birds delivered a loaf of bread to—Mrs. Schmidt, let's call her. She and her husband are American-born. I know them both, they consider themselves Americans, and no maybe about it.

"One day the bread distributor stopped to chat with Mrs. Schmidt as usual; and while they talked her Jewish cleaner brought back a dress. When he had gone, the Nazi agent reprimanded her for patronizing a Jew.

"This was too much for Mrs. Schmidt. She told the Nazi sharply it was none of his business whom she patronized or what she did; she said she no longer wanted his bread—and she slammed the door in his face.

"When Mrs. Schmidt told her husband, he thought she had done just right. The nerve of the so-and-so! He and I work in the same shop; and the next day he told me about it.

"About a week later a stranger called on them. He spoke good English without an accent and gave his name as Schlick or Schick. He lost no time in coming to the point: Mrs. Schmidt's 'unfortunate' behavior toward the driver of the bread truck; the man was a 'good German' and had had her interest at heart when he advised her not to patronize 'that Jew.'

"This got up the dander of both the Schmidts. She said, 'Say, who do you think you are!'—and her husband was ready to throw the intruder out of the house. But the man drew out a sheet of paper and began to reel off a string of facts about their families here and abroad. Some of his information was not strictly accurate, but it was specific enough to impress them. He mentioned all their close relatives in Germany and a good many dis-

tant ones. Then he said that their Hamburg and Leipzig
kin would 'suffer,' without indicating how, unless the
Schmidts promptly and thoroughly revised their attitude
toward Nazi ideas. They '*must*' dispense with the serv-
ices of all Jews and Jewish establishments, and they
'*must*' resume taking the bread which their well-meaning
friend, the truck driver, was accustomed to deliver to
them. And he smiled and left. . . .

"The Schmidts have been in a terrible state of mind
ever since. They gave up their Jewish cleaner, and they
hate themselves for it. The Nazi driver delivers their
bread. Mrs. Schmidt tries to avoid him, but it is hard.
He is very polite and pleasant, but they know he is spy-
ing on them. . . . Neither of them has ever seen any of
their relatives in Germany, but naturally they don't
want them to 'suffer.'

"The other day the little Jewish cleaner came around
to inquire why they don't patronize him any more. 'Is it
because I am a Jew?' She answered, 'No, no!'—and felt
like a louse. ——"

I met the Schmidts. They begged me to promise them
not to write up their story; at least not at once. It might
be dangerous even if I disguised their name. (Since then
they have moved to another city; Mr. Schmidt is a
machine-tool worker in a factory filling Defense orders;
and I see no reason for not relating their experience with
Nazi agents in October 1938.)

The Schmidt case probably was typical of many the
country over, then and later.

In Pittsburgh I talked with Slovenian and Croatian
Americans who had been intensely pro-Czech during

Munich and were now not only anti-Hitler but acutely anti-German—and their attitude took in also German Americans. I heard of a Yugoslav society which had canceled a performance scheduled to be held in a German hall.

I spoke with a Catholic priest, the American-born son of Austrian-German immigrants, who feared that the widespread anti-German sentiment in Pittsburgh and vicinity was apt to drive many Germans and German Americans into the nets of Nazi propagandists. He was himself anti-Nazi, of course, but he felt—in spite of himself—an occasional resentment toward those who hated everything German. Who wouldn't? He was human. He thought the Jews were especially unwise . . . and, although he tried to "see the thing from their angle," he confessed to momentary feelings against them; then he hastened to add, too self-consciously, that he was not anti-Semitic and disapproved of Hitler's treatment of Jews in Germany.

I spoke with a Jew in Pittsburgh. He was worried. There was "a lot of anti-Semitism." Much of it was purposely stirred up by Nazi agents. This could be proved. In the Negro sections, for instance, they were fomenting anti-Jewish feeling with some rather cunning tricks— such as sending "Jewish-looking" individuals who were not Jews into Negro homes and places of business to behave obnoxiously toward Negroes of standing and influence whose just resentment then spread through the Negro community. . . . What could the Jews do? . . .

It was my most disturbing trip through the United States up until then—and I had made several before.

I Begin My American Project

There was no precedent for the "Plymouth Rock and Ellis Island" project whose magnitude I did not at first realize. Its scope unfolded as I went along.

I found a method, the core of which was my so-called "broadside" (reprinted at the end of this book), which was simultaneously a tentative statement of what I was after and an extensive questionnaire. It probed into the attitudes of new immigrants and old-line Americans toward one another and toward America as an idea, toward the American way of life, toward the "old country." From January 1939 to July 1941 over a quarter of a million copies of the broadside were sent out and replies, comments and autobiographical letters have been pouring in ever since. At times during '39 mail arrived by the bagful.

Letters of two, five, ten, twenty, fifty, a hundred pages came from all sorts of people living all over the United States—immigrants, naturalized and alien; second-generation people; old-stock Americans, Indians and Negroes. Bundles came containing scrapbooks and obscure pamphlets and volumes. Everything was read, then filed (very little of it into the wastepaper basket). Nearly every piece of mail was acknowledged, usually with further questions which evoked more information from my correspondents. Assistants assembled data and prepared memoranda; and in the last three years we traveled over two hundred thousand miles through the United States, interviewing singly and in small groups thousands of people. About eight hundred became my "key people," especially interested in the project, who wrote frequent reports on pertinent matters in their communities.

In 1939–'40 I delivered over a hundred lectures and informal talks on what I was about. I was active too in an old organization known as the Foreign Language Information Service, renamed late in '39 the Common Council for American Unity; and the following year began to edit a new magazine, *Common Ground*, one of whose chief purposes was to develop writers interested in the vast "Plymouth Rock and Ellis Island" materials which were badly in need of authors.

The work was untellably interesting—fascinating. I felt I was getting at something; at the inside of America.

There rolled in upon me an immense story of courage and fear; of fear and hope and doubt; of welcome and rebuff, good will and misunderstanding; of effort and struggle and achievement; of aspiration and frustration; of meanness and greatness; of human flowering and decline; of degradation and beauty ——

By the middle of '39 I realized there was material for an indefinite number of books. I hoped to write a few of them, independent of one another: the Nation of Nations Series—after Walt Whitman's description of the United States as "not a nation but a teeming nation of nations."

From Many Lands, the first book in the series, came out in the autumn of '40.

In the spring of '41 I began to write *Plymouth Rock and Ellis Island*, intending to publish it early in '42; and by mid-July more than half of it was written . . . when America's profound involvement in the present world crisis impelled me to interrupt it in order to write this book.

THE PASSAGE HERE

A Man from the Black Forest

One day a letter came from Mr. John G. Gaiser, of
Yakima, Washington. He had got hold of a copy of my
broadside and wanted me to visit him if I ever traveled
in his part of the country. He said he was an old immigrant from Germany long in the United States. His
native village was in the Black Forest. He came of the
branch of the German people knows as Schwabians. ——

Some months later when I was in the Far Northwest
I turned up at Mr. Gaiser's modest fruit ranch and found
him a thoughtful and articulate man, well preserved for
his seventy-odd years. We chatted awhile. Through his
mind ran a strong current of reminiscence.

"To understand an immigrant and what America
means to him," he remarked, "you have to know something of his old-country background. Even the immigrant, if he is ignorant about his native land, will experience moments when he doesn't understand himself."

I nodded. Then I just listened.

"I was barely sixteen when I came to America," the
old gentleman went on, "but I know a little something
of my own story in the old country. Strangely, now that
the years are a burden, my clearest remembrance reaches
back to a day sixty-eight years ago, when I was not yet
seven, in the village of Baiersbronn. Perhaps it is so

29

clear because it is the only one that includes moments whose texture is pure happiness.

"It is early in the afternoon on Christmas Day in 1872. We have just eaten our best meal of the year. Through the rest of the year our food was miserable; a good dinner was an event to be remembered . . . and my full stomach doubtless had much to do with my enjoyment of the afternoon.

"It is a beautiful day. The sun is still high in the pale blue sky. It is at its weakest in warmth, but very bright. A wind blows down the valley. It swoops up and around the ridges, and sends little whirls of loose dry snow into our faces. This adds to the keenness of the moment. The world is as close to perfection as can be.

"The snow is two feet deep, but the road curving three and a half kilometers up the mountainside in back of the village is smooth, hardpacked by the ox sleds that hauled logs and cordwood out of the forest the week before; and a dozen or more of us village boys are digging our heels into the side of the road, where the snow is not quite so hard, and we are making slow progress up the incline. We tug at a hand sled used by our fathers and uncles and neighbors to move cordwood down the too-steep parts of the ridge to the road, where the large ox-team sleds cannot be used. Although upgrade all the way, it is an easy pull for so many boys—but a long pull, perhaps an hour and a half from the bottom to the top. Scampering behind us and between our feet is the canine population of the village. My own dog, just a pup, is along. For him, as for me, this is the first trip all the way up the mountain road.

"I am the youngest in the group; not yet seven. I was included because two of my older brothers are along, and my father built the sled.

"Most of us are poorly clad, some without mittens, and we are at once cold and warm: do you know the sensation—the color of young cheeks in such bracing weather? . . .

"Well, we get the sled up to the edge of the top of the plateau; then . . . then we have fifteen minutes of exhilaration going down. We go thirty kilometers an hour, even forty on stretches where the road is straight and the grade sharp. The soft loose snow, blown by the light winds, stings our young skin. The combination of bright sun and clean white snow almost blinds us. But no matter. We half close our eyes. We are packed tight in the sled, one on top of the other. I am wedged between two older boys. The dogs are running yelping way behind the sled.

"Down the mountainside we go, and at the end of the long but too brief slide, as we tumble out of the sled in front of a crowd of village folk, our feelings are a fusion of deep disappointment and extraordinary achievement. Do you know what I mean? It is the whole of life packed into a moment. Life at its best. Something to remember.

"It is a moment all the more keen because I am not entirely happy. My vest and jacket are of crude, rough homespun, not much better to look at than burlap in America, but warmer and more durable. My pants, however, are calico, made from an old skirt of my sister's. I do not especially relish this. They are somewhat threadbare; and crawling onto the sled on top of the plateau I ripped the crotch and seat . . . so now when I get off, I am at once desperate, humiliated and amused. I hold my pants together with both hands. The fact of the matter is, I wear no underclothes.

"My mother, who is in the crowd at the foot of the slide, notices my plight, picks me up, and starts for home, some distance away. Now we both laugh at my predicament. She laughs so hard tears break from her eyes. . . . This is the only time I ever saw her really laugh. She was never so amused, so happy. . . . I am her last child. She is now in her late forties. Although I am a considerable chunk of a boy, she carries me easily. We pass by the winehouse; men are singing inside. It is Christmas Day; a day of days. . . .

"We were a large family: six girls and four boys— and a respectable family, but, like most folk in our community, very poor. I said that on that memorable Christmas Day in '72 I wore no undergarments; the fact is, I had none till I was fourteen, although the temperature in winter was often sub-zero for weeks at a spell.

"Father's main business was turning cordwood into charcoal. It occupied him nine months out of the year. The other three he spent sledding wood and grubbing out old stumps for firewood—one of the hardest jobs when you must do it without powder or dynamite. That is to say, Father followed these occupations in the daytime; evenings, by dim lamplight, he built churns and washtubs, or hand sleds strong enough to bring down half a cord of wood. At most of these tasks he had the assistance of my older brothers. He was an assiduous, thorough and excellent worker, as are—or were at that time—many Central Europeans.

"My mother and sisters worked our four acres. But in that altitude the growing season was short, the soil not the best, and even the most intense efforts yielded meager results. The family exertions, it seemed, could make no dent in our poverty. There were taxes. There was an old debt on the place. Whatever happened to go wrong plunged us into a crisis. We could stack up no reserves; there were no cushions on which to fall, no backlogs to hold us up.

"One year it rained so much the potatoes rotted in the ground, the hay rotted in the shocks, and the rye, which was brought in too damp, molded in the barn. In consequence, late that autumn and through the winter Father and my oldest brother had to make several trips over the divide to get sacks of turnips, potatoes and grain from relatives on the western slope where crops had been better. For months during that dire year we existed on the scantiest of diets: rye soup for breakfast, a turnip each for lunch, and for supper potatoes or turnips mixed with rye flour and flavored with a dash of vinegar. To reduce the number of mouths, a sister hired out as maid to one of the few well-to-do farmers in the valley. She received the equivalent of thirty dollars a year and keep—but the keep barely kept her in strength from day to day.

"In those days, when people in the village hired out for any kind of work, their wages ranged from thirty-seven to seventy-five cents for twelve hours. In the spring the forest authorities called the peasants to plant seedlings, paying them two loaves of rye bread a day. What they did not eat on the job, they brought home. In hard times, Father returned with at least one full loaf.

"At seven and a half I was hired out to a farmer to herd cattle two hours in the morning and four in the afternoon. My wages were two meals a day (although in America they would not be called meals) and a pair of pants. The same year I started to school, but was able to do my job too.

"In early fall and after the spring thaw, first-graders attended school only from ten to twelve, and higher-graders from eight to twelve, so youngsters could work in the afternoon—gather grass in the clearings for the cow, pick up dry twigs for kindling, and rake leaves and pine needles for the cow's winter bedding. In July and August we worked as hard as our elders from morning till night; if at nothing else, picking huckleberries, which our parents sold for about sixty cents a bushel. In winter, school lasted from eight in the morning until four in the afternoon, with an hour for lunch, which in comparatively good times consisted of a big piece of dry bread—but I often consumed it while walking the four kilometers to school.

"In my seventh year at school, my parents were urged to send me to a teachers' lyceum, but there was not enough money. Although we had had a couple of fairly good years, Father was cleaned out. That autumn he had sent one of my sisters to the United States—to Missouri, where, according to report, there was a shortage of girls among German immigrants.

"I wanted to be a sawmill operator. But as we could find no opening for an apprenticeship, I spent the summer with my father and oldest brother in the woods producing charcoal for the King's ironworks, which were in an adjacent valley.

"We lived in a temporary lean-to, which Father put up and took down as we moved from forest to forest. We slept on benches with a layer of dried moss for mattresses and no covers. Father said if we slept too comfortably under blankets we might not wake up the necessary number of times a night to see that no fire broke out in the kilns turning the wood intended for charcoal into ashes.

"I was going on fifteen then. A thought came to me: why couldn't *I* go to America, too? I said nothing to anyone. Our sister wrote that nearly every German immigrant in Missouri, herself included, was doing well. Soon she would send money for another sister to follow her.

"In the late autumn, a distant relative on the other side of the divide offered to take me as an apprentice into the sawmill he supervised. I jumped at it, thinking they might need sawmill men in America. For fourteen months I worked from two in the morning until six in the afternoon, mostly trimming or shaping-up lumber. The first year I received only board, which was sufficiently scanty to prevent me from becoming dyspeptic. I was supposed to get meat twice a week, but it was always served as stew with turnips and potatoes—a kilo (two pounds) of beef or mutton for *nine* boys! With the start of the second year I began to receive about twenty-five cents a week.

"By now—the early 1880s—three of my sisters were in Missouri. The dollars they sent from America largely supported the family, for Father's health had broken down. Unable to work any more, he sat in a chair in the house, his work-inured hands, trembly and idle, grasping at the air. He had me quit my apprenticeship at the saw-mill and come home to help my brothers finish a charcoal order he had taken before his collapse. Father was that sort of man: fulfill every obligation. . . . He lived a few years longer. He realized that, because of the hopeless struggle in which he had engaged, his health and strength were finished at fifty-eight, and he developed a passion to see as many of his children as possible go to the 'Land of Opportunity.'

"This was in line with my own idea. One day I said I wanted to go to America, and Father nodded.

"On the advice of the sisters in Missouri, two of whom were married by now, it was decided that another sister, who had learned the trade of seamstress, would next go to the United States and take me along. I was sixteen. The emigrated sisters claimed that my youth would be of great advantage to me in the New World; I would have less trouble getting adjusted (which was sheer wisdom), while it would be immaterial, from that point of view, if the older brothers emigrated a year or two later.

"In March came word that our tickets were at the Methodist Emigrant House in Bremen, and my sister and I got ready to depart. . . . It was a difficult leave-taking. Now five of us ten children would be gone. I think it was especially hard for Mother to see me go, her youngest. She insisted on packing our carpetbags— the last thing she could do for us. Father looked on. Then Mother rested her still strong and steady hand on his shoulder. Suddenly seeing them so, I didn't want to go—but I knew I would. Father made a motion with his limp, shaking hand: *be on your way!* As I see it now, working in him was the strong purpose which stirred in others all over Europe and became a part of the dynamics of America. In a cracked, unnatural voice, he said to us: 'I don't count. Don't worry about me. You go! Go with God!' . . ."

John Gaiser's next dozen years make a story of experiences typical of thousands of young immigrants between, say, 1865 and 1914.

He worked for farmers; some treated him well, others abused him. Then his brother Lui, who was preparing for the ministry, ignited in him the desire for education.

He worked his way through Ottawa University, in Kansas.

By the mid-'90s all the Gaiser brothers and sisters were in the United States, except one brother who refused to come. "A quiet man, his thoughts locked within him, he took over the poor ancestral homestead in the Black Forest, married, and went on turning cordwood into charcoal.

"Father was dead. Mother lived at home and often wrote to us that if she could once more see one of her 'American children' she would die happy. So in the summer of '96, when I graduated, I was elected to go 'home' and find out if she might like to join us. . . . Her eyes could not have enough of me.

"I was 'home' nearly two weeks. I scarcely saw the brother who had stayed behind. He was on a job in the woods. When we met, he had nothing to say. He welcomed me with his smile and eyes. His wife I had not seen before—she was from across the divide.

"I took a good look at the village. There was apparently more money than there had been ten years before, and I found that most of it came from America. At least every third family had someone in the United States. We Gaisers had started the emigration. . . . And, looking at it as an American with a little education, I saw that the village, with all its limitations, some of which verged on the tragic, had its points. Though poor, many people were happier and, how shall I say? more clear-cut as men and women, or as young people, than almost anyone I knew in the United States. There was great (perhaps too much) stability there. Definiteness. There was character (perhaps too rigid). The life of the community was closely (perhaps too closely) woven together. Under the texture I sensed an unrest; I couldn't define it; I still can't; it was subdued, controlled.

"But I knew I would never want to live in my native village again for any length of time. I was an American. I spoke English with a slight accent, but otherwise as well as, or better than, most Americans. I was a citizen of the United States. I liked America better. Kansas and Nebraska were flat and not beautiful as was the Black

Forest . . . but the possibilities and promises there! The freedom of America! . . .

"Mother, however, was a different story. I was young; she was seventy. She had aged greatly. She was part of the village; it was part of her. Nearly everybody was her friend. She heard familiar speech and sounds. Of course she missed her 'American' children. But wouldn't she be much lonelier in Nebraska or Kansas, where we would be busy most of the time? After the first few weeks we might possibly be too busy to talk with her and explain our new ways of life. Wouldn't it be better if she stayed at home and one of us came back for a visit every couple of years?

"I told Mother some of these thoughts. She brushed them all aside. In her was the same frustration I had seen so clearly in Father when I left for America. The village had failed her; it could not support her children, and all but one had gone. She had not seen the wedding of any of her daughters. She had never seen her sons-in-law and grandchildren. Now she wanted to leave the village too. When I repeated my warning that in America she might be unhappy after a while, she shook her head as if it were irrelevant, and said over and over again, 'Son, I am going with you!' . . .

"She was happy for about six months as she visited around with her daughters and sons-in-law and grandchildren, and with her two other 'American sons,' especially Lui who had married and was a preacher with a pastorate. Then, as I had feared, she got lonely. Most of us talked English at least part of the time, and she could not learn a dozen words of 'this American language,' as she put it. She tried living with each of her children awhile, but did not feel very comfortable. Everything was so different. Her grandchildren, native Americans, thought her 'funny.' They gaped and giggled at her.

"But she was never homesick. She made it clear repeatedly that she did not want to return to Baiersbronn. But she was miserable because of the gap that America had placed between her and her children. We had changed; she was the same. She did not feel at home in America, but she sensed that we were, and that our children would not have to emigrate in order to live. There was plenty here.

"She died two years after I married. . . ."

John Gaiser went west . . . and by 1903 was known as one of the best pedagogues and school administrators in western Washington. He owned a ranch and engaged in a little conservative land speculation, which supplemented his small salary and enabled him to support comfortably his family, which in the course of years increased to six children. Off and on, also, he quit school work in disgust at politicians who wielded ignorant authority over education, and returned for a year or two to farming. He was not what might be called a radical, either as an educator or a citizen, but he was uncompromising—almost to a fault—in his attitude toward individuals who lacked any educational qualifications yet presumed, and too often had absolute power, to run schools and school systems.

In the fifteen years preceding 1917 he held half a

dozen teaching and administrative jobs, some of them elective, along Puget Sound. In one or two he was supremely happy for a while. In most of them, sooner or later, he came up against the "old curse"; there was a blowup; he crystallized the issue, and sometimes he lost and sometimes he won.

But in spite of these ups and downs John Gaiser might have spent the rest of his active life in education, had it not been for the anti-German hysteria which broke out in the United States even before 1917, deeply affecting the careers of many German Americans who were among the best citizens of the country. During the fights and squabbles over educational principles and methods he had sometimes been called a "foreigner" or a "Dutchman" or "that German," but it had not been serious. After the United States entered the war, however, he was accused of being a German sympathizer.

Feeling in the country ran so high that it did him little good to protest, to point out the reasons for his emigration from Germany, and to the fact that his oldest son was serving as a volunteer in the American Army. He was accused of being a German sympathizer because years before, in casual conversation, he had spoken favorably of certain qualities of life in his native Black Forest village, although he had never said anything that could sensibly be construed as devotion to the German state or its ruler.

John Gaiser was at the time an eighth-grade teacher in a small town. He was forced out of his job and replaced by a man whose sole previous connection with education had been as a baseball coach.

Thanks to his good business sense in land deals, Mr. Gaiser was better off than ever before. He bought a small ranch outside Yakima and decided to "retire"— to live calmly, read Homer and Goethe and Balzac and Emerson, raise fruit and chickens, and devote himself to his family.

The Gaisers have made a good job of raising their four boys and two girls. One daughter taught school for three years in Seattle, then married a Norwegian-Scottish American, who is a civil engineer. The other girl is also married, to a young tungsten-mill superintendent of Italian parentage. The oldest son, now in his early forties, is plant manager of the two Yakima Valley Creamery co-operative plants; he and his wife, who is of Swedish-English derivation, have a son. The other three Gaiser boys are single. One, in his mid-thirties, a graduate of Reed College, is assistant manager of a big transportation farm in Portland. The next works as a straw boss in a fruit-packing house in Yakima. The youngest went to the State University and now has a job in the Government Engineers' Office at Coulee Dam. . . .

Twenty-odd years have elapsed since John Gaiser's withdrawal from educational life. He feels no bitterness. He is essentially the same man he was at fifty, in 1917; a little mellower, to be sure: an *American* of Schwabian origin. Prior to the spring of 1940 he had almost never discussed the trouble of the German American element during the First World War. He seldom referred to his own experience. He had understood: in politics and war people say and do nasty things to each other, that was all.

"But now," he said, "I am a little uneasy. The United States is again taking a definite stand against Germany, and inevitably loyal to America—as I was in 1917–'18—I am afraid that hysteria is springing up again which will touch many Americans of German origin and descent. I don't doubt there are actually or potentially disloyal Germans and German Americans in the United States, and I realize that for Americans of other backgrounds it is difficult to separate the sheep from the goats, but I am sure that—for reasons as vital as my own—most of them are either firmly loyal or bound to swing with the rest of the country as events develop.

"I wrote to you thinking you might be able to do something about it; point out the danger if nothing else —point out the confusion which must exist among German Americans throughout the country. I have no contact with German Americans, for I know people as people; but, remembering 1917–'18, I don't doubt that many of us immigrants from Germany and also some of our American-born children are mixed up emotionally. I think that most of us are, or want to be, pro-United States first, last and always. Both as Americans and as natives of Germany, we are traditionally anything but pro-British. This does not mean that we cannot see the reason for aid to Britain. But we cannot be anti-Germany as a country: how can I be against my boyhood in the Black Forest, against that sled ride on Christmas Day in 1872? How can I repudiate *that*? How can I possibly erase it from my life? . . . Things like that exist in the make-up of other German Americans; only lots of them perhaps cannot think and talk about them and thus straighten themselves out as Americans. Many people, born on both sides of the ocean, have already been discharged from jobs in different parts of the country because they are 'Germans'—just as I was turned out of teaching in 1917. How can they think calmly and be firmly American? They need help—perhaps from 'outsiders,' from non-German Americans.

"I try to be calm; I think I *am* calm. I don't like to talk of my own troubles in 1917. I was called a 'dirty Hun' in private and in public, but my experiences were less humiliating than those of some other German Americans I knew. . . . A preacher, for instance, on a salary of six hundred dollars a year was asked to buy a one-hundred-dollar Liberty Bond when it meant choosing between this demonstration of patriotism and feeding his family. He was accused of disloyalty and ordered to appear in court, over a hundred miles away, only to be excused; his accuser was not even required to appear.

"Another case I know about personally was that of a German tailor in Spokane who employed eight men in 1916. When the United States entered the war, his patronage rapidly dropped to nothing. Even his fellow lodge members stopped giving him work. He had to discharge his men one after the other, then close his shop. Finally he sold his house and bought an orchard out by Soap Lake in the Grand Coulee. God knows what became of his former workers, who, I think, were also German immigrants.

"The children of a friend of mine, who was a naturalized citizen, were called slackers and 'little Huns' even by the principal in school because they had no baby bonds. Not until President Wilson said, 'A boy who raises a pig or a sack of potatoes is just as loyal as if he bought a baby bond,' and until they proved that they were raising food, did the teachers and the principal let up on them.

"Then there was my brother Lui (he died in 1939 at the age of seventy-six). One after the other, his seven sons graduated from Whitman College at Walla Walla. Three are school superintendents now in various parts of Washington. One teaches in Oregon. One is a doctor in Spokane. One is an attorney in Washington, D. C. The seventh is with Standard Oil. His two daughters also taught school before they were married; one lives in Spokane, the other in Portland.

"This family was reared on a salary beginning at three hundred dollars a year and rising to nine hundred at the height of Lui's career. To make ends meet, he used to buy groceries wholesale. During the war years he was district superintendent for the German Methodist Episcopal churches in Washington, Oregon and Idaho. In 1917 he was still in Ritzville where, as was his custom, he bought several sacks of flour which the family took along to Spokane when he was obliged to move there. About that time the anti-hoarding law came into effect, and he offered to turn the flour over to a grocer in Spokane, although the law required you to 'take the goods back where you bought them.' But the Spokane grocer said he had plenty of flour and refused it.

"Lui intended to ask a lawyer if he must ship the flour back to the grocery in Ritzville, but just then he had to go East as a delegate to the General Conference. His wife went with him. In their absence a snooper came around and saw the two or three sacks in full view on the pantry floor. The next day papers all over the West carried front-page headlines: 'GERMAN PREACHER CAUGHT HOARDING FLOUR.' The news spread East, and at the General Conference the pastor of an English-language church in Spokane refused to shake hands with the 'Hun hoarder.'

"My brother returned to Spokane baffled and heartsick—for at that very time five of his sons were in the United States Army.

"He presented himself to District Federal Judge Webster and explained how he had happened to have the flour. The judge was one of the small minority who had retained perspective; he inquired into Lui's life in detail, and was amazed to learn that he had raised so large a family on his preacher's salary. He exonerated him and ruled that the confiscated flour be returned to him. The next day a few papers carried a little news item under such headings as 'JUDGE EXCUSES HOARDING PASTOR'—on the inside pages, tucked among the ads.

"In his own small way, Lui had given most of his life to the education and advancement of immigrants. Now he had to resign and retire; the damage was done—worse than to me—and there was no way of repairing it.

"I would hate to see this sort of thing happen again. ——"

America Is Escape from Europe

From the beginning up to the present, migration from Europe to North America has been an escape from the undesirable to the promising.

The Pilgrims left a homeland which was no longer home to seek in the New World a freer, more rewarding and abundant life. So did most of the Jamestown Colonists and the subsequent Colonial settlers—English, Dutch, Scotch, Scotch-Irish, the Germans who became known as Pennsylvania Dutch, the so-called Moravians, the Sephardic Jews, Huguenot French, and North and South Irish.

Today refugees are in flight from other shores to these.

For three centuries now individuals and groups that migrated to America have been getting away from something, to come to something they hoped would be better.

This was true of the early waves of the New Immigration which began to roll this way about a hundred years ago: say in the 1840s. The South Irish who started to come over in large numbers in that decade were running away from famine. The Germans who arrived in the '40s and '50s were getting away from the consequences of the collapse of their revolutionary movements. The Hollanders who started communities in Michigan and Iowa in the last half of the '40s left Holland because they were

47

not free to believe and preach their particular kind of religion. The Poles who settled in Texas in the mid-'50s had slipped from under the "iron heel" in Prussian Poland. Late in that decade "Russian" and "Swedish" Finns began to emigrate here because they did not like where birth and fate had placed them. Swedes and Norwegians sought refuge in the United States from the cramped circumstances of their native countries.

This is history which has been elaborately recorded.

But the same thing is true of the immigrant groups which have come in noticeable numbers during the last seventy years—the eight or nine different kinds of Slavs, the Danes and Belgians, the Italians, French, Hungarians, Rumanians, Lithuanians, Greeks, Syrians and Armenians, the Austrian, Bavarian, Low and Bohemian Germans, and of course the Jews from Russia, Poland, Austria, Hungary, Bohemia, Rumania, the Balkans, the Near East and elsewhere.

The stories of these groups have not yet been adequately told. But my files bulge with statements—most of them autobiographical, many resembling the John Gaiser narrative—which indicate that the vast majority of the thirty-five million individuals who reached the American shore since the 1870s were running away from one thing or another that rendered their existence in the Old World relatively intolerable.

They were getting away from political oppression, terrorism, pogroms and massacres; from traditional compulsory army service, militarism and wars; from life in ghettos . . . from old-maidhood . . . from actual or potential economic, social, cultural or personal frustration.

Also America actively lured them. She needed more man power to get under way as a material empire. In the '70s or '80s there rose the "America fever," the germs of which were tales of incredible well-being in "the Land of Promise." They spread over skimping, tight-drawn Europe like an epidemic.

But with few exceptions, the "fever" seized only the poor, the discontented, the practically despairing people like the Gaisers. The well-to-do, functioning elements in the old countries were largely immune to it.

Emma Lazarus, herself a daughter of New Immigration, knew whereof she spoke when she wrote the lines which in 1886 were affixed to the base of the Statue of Liberty:

> *Give me your tired, your poor,*
> *Your huddled masses yearning to breathe free,*
> *The wretched refuse of your teeming shore,*
> *Send these, the homeless, the tempest-tost, to me:*
> *I lift my lamp beside the golden door.*

America has always been—and is now—a mass and individual escape from Europe, from life in the Old World.

Or perhaps I should say that America was *attempted* escape from life in Europe. For you can't escape from life, individually or *en masse*. As a person or as a country, you can't get away from what has gone into your formation. You can ignore it; you can refuse to look back; you can put a screen or distance between yourself and it, but sooner or later it catches up with you, seeking its place in your inner balance . . . or confusion.

Now European life has caught up with us Americans —with us who in a sense are the escaped, the escapist Europeans, directly or by descent.

Now we can't escape from it any more. Here it is. We must deal with it.

Of course, from different angles at different times, the Atlantic Migration—to use the title of Marcus Lee Hansen's fine book on the subject—was many things.

It may be regarded from an American point of view as escape from Europe. From the European standpoint, emigration was the same thing in reverse, the other side of the coin: a syphoning off of discontent which postponed decade after decade, year after year, the violent explosions to be expected from the fermentation brewing in the various overcrowded old countries and on the continent as a whole.

This seemed clear to me in 1932–'33 as I visited scores of villages in Yugoslavia, studying their human circumstances. My current project confirms it.

Eight or nine years ago even in some of the most advanced Croatian, Serbian and Slovenian villages from one half to two thirds of the inhabitants were not really peasants, but soilless village proletarians who barely existed—*siroté*, or paupers, dependent upon the meager resources, the charity, of the upper half or third.

Ten, even five, years earlier—say during the early and middle 1920s—a large proportion of these village proletarians was directly or indirectly affected by emigration to the United States. Every year for six or seven decades before the First World War, while the United States was rushing blindly to its industrial heights, hundreds of thousands left Europe for America seeking to better their lot. Millions of their kin who remained in the Old World hoped eventually to be in a position to follow—to escape. And the very hope of "crossing the big pond" some day was enough to keep most of them from political activity hostile to their perennially inadequate home governments.

The hope as well as the fact of emigration was a vent for much social inquietude and vexation of spirit.

Not only did America absorb countless shiploads of hitherto dissatisfied humanity, but the emigrants sent back one fourth to one half of their wages to relatives in thousands of European communities. And this money from America was even more important than the syphoning off of a sizable portion of the population. Millions of escaped Europeans laboring in American mills, mines and forests not only supported themselves in the United States but helped to feed and clothe their relatives back home. Mr. Gaiser observed this when he visited his native Black Forest village in 1896. It was true in his family before he emigrated. It was true in any number of European communities for a century.

Incredibly often the immigrant worker in America paid off the enslaving debts of his family. He paid the ever-mounting annual government taxes on the old homestead. He provided the dowry for his sister's marriage. He helped his friends and cousins to follow to America, whereupon they in turn helped others.

The three or four hundred dollars he annually sent

from America, when translated into kronen, dinars, zloty, levi or rubles, worked wonders in the old country. Year after year they ameliorated millions of family and individual crises, and thus smoothed out many a political wrinkle, abated many a political storm in many a European country. They relieved dire social conditions which would otherwise have produced gradual political changes. For decades they were instrumental in keeping in power the traditionalized, conservative ruling classes incapable of any other dynamic action than war. They were partly responsible for the leadership of Europe during the last thirty years. They were one reason why progressive and socialist forces could not develop sufficient strength to dislodge it before it brought on the war in 1914: for it is a truism that in the '90s and 1900s the hard-pressed, discontented European either became a social revolutionary or emigrated to America—or hoped to emigrate, which, as I have said, was also effective in keeping him politically innocuous. If he went to America, or could hope to go eventually, the forces of social progress were weakened by the loss of his smoldering protest generated by the conditions of his life—insofar, that is, as it might have been intelligently directed by progressive leaders.

The dollars which immigrants sent from America spread their balm beyond the family, beyond the village; they penetrated the entire economic life of the old countries. Yugoslavia, for instance, even after emigration to the United States was restricted, received from her people there from twenty to forty million dollars a year. This sum was a boon to the Belgrade regime. It helped

to keep it in power. It enabled the government to pay
foreign debts and the interest on them, cover trade bal-
ances, maintain the value of its currency on foreign
exchanges, pay its diplomatic corps, and hold taxes
lower than they would otherwise have been.

But eventually the United States was compelled by
its own internal problems to efface its world-famous
"Welcome" sign almost completely. In 1932, for instance, only thirty-five thousand immigrants were admitted, compared to over a million twenty years earlier.
Most of the thirty-five thousand, moreover, were wives
and children of men already established in the United
States. In '33 many more foreign-born returned to Europe, both voluntarily owing to the Depression and by
deportation, than came in as immigrants seeking a per-
manent home. This was before Hitler created the great
refugee problem; since 1935 the bulk of new immigrants
have been people forced to leave Europe overnight in
order to save their very lives. . . .

Also the thirteen million foreign-born in the United
States were hard hit by the Depression and were therefore unable to send their relatives as much money as
formerly; many stopped the remittances entirely.

That the United States had all but pulled down its
"Welcome" sign and that its great expansion drive was
stalled in a depression were facts important to Europe
when I was there in the early 1930s, and they had doubtless been serious for years. A sharp realization was grip-
ping the minds of the "wretched refuse . . . the home-
less . . . the tempest-tost." Something had gone wrong

with their dream. America could not take them and they must stay at home.

I suspect that this devastating realization was one of the main recruiting agents for Hitler's storm troops in Germany and for Communist ranks all over Europe. Young people, among them some of the finest, most eager and energetic human material in Europe, suddenly veered to extremist ideologies and causes—to violence. Their minds and instincts told them that any social progress—long postponed by the syphoning off of people like themselves to America—had now to be brought about quickly if they were to enjoy it in their lifetime.

These sudden tendencies to the extreme, and the reactions they engendered, produced new leaders everywhere; Hitler was merely the most able and successful, working in the likeliest country. He was but the most obvious symptom of the European disease—the disease that is a sort of madness born of mass and individual anxiety, a desperate attempt to catch up with problems which the World War, with its resultant Versailles Treaty and four or five new national states, had only aggravated: basically they had all existed for generations. To mention but one problem: it is a scientific fact that each active mature male requires three to four thousand calories a day to sustain physical and mental health, and a sedentary female twenty-five hundred calories, while most Europeans were getting far fewer. . . .

A blind figure in the darkening maze, King Alexander of Yugoslavia, with whom I talked in March 1933, was afflicted with the contemporary European disease, as were many other South Slavs and some of the Hungarian,

Czech, Polish, Rumanian and Austrian politicians, jour-
nalists and "intelligentsia" whom I met about the same
time. They had will and energy, and were capable of
ideas, but they were trapped, up against it, on the defensive; attack, destruction seemed to many the only
action possible, the only way out.

Without admitting it, the upper crust was frightened
stiff—into idiocy. A banker appointed to Yugoslavia's
sham Senate by the dictator, King Alexander, admitted
to me casually one day that, yes, overpopulation in the
Balkans and elsewhere in Europe was a serious matter.
What was needed was another war. It had to come—
"there are too many of us. America has slammed the
door; so, my dear sir, what can we do? If poison gas
were used on a large scale, perhaps fifteen or twenty
million men would be killed, solving temporarily the
most pressing European problems."

Later I quoted him to a journalist who had just ended
a two-year assignment covering the League of Nations
at Geneva. He remarked that such statesmanship was
not uncommon in Europe.

The Europe of the '30s was whirling in a vortex.

There was the intense fear and sound resentment of
rapidly growing numbers of individuals who wanted to
remain individuals against the steady convergence of
European affairs which, on its way to a super-crisis, was
pushing them into a negative homogeneity, a uniformity
of plight, a mass surge toward a chaotic future. It was
violating their selfhood, their sense of individual identity.

They were essentially the best Europeans, these fearful and resentful people. They belonged to all nations and economic levels; they were the potential balance of power in the situation. But with their fear and resentment—and little or nothing else that counted at the moment—they but heightened and hastened the climax they feared and resented.

They were in the vortex. There was no escape.

Let me stress: not the least of the factors in the complex European situation in the '30s and before was the abrupt closing by the United States of the century-old vent and the consequent intensification of long-neglected problems in an asphyxiating Europe.

Apparently at odds but actually closely connected with the two preceding ideas—that America is an escape from Europe, and that it was Europe's vent—is the further idea that the "old country" has had an enormous share in the formation of most Americans' mentality and emotions. The "old country" is present in us all, particularly in times of international crises—and very particularly right now in 1941.

Professor Horace M. Kallen was on the trail of this truth when he said that "the United States is a young country with old memories." The Gaiser story shows it clearly. And it inheres in thousands of statements sent me by immigrants. It does not, in the overwhelming majority, impinge upon loyalty to the United States; but rather deepens it, infusing it with a more profound meaning.

The "old country"—the "homeland," the "Mother Country," the "fatherland"—is important not only in the psychology of immigrants. At critical times England is as alive in the minds and feelings of many old-stock Americans as is, say, Rumania in the minds and feelings of many Rumanian immigrants and some of their American-born children. I know Anglo-Saxon Americans in the seventh and eighth generation who never took the least interest in King Carol's relations with Madame Lupescu, but who suffered almost a personal shame when the King Edward-Wally Simpson affair broke on the world.

That the American people have fought two wars against the British, that their diplomatic relations with London have not always been the best in times of peace, and that there has always been an acute trade rivalry between the two countries, are relatively slight factors in many old-stock Americans' attitude toward the "Mother Country" even in normal times. The difficulties of the past are like family quarrels, to be swept aside in times of emergency, particularly in these critical days when the very existence of England is threatened. Also of small weight is the memory of England's role at Munich and in the whole of Europe prior to that awful episode. I am sure that even those who reacted to Munich as did Humphrey Cobb have now forgiven if not wholly forgotten.

The numerous aid to Britain movements did not get going primarily because Hitler menaced the Western Hemisphere, because he might get hold of the British Fleet and thus place the United States squarely in the middle of the most terrible predicament of its history— but simply because vast masses of the dominant old-line-American strain reacted instantly and passionately to England's sudden and extreme danger—England: the home of Magna Carta, of Shakespeare and of Milton and Keats and Shelley, of the King James version of the Bible; their imperishable "home." It did not matter that Hitler was in part a creation of British diplomacy, that the war was Britain's fault almost as much as any other nation's. What did matter terrifically was that Hitler was bombing London, Dover, Southampton and Plymouth; that he threatened to invade the island and subjugate its people, whom he had led into a trap. When Churchill began to utter his honest, dramatic phrases, when the R.A.F. beat off the Luftwaffe and the people in English cities behaved so greatly in their ordeal, the Anglo-Saxon Americans' most vital chords were touched.

Many of the rest of us in the United States strongly sympathized with Britain's plight and stood in admiration before her newly regained soul. With us non-Anglo-Saxon Americans it was not a matter of blood, of direct heritage. We admired the R.A.F. boys, the Londoners, and the aptness of Churchill's eloquence, but with many of us the paramount consideration was not England or Britain and her empire, but the safety of the United States. I know this was my own reaction in June 1940, and I know it was so with hundreds of my non-Anglo-Saxon American correspondents and friends. Few of us read Alice Duer Miller's *The White Cliffs*; it was the old-line Americans who made that poem a national best seller and who thrilled to it when it came over the radio.

It was an old-stock American, Governor Robert O. Blood of New Hampshire, who in mid-February of 1941, presenting John G. Winant, the newly appointed Ambassador to the Court of St. James, to his State Legislature, called him "the man who is going over to represent us in our fatherland." Seven members of the Legislature protested to the Governor that England was not "our fatherland," that "we Americans cannot have two fatherlands"; but the Governor, so far as I know from the press, made no reply. Nor were there any other repercussions worth noting. The official reference to "our fatherland" by the Chief Executive of their State was all right with New Hampshire's dominant, articulate element.

Anglo-Saxon Americans and their closest kin in point of heritage, the Welsh, Scotch, and Scotch-Irish Americans, have exerted much effort to "Americanize the foreigners," as they are in the habit of calling continental immigrant groups. Their chief aim was to wean them away or abruptly disconnect them somehow from their "old countries." Not that the "Americanizers" knew very much about them; they were "foreign" lands and therefore not so good, and the newcomers ought to be purged of everything that smelled of them.

This sort of "Americanization" seemed to work with some immigrants, but fortunately by no means with most. Where it worked, the "Americanized" foreigner usually did not become an American in any essential way. He merely succeeded in appearing to be no longer what he had been. He became a cultural zero paying lip service to the United States, which satisfied the "Americanizers," most of whom were unconsciously only after appearances anyhow. He was a man drained of his own history, with no inner continuity.

On the other hand, "Americanization"—with its narrow definition of Americanism, and its demand that everybody remodel himself to fit into it—was instinctively resented. It only strengthened the non-Anglo-

Saxon immigrants' natural, inevitable impulse to form "colonies" of their own—"foreign sections," the old-line Americans called them—which were partial carry-overs of the "old country." As immigrants poured in they segregated themselves in hundreds of Little Bohemias and Little Italys, Germanias, Hungaricas, Polonias, Slovenias, Hunkytowns, Finntowns, Wop Roosts, and ghettos—for the same obvious reason that Iowa continues to be important to Iowa farmers and small-town folk who have moved to Southern California, where they now enjoy Iowa Society meetings and picnics. In fact many Iowans in Los Angeles are more conscious of their home state than they were in Iowa.

This has always been true of people in "foreign" colonies. Many came from politically oppressed lands. Here they found freedom. By and large, they could do what they liked, even though some "Americans" disapproved. They subscribed to foreign-language newspapers. They joined fraternal and cultural societies. These were American newspapers and American organizations; they were started here for immediate, practical purposes by people who intended to remain in America. But since they were founded by and for groups who had come from Poland or Croatia or Armenia or Italy, they had strong old-country underpinnings and overtones, and they were called "Polish," "Croatian," "Armenian" and "Italian" papers, societies and clubs.

Sometimes the immigrants started more newspapers and organizations than they actually needed, for it was something to be free to do so. Also it was something to be an editor or publisher, or a president or secretary.

This produced rivalries which in turn led, among other things, to an overemphasis upon the "old country." It was a sentiment that editors and officials found easy to play on. For the act of leaving his native land had already enhanced its psychological importance to the average immigrant.

It is a proclivity of the human spirit to dwell on pleasant experiences; and when our immediate surroundings leave something to be desired, we are apt to invest the past with illusory happiness. From the beginning, we left Europe because we didn't like it there. When we got here, however, most of us stepped into anything but a utopian environment, and our memory began to tinge past events with more pleasure and less pain than they gave us at the time they occurred.

When the Pilgrims plunged into the New England wilderness and encountered extreme hardships, their minds went back usually to the agreeable things in England or to those which they began to remember as agreeable. The peasant immigrant from Eastern Europe who suddenly found himself in the industrial jungle of Pittsburgh recalled chiefly the good aspects of his native village. His nostalgic propensity then enlarged the virtues of his homeland, and thus he acquired a somewhat fanciful "old country" which he enjoyed in his daydreams or when he talked with fellow immigrants over a pail of beer. Had he been threatened, say, with deportation, his recollections of the "old country" would very likely have rapidly shifted.

Then too he had a touch of guilty conscience. Having escaped from Europe's inadequacies, he felt badly over the people he left behind; and to soothe his conscience, as well as to rationalize his failure to send them more money than he did, he told himself little by little that things weren't so bad "back home" after all.

Again, he remembered mostly the nice things and compared them with the least attractive aspects of his circumstances in America. The villagers in the "old country" did not have to breathe smoke and dust that enveloped Pittsburgh; they smelled clean air and looked on green fields and meadows. . . .

The editors of his newspapers and the leaders of his organizations, themselves nostalgic and therefore selective in their remembrance, exploited the average immigrant's homesickness for all it was worth to them, him and the "old country." In print and in picnic speeches they told him about the glories of his background . . . and about the unjust centuries-long sufferings of his people "back home," keying him up to become a "patriot" and to give money for the "old country" cause. Usually he gave . . . and thereby also salved his guilty conscience over having escaped from Europe while his kin remained there.

Meanwhile the perturbed "Americanizers," watching all this without understanding, prompted naturalization judges to caution new citizens to forget Greece, Italy, Bulgaria, Poland, Sweden, Finland and Hungary. But it had little effect—such things do not depend upon reason. They are bred in the bone, as the conduct of a Pennsylvania judge with Welsh blood demonstrated. After a regulation admonitory lecture to a group of Slavic and Italian immigrants he had just sworn in as citizens, His

Honor spoke glowingly of Wales at a public dinner given by a Welsh American society at which special Welsh dishes were served.

Groups from countries under foreign or oppressive rule founded special newspapers and organizations to work toward the liberation of their native lands. The people in these movements were both aliens and naturalized citizens; the activity of the latter on behalf of the "old country" probably did not seem to make them more effectively American, but neither did it seriously interfere.

It implied no disloyalty to the United States. By and large it was good. In a way it was a compliment to America. Here was freedom; and these people felt free to feel ardent. Naturally they could feel ardent only about something that was vital within them. They could get excited only about what they knew well, or thought they did: the "old country." Coming here had given them a perspective on the "homeland"; now they felt they could do something about it. They had as yet no perspective on America, and did not presume to know what ought to be done about this country if anything. Many it suited perfectly. So they devoted themselves to the cause of the "old country." . . .

In 1914–19 these American-born movements assumed world importance. They influenced the Allied-American victory. They were instrumental in destroying the German, Austro-Hungarian and Turkish empires, and in the creation of Poland, Czechoslovakia, Yugoslavia,

Finland, Lithuania and—last but not least—the Irish Free State.

Not that they were an unalloyed good from every American angle. For one thing, the Slavic movements added greatly to the anti-German hysteria in the United States which Mr. Gaiser mentions. But they were in a very real if subtle sense genuine *American* movements. They were established here; most of their energy and intelligence gained momentum under the influence of America, in line with the best American traditions, even if they were conducted largely in tongues other than English.

The papers of President Wilson and Colonel House indicate that they realized the nature and importance of these immigrant movements. Lincoln would have understood them. Once he said: "I have often inquired of myself what great principle or idea it was that kept this confederacy so long together. It was . . . that sentiment in the Declaration of Independence which gave liberty not alone to the people of this country, but hope to all the world, for all future time."

These movements and the immigrant's nostalgia for the "old country" caused him to talk to his American-born children about "how it was back home." The majority of the young people did not seem very much interested at the time. Some appeared a little uneasy. Sometimes they were apt to ask why he had ever left such a wonderful country to come to this shabby neighborhood in Wilkes-Barre or Youngstown.

But often his nostalgic talk had a profound effect, to appear later.

In the 1920s and early '30s a great many older immigrants ceased to worry about the countries of their birth—at least insofar as they were aware. They felt they had done their bit, having helped to free them; now they meant to be Americans. Their native-American children wished even more strongly to shed whatever stamped them as "foreigners." And gradually, in conjunction with other forces which I shall not mention here, the "foreign sections" began to break up . . . or so it seemed.

What prompted this was somewhat negative. It came from the to-hell-with-Europe attitude, which is kin to the old-stock Anglo-Saxon Americans' superficial attitude of to-hell-with-England, or the Westerners' to-hell-with-the-East! It came also of inferiority feelings, especially in the sons and daughters of immigrants who were hell-bent to turn themselves—somehow—into standard Americans. Many changed their names and "passed" as Anglo-Saxons, but few were happy about it.

Abreast of this, however, there began the contrary tendency to look back to one's beginnings and heritage. Thomas Wolfe called it in another context: "Look Homeward, Angel." Thousands of young Americans of recent-immigrant derivations started to replace their shame with pride about being "Finns," "Swedes," "Wops" and "Hunkies"; they read up on their parents' old homeland or took trips abroad and visited their folks' native villages. Some got terribly excited about what they discovered and became almost chauvinistic "Finns," "Swedes," "Poles" and "Czechs"; then they slowly settled down into a balanced feeling about their backgrounds and became matter-of-fact Americans of Finnish, Swedish, Czech, Polish (etc.) descent.

Of course most immigrants, whether naturalized or not, kept up a close interest in the "old country" right along. But their numbers were decreasing. More and more they fell into the mood: let Europe get on as best it can without me; I'm busy *here*. They took on the traditional American isolationism; in many cases with a vengeance. They were ready for it. They had come to America to get away from European conflicts. They acquired some of the fear of the "Americanizers"—the fear that Europe was coming over and might ball up America—the fear of the escaped European: that Europe might catch up with them.

With Hitler's ascent to power, however, the to-hell-with-Europe trend turned sharply. America in general became absorbedly interested in the old continent, and the new-immigrant groups focused their anxiety on their respective old countries. The "old country" still meant something to them; in fact as much as ever. Even the second and third generations were affected by every new episode in the Old World.

The resurgent attention to the old "homelands" reached its first climax at Munich; its second at the invasion of Poland; its third during the fatal spring of 1940. Since then it has swept the country, seizing upon almost all Americans regardless of background.

Now millions of Americans are aware—many acutely —that they are Anglo-Saxon, Irish, German, Jewish, Italian, Czech, Slovak, Slovenian, Croatian, Serbian, Polish, Hungarian, Finnish, Swedish, Norwegian, Dutch, Lithuanian, Rumanian, Ukrainian, Armenian, Greek, Syrian Americans — Americans without a hyphen; "Czech" in "Czech American," for instance, is only an adjective. It means that this particular American stems from the Czech nation but is not of it in any sense which hampers his being an American.

Millions of other Americans have become conscious that their blood is mixed. But I have noticed that Americans with, say, French and German ancestors are inclined to stress the French strain.

No groups are more conscious of their background than are the German and Italian American. Many are self-conscious, uncomfortable about it; a few pugnacious. But many too—Wendell Willkie, for example, or Professors Arthur Schlesinger and Taylor Starck of Harvard, or Dean Christian Gauss of Princeton, or Judge Ferdinand Pecora—are quite at ease as German or Italian Americans most of the time.

Off and on something moves in native Americans of new-immigrant origin even in normal times. Usually quite suddenly. Something extremely deep and so subtle that even the most intelligent do not quite understand it. They are mystified by it. The experience of Judge Otto Kerner of the United States Circuit Court of Appeals in Chicago, who is a son of Czech immigrants, is a case in point.

He told me that when, in the course of a trip to Europe in the late 1920s, he crossed the border from Austria into Bohemia, which he had never seen before, tears suddenly filled his eyes. "I don't know what it was," he said.

I think it was simply that blood is not water; also that while growing up in Chicago he had heard a great deal of talk about Bohemia, much of it nostalgic, by his parents and their neighbors . . . and probably by his friend, the late Mayor of Chicago, Tony Cermak.

That the "old country" complex is strong in Americans of the oldest stock, as well as in the newest citizens, was recently illustrated for me by my friend Ross Wills. For many years a Californian, he was born and raised in Missouri. But his paternal forebears had lived in Kentucky for generations. This summer Ross visited Kentucky for the first time in his life, and this is the way he describes the trip:

"As you know, I love Missouri; no other state could displace it in my affections. But I had the strangest, most unexpected experience recently in Kentucky. Driving East, I decided on a mere impulse to come through Kentucky, perhaps just to try a Louisville mint julep. My people had come from there, but I wasn't thinking particularly about that. As a kid in Clay County, Missouri, I had been too active and too much concerned in my own affairs to listen very acutely to any family stories about life in pioneer Kentucky. Moreover, I have never been very 'family' conscious, save for a certain regard for my paternal grandmother who died at ninety-five several years ago. . . .

"I crossed the river just east of Poplar Bluff, and was in Kentucky. It was about eleven in the evening, but there was a full moon and it was a clear, calm night. 'Well,' I reflected, 'so this is Kentucky; this is where that Wills clan came from—some eighty years ago; why, it looks just like Missouri.'

"But I began unconsciously to drive more slowly. As you well know, I am the least sentimental of persons, certainly not susceptible to the vagaries of the moonlight! I had planned to hurry, I was tired, and wanted to get up to Paducah and to bed. But something more powerful than I was slowing me down to a stop.

"I pulled up by the side of the road, and got out of the car and stood there and looked out over the land of my forebears. I had never been in Kentucky before, but it was here that my father was born, and his father, and his father before him, and my father's mother and her mother. . . . I climbed through a 'bob-wahr' fence and went over and sat down in a field. The moon hung over a border of trees at the edge of the field, and a pure-white cloud shaped like an enormous arrowhead was drifting by. . . .

"The past is but a moment back!

"I had come back to a place where I 'belonged,' and never expecting it, or being consciously prepared for it, had sensed it almost at once and felt it overpoweringly. No European able to trace his own heritage back in a straight line in the same land for twenty generations could possibly feel more 'at home' than I felt on this occasion. . . .

"There is some deep force in man that relates him intimately to his real, his only source, the earth; and, uniquely, to the particular part of the earth where he originated, where his forebears lived. . . . If we could grasp and comprehend this force, if we could adequately understand our heritage—in whatever land it lie—we might even realize civilization in the world."

The Armenian poet Eliche Charentz expressed the power of the "old country" in his poem "To Armenia," well-known among Armenian immigrants in the United States and their American-born children. I find a translation of it—by Hope Kassabian, a native American—in the August 13, 1941, *Armenian Mirror-Spectator* (New York):

Armenia mine, 'tis well I love thy sweet, sun-flavored name,
Thy time-aged zither's saddened tones I love,
Thy fragrance of thy blood-red roses sets my heart aflame,
Thy demure maidens' graceful dance I love.
Dear to my eyes thy deep blue skies, thy waters, rippling
*   clear,*
Thy crystal lakes, thy summer sun, and winter's hissing
*   storm,*
The humble, blackened walls of thy thatched huts to me are
*   dear,*
Thine ancient cities' rocks, which all the ages could not harm.
Roam where I may, I'll ne'er forget thy sad-toned songs and
*   airs,*

Thine aged, sacred books, their very letters changed to
  prayers,
Pierced be my heart, no stabbing wound my loyalty can kill.
Orphaned, bleeding and sore distressed, I love Armenia still.
No other legend fair my aching heart can ever soothe,
Like Naragatzi's and Koochag's there's no other haloed
  brow.
In all the world, like Ararat no mount's so white and
  smooth,
The glorious road to Massis' icy peak I long for now.

The European-American Idea of Unity
Within Diversity

I want to mention another thing about Judge Otto Kerner.

He is one of the ten or eleven highest-ranking judges in the United States. He is a leading citizen of Chicago and the Middle West. He is at home in Chicago, in Illinois, in the United States. He is an American. This is his country. . . . A man with an interesting mind and social charm, he goes out a great deal, is always at ease.

"But, you know," he told me, "I enjoy myself best when I get together with people whose background is Czech. When I'm with them, there is something special for me in the atmosphere. A group of us Czech Americans have a little organization; we meet every now and then, and without fail I have a good time, although nothing much ever happens. The way things are said or done evokes deep down in me an echo which is not something you can put your finger on but is completely satisfying. . . . I am, of course, not reflecting on any of my non-Czech American friends. I know that some of them who are Polish or Jewish or old-stock or German Americans have essentially the same experience in their own group. . . . It probably is the way it ought to be."

There is a close connection between Judge Kerner's emotion when he stepped on Czech soil and the differ-

74

ence in his feeling which rises from being with Czech Americans or with those of other strains. The fact of the matter is that he *is* a Czech American and therefore naturally different from non-Czech Americans.

And that is all to the good.

What Judge Kerner told me about himself is, I think, a vivid illustration of the importance of the "old country." I know there are people in the United States who will be uneasy about it. But they will be wrong. Working in Judge Kerner—and in millions of other Americans —is the simultaneous two-way disposition of man toward homogeneity or unity and toward its opposite. I say "its opposite"; and they are opposite in point of direction. But this two-way impulse springs from one central source. It is essentially the age-old search for a balance point between the claims of the individual and those of society.

Consider a thermometer. "Hot" is the opposite of "cold," yet who can mark the point at which absolute heat becomes absolute coldness. If it is difficult of a relatively objective thing like temperature, how much harder is it to indicate the boundary between heterogeneity and homogeneity. My guess is there is no boundary; they interpenetrate, they are interdependent. The problem is to encourage the flowering of valuable individual qualities and impulses without impairing the equally valuable functioning of those we hold in common. In other words: the problem lies in finding the point of balance between the two so neither will be crushed.

In an essay entitled "The Unity of Europe" in the

April *Atlantic Monthly*, José Ortega y Gasset discusses
this two-way human disposition as it appears to him in
the Old World. He says in effect it is Western man's
everlasting impulse to seek a common ground with
others unlike him, to pool his ideas, manners and en-
thusiasms with theirs, and at the same time to hold onto
his own particular values and characteristics. It is his
wont to jump like an acrobat "endlessly back and forth
between the affirmation of plurality and the recognition
of unity."

I believe Ortega y Gasset is wrong in limiting his
concept to Western man. I think it is a general human
impulse. It exists in China and Japan as well as in England and Belgium. I know firsthand that it exists in
Chinese and Japanese (*nisei*) Americans.

It was this human two-way impulse which, with other
things I have mentioned, enabled the new immigrant to
resist "Americanization" drives. His attachment to the
"old country," or to his magnification of it, was an instinctive means to evade being pushed into the standard-
izing Melting Pot under which some hasty, frightened
old-stock Americans had built a fire. It was an unconscious, traditional stratagem against designs to fry his
individuality, his notions, his passions out of him.

Often the new immigrant, the escaped European of
the last several decades, made an unfavorable impression on Anglo-Saxon, early-Dutch, Welsh and Scotch-
Irish Americans who had staked out priority claims, and
who regarded themselves as standard Americans. They
thought him a contrary-like creature. Sometimes he
seemed to refuse to learn English. Sometimes he did not

become a citizen. Generally speaking, however, even when he seemed most ill-mannered and "ungrateful" to those who strove to overhaul him quickly and neatly into a standard Anglo-Saxon American, he was anything but opposed to unity. Indeed he yearned for unity: that is implicit in many of his statements to me. He was not always consistent; he had his misgivings and deviations; but essentially he was for American unity or any other kind, even world unity.

But he meant *unity*, not uniformity. He was against uniformity.

I say he "meant *unity*," but of course not necessarily in his head. He was usually not educated, not an intellectual, not used to stating his views and giving his reasons. Perhaps he was just a peasant, or only what I have called a village proletarian. But often he was a very definite person. Like Popeye the Sailor, he was what he was, and he meant what he meant with his manner, his eyes, his bones; with the way he was put together.

He was for *unity within diversity*, as distinct from uniformity which usually means what is left of you after you have been under pressure to change and you have yielded; as distinct, that is, from standardized mediocrity which—anticipating Hitler—was the unconscious aim of ill-conceived, fear-motivated, "Americanization" drives. Unity within diversity is not only an old American practice with continuous, if imperfect, results; it is, as Ortega y Gasset points out, also a European practice of long standing, with sharp ups and downs, and so far without success. This is due, I believe, to the apparent inability of Europeans till now to synchronize the two simultaneous impulses toward homogeneity and heterogeneity.

The interplay of unity within diversity is the source of vitality and originality in the human world; it underlies the ideals of freedom, justice, democracy; but it is extremely difficult in conscious practice. Its paradoxical nature needs recognition.

This paradox has been operating in Europe, says Ortega y Gasset, for two thousand years, ever since the "swarm of Western peoples . . . set out on its flight through history from the ruins of the ancient world." There was a steady increase of European homogeneity, which eventually inspired Montesquieu's remark that "Europe is only a nation made of several" and Balzac's about "the great continental family whose efforts reach toward I know not what mystery of civilization." At the same time there was in Europe an increase of differences, out of which came most of the Old World's cultural stirrings. In fact, as "a crowning paradox of this destiny," the growing European homogeneity augmented its heterogeneity, for "in this case the two were not alien. On the contrary, every new unifying principle served to fertilize [the] diversity. The idea of Christianity engendered the national churches; the memory of the Roman *imperium* inspired the various forms of the state; the renaissance of letters in the fifteenth century let loose divergent literatures; science as the unitarian concept of man as 'pure reason' created the different intellectual styles which were to lend their mould even to the farthest abstractions of mathematics. And as a culminating point, even the extravagant eighteenth-century idea of prescribing an identical constitution for all peoples resulted in the romantic awakening of the differential consciousness of the nationalities, and thus served to push each towards its particular vocation."

To put it another way: Unifying concepts and developments were adapted by the various countries to fit their different backgrounds. Then they jelled in separate, different molds. But, thus divided, they no longer added up to the initial whole.

To put it in still another way: we may both listen to the same sentence; we may agree that we understand it. But because the experiences which have made me are not those which have made you, we are different from each other and the meaning I get from the sentence will not be quite the same as the one you get—although the words we hear are identical.

Similarly, while the paradox went on working its wonders in cultural matters, the growing differences within each nation simultaneously inspired a violent impulse to create and then maintain a definite, rigid government and a standardized national attitude. Unfortunately, the impulse to homogeneity somehow failed to produce clear, feasible, organic ideas for a pan-European setup. And now "European society as a whole . . . is obviously less advanced than that of its component parts, the nations."

Ortega y Gasset vents his great distaste for the demagogues who have been in charge of European nations in recent years, including of course Hitler who is in control of almost the whole continent at this writing. But Ortega seems to consider that the demagogues would not have arisen had it not been for the "revolt of the masses," to which he, an upper-class European aristocrat, objects.

I think "the revolt of the masses" against poverty and frustration was inevitable and not anything to bemoan. The current crisis cannot be blamed on the "masses." Besides, why waste time looking for those to blame. The crisis is here; the critical question is: how are we going to deal with it?

Señor Ortega has one answer which I consider sound. He predicts "a possible, a probable unification of the states of Europe," but gives no hint when or how that tremendous step is to be brought about.

America had a share in the European progression toward the present crisis. America was Europe's vent. It drained Europe of its most actively discontented, which is to say its most dynamic, unfatalistic people. It thus helped to continue in power the intellectually bankrupt classes in Europe. They in turn brought on the futile but disastrous First World War in which were killed off some of the best potential leadership for two decades. This step in the vicious process cleared the way for Hitler and his ilk.

I must also return to my ideas about America as an escape from Europe and about the importance of the "old country" to the United States. Concern over the "old country" was largely responsible for our getting into the First World War. We helped to win that war; we even gave Europe the concept of the League of Na-

tions; then the escapism—isolationism—in us impelled
us to withdraw instead of helping the Old World, for
our sake as much as its own, to construct a practicable
continental system of government.

But, as I have also said, there is no escape from anything—not really, not in the long run. Things catch up
with an escapist country as well as with any escapist individual. Europe has caught up with America once
more. Europe is upon us. We are again neck-deep in the
whole difficulty. Inextricably.

Now ——

Now we'd better not try to escape from it. In fact,
we'd better go into it much further than we did in 1917–
'18, not only to rub out Hitler and his "new order" (that
is a detail), but to help the Old World—and help ourselves at the same time—to organize itself so that it can
be at once diverse and united: in short, human. If we
try to escape again, our chances for remaining diverse
under the same flag will swiftly vanish. And then the
only possible homogeneity will be that of general chaos.

EUROPE IN AMERICA

The Psychological Civil War

If any country has the right to call itself a democracy, it is the United States. I am aware of course of numerous undemocratic phenomena in American civilization. But certainly this country is what Henri Bergson called an "open society"—one in which all things are possible, the best imaginable and the worst.

There is freedom here backed by a long and strong tradition. No other people has ever been freer for as long a period of time. Aside from the potential effect upon us of extreme international changes, we Americans are free within the bounds of natural laws to do what we wish with the immense land between the Atlantic and the Pacific, between Mexico and Canada. We are free, within psychological laws, to make what we wish of ourselves. We can continue and improve our democratic system, our open society, or we can let it degenerate and forfeit our freedom. We have these two tremendous alternatives.

Our system is largely dependent on the character and intelligence of the individual. The average American was well able to cope with the problems of life when there were still physical frontiers. Now that they have vanished, his character and intelligence—his ability—must rise to cope with other problems. Should he fail, he will rapidly lose his free or "open" society. An inferior citizenry is bound to hand over its rights and duties to demagogues and "bosses," and in so doing to sacrifice "government of the people, by the people, and for the people."

About the middle 1930s—as I traveled about, meeting people on Main Street, Tobacco Road, Park Avenue, Pennsylvania Avenue and in side alleys and rural corners and crossroads, at roadside camps, in factory towns and in "foreign sections"—it began to appear to me that there was a slackening in the character, intelligence, standards and purposes of too many Americans in all walks of life, of all strains and backgrounds. It was nothing you could put your finger on or translate into headlines. It was intangible but, nonetheless, I thought it was there.

I tried to get at it with the help of various terms and concepts. It was a deep confusion; vast numbers of people didn't know whether they were going or coming. It was the Depression. We were in what the pundits called a transition, the end of one epoch and the beginning of another. Sociologists talked of "social lags"; others of the collapse of old-fashioned religion and morality. Why the country was going to the dogs was explained by the 1917–'18 war, "Coolidge prosperity," and all the other things of "only yesterday." Industrialism was the villain of the "Southern agrarians," some of whom lived in Greenwich Village or on the campus at Princeton and North Carolina. Some blamed whatever didn't seem quite right to them on the "revolt of the masses," and on the New Dealers who insisted on the "general welfare" mentioned in the Constitution; on relief, on That Man, on the Supreme Court, on the C.I.O. and the Communists ――――

Most of these theories and hunches had something in them. American society *was* in a terrific flux; almost anything you said about it was apt to be true. It was not only an "open society" but wide open. This was bound to continue; America was a process, a continual revolution. Essentially and in many details it was all right. But when a thing like America gets going only-God-knows-where at an accelerating speed, and at a time when much of the rest of the world is about to commit both murder and suicide, there are dangers ahead.

Economic and industrial problems, labor, education, trends in writing, the theater, architecture and other arts were attracting a lot of attention. They interested me too. But little heed was paid in print and on the platform to the United States as a conglomerate of peoples —the result of a vast migration. Little attention was directed to the intricacies and maladjustments which grew up in its train. There was little realization that in the process cultures were being shattered.

This last fact appeared to me most important. The old-stock American cultural patterns of a hundred years ago clashed with the Old World ways (as revised by the slum and the factory) of new-immigrant groups and partially destroyed them. It was a negative business. Many values, both old-American and new-immigrant, were not adjusted to the needs of contemporary America. Nor did they fuse or merge. They were simply ground out, pushed aside, scrapped, without giving rise to new values. They either went down through lack of character, through irresponsibility and vulgarity, or they were clung to desperately, in toto—and thus perverted and devitalized. They became a stubborn, crystallized defense of "foreign sections" and Boston's Back Bay alike.

This negativeness, this defensiveness worried me. It could lead only to "against" attitudes in all sorts of other situations. Yet it was largely traceable to the sound, simultaneous, paradoxical human impulse toward diversity and homogeneity. What had gone wrong?

The difficulty was complicated. It looked different from different angles. It could be said to have begun with the "Americanization" which attempted to turn "foreigners" into imitation old-stock Americans. (Jonathan Daniels, in his *A Southerner Looks at New England* has called the Yankees the most "unassimilable" element in the country.) Or it could be said that it began with the "foreigners'" stubborn tenacity which led them to bristle against the very idea of so narrow an "Americanization."

However it came about, the "Americanization" idea and the immigrants' reaction to it became part of the American atmosphere. The "foreigners'" defensive refusal to try to become "standard" Americans put many old-stock Americans on the defensive too. The result has been an American psychological civil war, which is a *sitzkrieg* most of the time with frequent outbursts of the anti-alien, anti-Semitic, anti-old-stock-American *blitz*.

Like the peoples of Europe, we in America have not yet completely synchronized the two-way impulse to homogeneity and diversity. We have experienced both but, as our sporadic psychological civil war with its several fronts demonstrates, we have not achieved a steady, continuous balance between them. When we examine our resemblances we find that one of them is our common against-ness; when we look at our differences, most of them charged with potentialities for good, we see that all too often they function defensively against other differences. ——

Where can this take us?

Basically, I think, it was this that led me into the "Plymouth Rock and Ellis Island" project. I wanted to ask this question. Also I wanted to uncover and publicize any evidences of a positive homogeneity—unity within diversity—which might suggest a productive future.

I came upon an instance of it almost at once.

Early in April 1939 a friend in St. Paul wrote me about the "Festival of Nations" to be given that month under the auspices of the St. Paul International Institute, "an organization which is really doing something about the Plymouth Rock and Ellis Island situation." He urged me to come and see the Festival . . . and I went.

The interior of the City Auditorium, with a capacity of ten thousand, its floor space running from street to street, was transformed into a market square in a composite Old World city of about the year 1850, when modern immigration to America began in earnest. Around the vast open space in the center was a stage-set —one of the largest ever produced—suggesting the architecture of two dozen European and Asiatic countries. A committee of people from different backgrounds decided upon the scheme for the set, which was designed free of charge by a local architect. The books and pictures consulted by subcommittees and individuals during the research period taught them much about their old countries.

The "buildings" and the long winding corridors were filled with booths for the display of old-country wares and symbols, or served as food shops offering 178 different kinds of food as prepared in more than two-score countries which have contributed to the present population of St. Paul. There were thousands of plants given by local florists, nurseries and city parks. The hostesses, cooks, waiters and ushers wore picturesque ancestral costumes. And the sum of it all was an exhilarating hurly-burly of color and movement.

For three days from ten in the forenoon till after midnight crowds moved about the "square" between formal programs, or sat in front of the food shops, eating Southern fried chicken and corn pone, French *crêpe suzettes*, Swedish waffles, Czech *kolace*, Mexican *tamales* and *enchiladas*, Cornish pasties, Norwegian open-face sandwiches, Swiss *kase brotchen*, Polish *barszcs*, Armenian *Lokoom*, Russian caramels, Greek *Keri*, Danish coffee, Finnish *Kallaa*, Scottish shortbreads, Irish *Barm Bracks*, Jewish cheese *blintzes*, Rumanian noodles, Austrian strudel, Italian spaghetti, Hungarian goulash, Chinese sweet and sour pork ribs, Syrian lamb with green beans and rice, German sausages, and Ukrainian *varenycky*, milk served from a Holland dog cart, and American wild rice and ice cream.

Each of the six performances had between one and two thousand participants. Each opened with a parade of the thirty-odd groups comprising the population of St. Paul in the order in which they came to live in the Twin Cities region—Indians, old-stock Americans of the Anglo-Saxon strain, Negroes, the French, Netherlanders, Scandinavians and Finns, the English, Scots, Welshmen, Germans, Jews, the Irish, Italians, Hungarians, Poles, Czechs, Slovaks, Ukrainians, Russians, Croatians, Serbians, Slovenians, Greeks, Mexicans,

Orientals, and the peoples from the Near East. Each group, as it passed the reviewing stand, which contained representatives of all the strains (and at one performance the Mayor and the City Council of St. Paul costumed as burgomaster and city fathers), was announced through amplifiers and given a hand by capacity audiences.

In fact hundreds were turned away. Except for about six thousand participants who had passes, all admissions were paid. The receipts amply covered expenses.

Following the parade were English May Day Dances; songs and stories in the Ojibway Indian sign language; dances, songs, and instrumental music by Ukrainains, Poles, Czechs, Serbians, Greeks, Negroes, Norwegians, Italians, Croatians, Rumanians, Hungarians, and French; songs by Welsh, Finnish, and combined Danish-Swedish-Norwegian choruses; Swiss yodeling, Irish jigs and reels, and Czech *Sokol* and German *Turnverein* drills. In point of beauty—and presage—the most significant number was a dance done simultaneously in three different rhythms to the same piece of Scandinavian music by three distinct groups—one Danish, one Swedish, and one Norwegian. (If stage and screen do not pick up this triptych dance idea, they will be missing something extraordinary.)

Between numbers, an old-stock American woman clad in a German costume of about a hundred years ago led the audience—with the aid of printed music and words— in mass singing of old-stock American, English, Scandinavian, German, Italian, and Slavic songs in the original languages. After the evening show there were two hours of dancing on the "square."

The mood of the Festival was one of spontaneity,

creative freedom, satisfaction in participation: democracy. Hundreds of families—parents, children, grandparents—spent nearly all their waking hours at the Festival.

During an intermission one evening a young lad in a Chinese costume ran into a little Ukrainian-clad boy. They bounced apart and fell over backwards. Then they laughed, got up quickly, embraced for a second, and ran off in different directions—to the audience's cheers.

A little later from the Mexican booth came a guitar-accompanied rendition of the moving peon song *Cuarto Milpas*.

After the show that same night I chanced upon a score of young men dancing the Virginia Reel. One was a Mexican; the others were American-born sons of Scandinavian, Italian, German, Ukrainian, Armenian, Greek and Chinese immigrants, all in costume. They had accepted each other in a spirit far different from the "tolerance" advocated by defensively-minded well-wishers.

The high spot occurred just before the final program. A strolling minstrel with a harmonica started a few people marching around the arena with their hands on the shoulders of the one ahead. Soon several hundred gaily costumed people were serpentining in and out, singing one another's songs. Finally, the hall could not hold them; they went out singing through the stage door, around the Auditorium and through a near-by park, till it was time to go on with the program.

The St. Paul Festival of Nations is a continuing project, managed by the Swedish American woman who started it, Alice Lilliequist Sickels, who has been director of the St. Paul International Institute since 1931.

Mrs. Sickels soon discovered that social case work, clubrooms for "foreigners," English classes and other aids toward naturalization only scratched the surface of "Plymouth Rock and Ellis Island" problems for a few thousand people a year. It was important, but not enough by a long shot. Routine social work did nothing to balance the paradox of simultaneous diversity and homogeneity. It did not touch the atmosphere of prejudice, antagonism, and fear to which all the racial, national, and religious elements (including the old-stock Protestant Americans) in St. Paul were daily contributing in their various ways.

Mrs. Sickels and her associates believed the city's inhabitants should be, somehow, brought together and helped to *accept* one another. Tolerance, which in practice means mostly that you and I refrain from insulting each other, was not enough. The thing to do was to bring all the different strains of contemporary human America together to let us have a look at one another.

The various groups would probably take pride in displaying their talents and treasures—particularly, if the so-called "American community" could be induced to partake in as well as to enjoy such a project. It would have a tonic effect on the city. It would help American-born sons and daughters of immigrants to feel better about themselves, to become more self-reliant, better able to fight their individual battles on the economic front. It might make old-stock American employers better disposed toward the new elements. It might lead to better understanding all around.

The first Festival in '31 was nothing to write home about. Nor the second. Most of the "Americanized" foreign-born were tragically ashamed of their Old World backgrounds. They had been made to feel that to be "good" Americans they must forget their origin. Others were rigidly obstreperous in their group egoism. Many American-born sons and daughters of immigrants, who had been called Dagos, Hunkies, Greasers, Kikes, and Squareheads in their childhood, did not want their parents to put on old-country costumes and perform before an audience which would include old-stock Americans. And many of the latter, resting on their sense of priority, were antagonistic to the whole idea: why encourage "these foreigners" to exhibit their foreignness? But the second Festival was better than the first, doubling the number of participants; and the third, while still falling short, was more successful than the second.

In 1935, wanting every part of every future Festival to be authentic, Alice Sickels visited thirteen Old World countries to study their folkways and folk arts. But most of the ideas were developed by the program committee as the work progressed.

Gradually, in the course of seven or eight years, the blocks that kept people from taking part in the Festival subtly dissolved, and in the process everybody connected with it realized that the show itself was not the thing. The thing was the preparation for the show—the long evenings of committee work when people of many strains really got together; when they discovered and

began to appreciate each other. Methods of working together in a creative enterprise unfolded, and to an increasing number this was a source of growing satisfaction. Eventually, many people of different groups who
met through the Festival became warm personal friends.

The festival idea grew organically out of the developing International Institutes, which exist in fifty-odd
cities all over the United States. But special credit is due
St. Paul: there the Festival, with its long preparatory
periods, became a continuing, inclusive and cumulative
communal affair run by the thirty-two races and groups
which produce it. After a decade it is still *their* Festival.

In 1937 the Festival of Nations Committee, a few of
whom underwrote the venture, determined that, with a
fair amount of luck, in '39 they would "really do something." They "sold" the idea to leaders of new immigrant groups and a large number of old-stock Americans,
to newspapers and schools. Then for two years, two
hundred twenty-seven committees, totaling nearly two
thousand people, worked out the details. Some committees consisted of people of similar backgrounds; the
more important committees, however—scores of them—
included representatives of many different strains and
persuasions. Some met once a month or once a week,
many two or three times a week. Most committee members were also performers (singers, dancers, cooks, ex-
hibitors, etc.) and about three thousand other men and
women, boys and girls came together frequently for
training and rehearsals. All this effort was voluntary,
without expectation of material reward. The only people

to receive a salary were a stenographer, a publicity man, and a photographer. The enterprise was nonprofit.

During the Festival's two-year preparation, events in Europe sharpened cleavages between groups almost everywhere in America, especially in big cities. St. Paul was an exception. There the Munich crisis in 1938 did not unfavorably affect relations even between German and Czech Americans, nor have any of the succeeding crises disturbed the friendly spirit between groups whose relatives abroad are in combat.

The St. Paul Festival enterprise is many things. It is very good fun. It is effective education. In it is the technique of communal self-discovery. Through it, these past ten years, St. Paul has been discovering St. Paul. "My goodness," I heard a woman exclaim, "I didn't realize we had all *this* right here in our city!" People saw for themselves that the heterogeneity of St. Paul (57 per cent foreign-born and of immigrant and mixed parentage) was not a grave handicap but an advantage—potentially a great and exciting advantage. This is an important realization, especially when it reaches the average busy citizen. It opens immense possibilities. It turns the negative homogeneity which exists on the basis of defensive diversity into a positive unity within diversity.

It suggested to the schools of St. Paul a way of breaking down the essentially defensive superiority attitudes of old-stock American and the defensive inferiority feelings of new-immigrant children in their relations with one another. In recent years Neighborhood Festivals and Homeland Exhibits have been held in nearly every public school in the city. Early in 1941, Paul S. Amidon, the St. Paul Superintendent of Schools, said that the influence of the Festivals "encourages those of our students whose parents were born in other lands to see in a new light the background of their fathers and forefathers. . . . They lose the sense of being . . . individuals apart, and feel that they and their families form an integral part of the United States. They get a sense of belonging."

To recapitulate: the Festival of Nations is a subtly effective method of communal self-analysis. It reveals the different parts of the community to the community as a whole; it lessens many suspicious fears hitherto rooted in ignorance under layers of prejudice—prejudice which often is not personal as much as secondhand opinion, usually to be found in a meager, unhealthy community atmosphere.

The Negroes, for example, shared in all parts of the Festival for the first time in 1939. All participants were supposed to be in the costumes their forebears might have worn about 1850. But the Negro group did not want to remind anyone of their ancestral slavery; they preferred contemporary clothes—black choir robes or starched white jackets and aprons. After seeing other groups in peasant and ghetto costumes, however, the leader of the Negro group appeared in the "Americans All" procession in what she called her "mammy clothes." She had shed her defensive inferiority and for the first time really accepted her own background. . . . At the end of the Festival, a Negro said, "We have never felt so completely included before."

There was a boy of Magyar parentage who wore a

Hungarian skirted shepherd costume and danced with vigorous skill the *csárdás* with a Danish American girl, although five years before he had begged his mother not to put on "that funny skirt" and go dancing "that queer foreign dance" where "Americans" would see her. Now on discovering that people thought the Hungarian dance and costume beautiful, he was at ease in a kind of smiling "so what?" attitude—a great step forward for him as a person and as an American. There were lots of similar incidents.

Many participants regretted that their two-year close connection with the Festival was coming to an end. But they hoped to continue their new friendships with people of different backgrounds. Several intermarriages had already taken place. An American-born girl of Syrian parentage remarked that her work with the Festival had made her feel for the first time in her life that she was an American. She had before felt at home only among "Syrians" and had therefore been a "Syrian." Mixing with all the other kinds of Americans made her consciously an American—an American of Syrian blood.

The significance of the St. Paul Festival of Nations lies in this sort of thing. It is a deliberately arranged show, but much more than a show. It includes things no one can arrange; they happen. It becomes real. It stimulates understanding; it breaks down fear; it gives personality a chance to develop organically. It synchronizes the paradoxical two-way impulse, strong in every human being worth his salt: to be like everybody else, yet different.

It furnishes an example to the United States as a whole.

But it has a significance also for Europe. Some of the participants in the show and people in the audience felt this with the peculiarly American mixture of naïveté and insight. I overheard remarks like these:

"Hitler ought to see this—the dope!"

"Go on; all Europe ought to see it. If this show could only go barnstorming through Europe!"

The problems of Europe and America differ considerably. Over there, generally speaking, each different group huddles together in a circumscribed area; while here, aside from large "foreign sections," such as New York's Little Italy or Buffalo's Polonia, Americans of various backgrounds are scattered thinly far and wide over the immense space between the two oceans. Both of these opposites are good *if* Europeans and Americans manage to find ways to make the most of them.

With their extreme and regionalized diversities, Europeans need our help to organize the divergent nations—which have a great deal in common—on a sound economic basis into a great continental political system, which might eventually become a part of a world state, and within which peoples' unique and joint attributes would find their own positive functions on the principle of live and let live.

In this country our political system is basically well-nigh ideal—"the world's best hope," Jefferson called it—but we have a long way to go to set right our economic system. And we have still farther to go in evaluating and employing for positive purposes our divergent backgrounds and the different qualities and ways and religions which stem from those backgrounds.

In this we Americans, we ex-Europeans, will discover that Europe can be of great assistance to us.

In the Spring of 1939

On the way to the St. Paul Festival, I stopped off in Cleveland where I chanced to meet with a group of my friends and fellow immigrants from Slovenia: Janko Rogelj, an insurance agent who devotes most of his energy to Slovenian American cultural affairs; Ivan Zorman, a church organist who is also the leading American poet writing in Slovenian; and three newspaper editors—Vatro Grill of the *Napredek* (Progress), Anton Sabec of *Enakopravnost* (Equality) and Anton Terbovec of *Nova Doba* (New Era).

We talked for hours—of things in America somewhat; but, owing to Hitler's recent seizure of what had been left of Czechoslovakia, mostly of Europe. Newspapers said that Hitler's forces had taken all the government gold out of Prague and were now shipping most of the country's food and other supplies into Germany, while the leaders of the Czech nation—not only government officials, but professors, writers, artists—were being liquidated and the treasures of Czech culture— monuments, old manuscripts, rare books, works of art —were being systematically destroyed.

The "next war" ——

What would it mean to *our* "old country"? All six of us had relatives and friends there. Some of our friends were outstanding men: poets, writers, artists. Couldn't

we do something about them? If Slovenia—a part of
Yugoslavia—went the way of Bohemia, they might be
the first to be killed. I was for creating a committee immediately and getting hold of fifty thousand dollars or
more to bring over—on visitor or artist visas—about
a score of the best Slovenian cultural workers, together
with irreplaceable Slovenian cultural treasures.

Rogelj, Grill, Zorman, Terbovec and Sabec thought
the idea good but impracticable. Where would we get
the money? Would we bring over just the writers and
artists or also their families? What would they do here?
Who would support them?

I thought we ought to constitute a provisional committee to explore the problem. But this was not a good
suggestion. We were all more or less of one stripe in
our thinking; and if we six came out as a committee, the
factions within the "Slovenian element" in America
who held different ideas would refuse to work with us.
And again, where was the money to come from? Few
people are willing to shell out in a hurry for anything
until after the catastrophe.

There were a half-dozen Slovenian-immigrant fraternal or benefit societies, each with resources running
into millions of dollars; couldn't they give five or ten
thousand apiece? That would be difficult, Rogelj told
me; benefit societies are organized under State laws
with rigid bylaws and financial supervision. Hadn't one
or two of them given considerable sums for Spanish
Loyalist relief? Yes; but those donations had had to be
approved by the membership. If I wished to push the
idea, there was only one thing to do: get it approved by

the organizations' executive councils who could then present it before their next conventions, scheduled for late summer or early autumn—too late if the war was to break out in '39, as the six of us agreed was probable, to say the least. But I was cautioned again: organizations like individuals don't give until after disaster occurs. There would be objections to the proposal; there were jealousies among organizations—and, I knew without being told, other difficulties peculiar to "foreign" groups which are ingrown and on the defensive. . . .

Well, we were not getting anywhere. Finally we agreed to think the problem over and discuss it again on my way back from St. Paul. ——

Returning from St. Paul, I stopped in Chicago . . . and saw my friend Vladimir Geringer, a native Chicagoan of Czech-immigrant parentage, whom President Wilson had sent on a mission to Prague in 1919, and who was publisher-editor of *Svornost*, one of the oldest papers in Chicago and one of the largest Czech-language papers in the United States. He began to talk about ex-President Eduard Benes of Czechoslovakia who, after his flight from Prague to London, had come to America to lecture on political science at the University of Chicago.

Geringer thought I ought to meet him . . . and took me to his hotel. The ex-President couldn't see us at once, so Geringer went on with what he had been telling me in the cab. The Czechs and most of the Slovaks in the United States (by which he meant Czech and Slovak

Americans) were organizing again to free the "old country." It was 1914–18 all over again. . . .

There was a fine view from the hotel. It was a windy, clear beautiful spring day. . . .

Benes ——

He must have gone through hell the previous summer and autumn; he must be going through hell now, what with Hitler and von Neurath in the Hradchany Castle. . . . And he doubtless had been one of the best men in Europe during the past ten or fifteen years. This wasn't saying much for him, but—he'd been important, certainly; not only president of Czechoslovakia in recent years, but before that, while foreign minister in Prague, he'd also been President of the Council of the League of Nations. . . . But now, waiting for him, I couldn't help thinking of a trifling circumstance.

In *The Native's Return*, published in '34, I had criticized King Alexander's terror regime in Yugoslavia. A Prague publisher wanted to issue the book in Czech translation, but was compelled to give up the idea: the Foreign Office of the Republic of Czechoslovakia "requested" his firm not to publish my book because it condemned the Yugoslav government. Benes was foreign minister then. No doubt it had been a routine matter of which he'd never heard. But it showed that Czechoslovakia, famous for its democracy, had been playing along with a dictator regime; had been more concerned with Yugoslavia as a government than as a people. It had not been actively interested in democracy in other countries. On the contrary, it had been closely tied to France, within whose ruling class a corrupt clique, including the French General Staff, had—according to a theory widely whispered in Yugoslavia—encouraged King Alexander to become dictator and later supported him. . . .

Of course Masaryk and Benes could not have helped themselves. Theirs had been a small country. It had been on the defensive like all European countries, large and small—even the Third Reich, which had been built up out of Germany's extreme defensiveness, and which was now preying on that weakness in other nations. Aside from certain phases of the Slovak problem, and from a few other such tremendous trifles, Masaryk and Benes had done as well by Czechoslovakia internally as they could have; and from that standpoint, they had been two of the best men in post-Versailles Europe. But the defensive streak in their national problem and in their mentality had pushed them into the thick of the corrupt, self-seeking, bluffing, tyrannical—and fruitless—game of European power politics which only Hitler and perhaps Stalin really knew how to play. In fact, as titular head of the League of Nations, Benes must have been fully aware of it.

He was essentially perhaps a good man, but . . .

Eduard Benes—a small middle-aged man, full of energy, with shrewd eyes and an eager manner, flawlessly barbered and dressed—did not look like a man who was going or had gone through hell. We talked for about half an hour. He mentioned some inside facts about Munich, and I suggested—naïvely—he write up

the story. He shook his head. *Collier's* magazine had
offered him twenty-five thousand dollars for it, but he
could not write it. He implied he had the future of
Czechoslovakia to think about.

I appreciated his position; he was his country's leader
in exile. But I thought that just now—in the spring or
summer of '39—his story might have some effect in
Europe. It might rouse France and England out of their
appeasement apathy.

Benes shook his head again. He was still the diplomat. War would break out in Europe by midsummer or
soon after, he said optimistically; then he would go to
London. The future of Czechoslovakia would depend on
a Franco-British victory. The implication was that he
had to play along with the powers that be in those countries—presumably with Chamberlain and Daladier; the
two men, I thought to myself, who had sold him down the
river at Munich.

I asked Benes if he thought France and Britain would
win the "next war." Benes had no doubt they would; in
fact he was the most optimistic man I had met in years.
What would Russia do? His shoulders moved in a slow
shrug, and he gave a vague answer. How did he visualize
a Hitlerless Europe after the next war? He spoke about
a Federation, the United States of Europe, a continental
system of free autonomous states. "I cannot imagine a
free Czechoslovakia," he said, "except in a free Europe."

But how would Europe be freed? What kind of economic system was necessary to make her free? He answered, "Some form of state socialism." I repeated:
How would a European Federation be brought about?

His answer was unsubstantial. I had difficulty remember-ing it an hour later as I made notes on the interview. It was something to the effect that Hitler and Mussolini were carrying nationalism to such extremes they were discrediting it everywhere. After the war—the "next war"—the peoples of Europe would be glad to get to-gether. I wanted to ask again, "But *how*, Dr. Benes? How will the thing work itself out?"—but didn't. How could he know anyhow? How could anybody know?

Instead I asked him what he thought Yugoslavia's role and fate would be in the "next war"? Benes spoke unfavorably of Belgrade's recent pro-Axis Premier Stoyadinovitch; now, fortunately, the country had a new government . . . and he had no doubt Yugoslavia would get into the war—against Germany.

Then he asked me what the "Yugoslavs in America" were doing about that? I said nothing at all; and men-tioned the committee I was trying to get organized to rescue the artists and writers and the irreplaceable cul-tural treasures of Slovenia before the war began. He nodded. Then he advised me to urge the "Slovenians," "Serbians" and "Croatians" in the United States to begin to consider the future of their old country.

It was a beautiful day outside. It was spring in America.

Also in Europe. ——

In Cleveland I reported most of my interview with Benes to my Slovenian American friends. To his sug-gestion that we "Yugoslavs" in the United States ought to do something with an eye to the future of Yugoslavia, they replied, "What?" They were full of misgivings. How could we "Slovenians" get together with the "Croatians" and "Serbians"? How could we overcome the universal human reluctance to bring out the fire equipment before the fire breaks out?

Caught up in the defensiveness common to all new-immigrant groups but sharper with the smaller ones, they knew more about the difficulties than I did, who was an outsider at the same time that I was one of them. I was discouraged. One of my friends kept asking: What would all those artists and writers do over here? Who would support them?

I said "we"—the potential committee—would keep them alive. Didn't Jewish Americans support thousands of Jewish refugees from Germany? Why couldn't we do the same thing on an infinitely smaller scale? If some of the Slovenian American fraternal lodges voted dona-tions for the Spanish Loyalists, why couldn't they give for this idea?

As to what the Slovenian artists and writers would do here—I thought of the St. Paul Festival of Nations. They could go to "Slovenian colonies" all over the United States. They would lecture, paint, mingle with people; teach them the valuable attributes of the old country, and learn from our immigrants and their American-born children what the United States means to them: what America is in human terms. Thus, I said, both countries would benefit. After the war the poets and artists would return to Slovenia with an insight into America and leave the leaven of their presence here. Oton Zupancich, for instance, was a poet who to my mind was comparable in some respects to Keats and Shelley, and in others to Robert Frost, the early Edna St. Vincent Millay and Edwin Robinson. Why not turn him loose among Slovenian Americans for a while? He might not click at all; on the other hand he might perform miracles. He might do what none of the rest of us seemed able to accomplish in a hurry. He knew English, and he might be able to restore self-respect to many young Americans who were uneasy about their immigrant parentage and their Slovenian name. They would become more mature, more balanced, and thus raise the level of American citizenry.

But — but ——

In the end it was decided that I, as an American writer of Slovenian origin, who did not belong to any Slovenian-immigrant organizations and was removed from intra-Slovenian-American jealousies, should send a memorandum to the heads of the large fraternal organizations, outlining the idea and urging the immediate formation of a special representative committee.

I wrote the letter and sent copies to most of the Slovenian-language newspapers in the United States and to a number of editors in Slovenia.

So far as I know, no paper abroad published it; they probably couldn't; but it roused interest by word of mouth.

In the United States it appeared in several Slovenian-language papers, in a few cases with comments by officials of the fraternal organizations publishing them. Two or three seemed to like the idea very much; "it should be considered even if nothing comes of it." It all depended, however, on the big organizations. One of them decided against it. I heard rumors of suspicions about my motives. What was I up to? . . .

This reaction prevailed. Only one or two societies brought my suggestion before their conventions. The committee was not formed. Nothing was done.

THE CRISIS ENGULFS AMERICA

A few facts and dates:

The army of the Third Reich invaded Poland on September 1, 1939. Two days later France and Britain declared war on Germany. On the 17th Russia—which a few days before had signed a pact of collaboration with Hitler—marched into Poland from the east. Exactly ten days later the Polish army surrendered unconditionally to the Nazis.

Then two months of *sitzkrieg*: France behind her defensive Maginot Line, England continuing her twenty-year-long week end, Americans beginning to talk about the "funny" war. Nobody of any consequence had any clear notion, apparently, what it was all about, except the top-flight group in Germany—and, it seems, Winston Churchill and Franklin Roosevelt.

On November 30th Russia invaded Finland, gaining territory with the "peace" of March 13, 1940.

More *sitzkrieg* ——

Then between April 9th and June 2nd of '40, to the general surprised indignation, Hitler with the greatest of ease successfully invaded Denmark, Norway, Belgium, The Netherlands and Luxembourg. Despite defeat, most of the British Expeditionary Force was able to withdraw from Flanders.

Mussolini took Italy into the war on June 10th.

Exactly two weeks later, with the Germans occupying the most important parts of her territory, including Paris, France accepted Hitler's terms.

The only flashes of light in the Great Gloom were Dunkirk, a suddenly awakened Britain, and a frightened United States.

Subsequent dates and facts are intimately woven into your daily life and mine. They have upset all our apple-carts. You are suddenly a soldier instead of working at your job and marrying your girl; your business is completely upset because you can't get materials; you are stripping the house of old aluminum, or you are on a Defense job in Washington or on "patrol" in the Atlantic——

When the President signed the Lend-Lease Act on March 11, 1941, the United States became officially and deeply involved in the Second World War. Up to the time this book is to go to press (mid-September) we have not yet declared war, but there can be no doubt that as a government, as a power, we have now been engaged in hostilities with the Axis, especially with Germany—in a peculiar, unprecedented fashion—for six months.

A great many of us Americans were involved in the war in various ways when it was still the "next war." During the Munich episode most of us got into it; some neck-deep, others only knee- or waist-deep.

And, so far, a preponderance of us Americans has never been on the same side. Our government with its enormous power is 100 per cent anti-Axis and actively pro-Ally, but we the people are not.

We are split.

A good many of us are intensely anti-Axis and pro-Britain and/or pro-Russia since the Soviet turned out to be anything but a pushover for Hitler's invaders late in June; but a great many of us, also, are not pro-British. Some of us are definitely (if not yet too openly) pro-Axis.

A good many of us are behind the government; some of us, while we trust his sense of timing and procedure, are even impatient with the President because he does not move faster against the Axis. Some of us don't know what to think. Many desire simultaneously to "stop Hitler" and to "stay out of war"—although, clearly enough, we are already in it. And some are against the whole foreign policy of the United States which has been slowly crystallizing under the Administration's leadership since June 1940, but which in many respects is still unclear, still in the groping stage, waiting for public opinion to push it along while large sections of the public are waiting for it to form and give them a lead.

Some of us are behind organizations like the Committee to Defend America by Aiding the Allies and the Fight for Freedom Committee, which advocates an immediate declaration of war on the Axis. And some of us belong to the America First Committee either because we are isolationist or because of our Anglophobia, or merely because the slogan "America First" serves to cover up our personal confusion, our group defensiveness, or our pro-Nazism.

Since June 1940 the cry in the United States has been for national unity . . . national unity . . . unity, unity. Some of it has gone up from hysterically stupefied throats; a primitive fear-inspired cry, not for unity really, but for uniformity.

We are not yet united—far from it.

We are instead profoundly confused as to the nature of the Second World War, its issues, and our present and potential part in it. On the surface, our national confusion manifests itself in the interventionist-isolationist debate and in name-calling. But this is only the surface.

We are achieving a surface unity of confusion.

Beneath it are divergent conceptions of what constitutes the democratic functioning of a people of a great country. These conceptions derive from hangovers of the old Jeffersonian-Hamiltonian debate, from the mass-versus-class orientation, from the traditional againstness of average-run people toward those on the top levels, and from the equally traditional pressing down of the average man by those on top.

Beneath the surface are deep cleavages within the American people. They exist largely on the basis of different backgrounds in the Old World—and on the basis of the entangled, still-veiled twin facts that most of us are escapist Europeans, and that the "old country" accounts for a great part of our inner make-up. The facts are twin, but they produce a conflict within us.

The international situation which has developed in

great part around the long-neglected European problem has got us in a vise, and as a people we don't know what we are able, or even what we would like to do, about it. We want to stay out of it, to be safe; we want Europe fixed up, but don't know how. We hope we can eat our cake and have it too, and we fear we can't. We say we come first, then we can't rest in peace—because of the "old country," because of the rest of humanity, because we are on Hitler's list. The threat to our "security" is something that many of us have secretly, unconsciously feared right along; that the country as a whole has feared; but we have never faced it, never set ourselves to think about it. We have shivered and turned away to a negative isolationism shot through with doubt.

June 1940 found us unprepared; not only militarily, but, what is more important, psychologically—spiritually.

Now when that which we feared has overtaken us, it is hard to decide in a hurry on a sound course of action.

Now it is hard to be objectively intelligent, to see beneath the appearance, to probe into our personal, group and national innards.

It is difficult to realize in a hurry that our current American confusion is but an old, old thing; that much of it we brought over in our flight from Europe.

It is hard to analyze the nature of our cleavages. It is hard even to admit their existence; harder still to accept their origin in the intricate, deep-down motive of our escape.

That the great Atlantic Migration was really the Great Escape is not easy for us Americans to take. The

history books put a different interpretation upon the
settling of America and the subsequent enrichment of
her population.

I have mentioned the direct personal and group
motives for the migration. They are true, but superficial . . . although not at all at odds with the fundamental reason for the escape of most of us, from the
Pilgrim Fathers to the recent immigrants.

That fundamental reason may be variously stated.
One way is to say that most of the emigrants, from the
time of the *Mayflower* to the present, were intensely
dynamic people. They not only wanted in a hurry a
better world to live in, but they were willing to uproot
and transplant themselves in order to attain it. Those left
behind did not seem to have sufficient initiative or
sufficient energy to face the unknown hardships of a
new country. And perhaps their roots were too deeply
buried in their native land. So they resigned themselves
and became fatalists. The emigrants, on the other hand,
took action, if only that of flight. Perhaps most Americans were Americans before they left Europe. And
perhaps America became what Europe wanted to but
didn't—couldn't—become because the urge itself emigrated in the makeup of the persons who came here.

When they got here, Americans did not have their
new society all figured out in blueprints. They didn't
know in their heads exactly what they wanted. But in
them was the great, endless human two-way impulse
to diversity and homogeneity: to be what I am and also
part of something bigger than myself, bigger than a
family, than a tribe, than a nation—the paradoxical

two-way impulse which had been frustrated in Europe as the countries there hardened into delimited, defensive sovereignties.

But most of us Americans had a lot of faults. We brought some over. Some we developed here. We were in a hurry. This vast new continent excited us. We wanted to build a great new civilization overnight. And, while we did not like the old order in Old Europe, it was in our very being. You can't discard part of yourself just by stating that it is now discarded. We had run away; now we greatly needed illusions—"happy endings."

We *did* make a new start here; we began a new human experiment—but it has been cluttered up by the unproductive aspects of our European experience and continuity.

If we were in a hurry before we left Europe, we were in a much greater one after we got here. Being escapists, and consequently a little unbalanced about what we fled from, we were afraid Europe would catch up with us. So we were in haste to create America before that happened. So we had no time to think. So we eyed with suspicion some of those who came after us, the "foreigners," especially if they were poor or somehow "different," for they might be the advance guard of the Europe we feared was coming after us. So, while we made a very good if rapid job of America, we made many mistakes.

No need to enumerate them all. But perhaps the most serious is that we have not yet learned quite what we have created and why. Nor who we are. Nor what our mistakes have been. Nor that in reality beneath our surface divergencies, serious as they may seem, and even when they are most serious, we Americans have a great deal in common and do get along in many respects a good deal of the time; we Anglo-Saxon, German, Polish and all other kinds of Americans.

So we are confused . . . when we can least afford to be; when our past has overtaken us . . . and in our confusion we run the risk of running amok in our newly created civilization—not only of harming or even destroying what we have done but of muffing a great historic opportunity.

Too many of us are thinking and feeling mostly about America or mostly about the "old country"; too few about the world of which we are a part and in which we collaborated for three centuries to produce the crisis that has now engulfed us.

One Saturday night in May '39 I went to a banquet in Newark, New Jersey, given by a Ukrainian American "youth organization" affiliated with a Ukrainian American benefit society.

In some ways, it was a very pleasant evening. There were colorful Ukrainian costumes. There was much spirited singing of Ukrainian songs. Laughter and gay talk.

But the majority of the fifteen hundred people present most likely had no notion of the behind-the-scenes content and purpose of the occasion.

There were speeches, some very long and impassioned. I understand only enough Ukrainian to know they were all about the "Mother Country" and the duty of "Ukrainians in America" to help free her from Soviet, Polish, Slovak, Hungarian and Rumanian rule.

The principal speaker, a leader of "Ukrainians in America," had just returned from abroad where he had met with European Ukrainian leaders. He got a big hand from the audience. And his report—frequently interrupted by applause—ended with another appeal to all "Ukrainians in the United States" to work for the cause to free the Ukraine.

The core of the cause had long been the so-called

Hetman and ODWU organizations. The initials of the latter stand for "Organization for the Rebirth of the Ukraine."

And on the face of it, it appears an excellent cause: the cause of freedom. Resembling those of twenty-odd years ago to free Czechoslovakia, Finland, Poland, Lithuania and Ireland, it attracts sincere and ardent adherents in both Europe and America. The great majority who believe in it in America do so in part because they awoke here to the meaning of freedom.

The trouble with the movement for a "free Ukraine" is that some of its leaders in Europe and in the United States are hand in glove with the Nazis—much in the same way, let me hasten to add, that Masaryk and Paderewski in 1918 were linked to the Allied-American side. Not that all or even most of the Ukraine leaders are themselves Nazis. Some are. But a good many who are not have long been collaborating with Hitler, the archfoe (except for the apparent interlude between August '39 and June '41) of the Soviet Union which held the biggest slice of what they considered the Ukraine.

Hitler was their ally—for his own good reasons; but they were his allies for their own reasons. No one else of any consequence was interested in the Ukraine; so the movement fell into Hitler's hands. And under his machinations the least scrupulous of the Ukrainian would-be leaders were elevated to top positions. Hitler has always been interested in able, corruptible people whom he can use in his Design for the Future. Potential Quislings. . . . So the movement, good in its initial

dynamic, became largely a Nazi-controlled affair in this
country as well as abroad—a fact with serious implica-
tions in view of the United States' definite anti-Axis
orientation since March 11, 1941, and in view of the
large numbers here—some say eight hundred thousand
—of Ukrainians and Ukrainian Americans, native and
foreign-born.

I assume the names of the ODWU and Hetman
leaders in the United States are known to the F.B.I.
Several have already been published in *The Hour* (100
East 42nd Street, New York) which—sponsored by
such anti-Nazis as Professor F. L. Schuman, Leland
Stowe, Hendrik van Loon and Wythe Williams—
devotes itself to exposing subversive movements.

Not all leaders of the "Ukrainian movement" in the
United States are scoundrels. Some are stupid. A few
are decent, not unintelligent fellows with a hope that
the end justifies the means and a talent for rationalizing
actions which are far from lily-white. All are figures in
the dark maze of our internal American confusion, the
confusion in which Hitler and Goebbels take a specula-
tive—and an active—interest.

And the precious pair has for a long time been
stirring up the "Ukrainian movement" in the United
States with a deep and cunning ladle. Nazi agents have
been busy among Ukrainian immigrants and their
American-born children since the middle 1930s.

A number of them were present at the Newark
banquet. One—a handsome blond young male—sat at
the same table with me. He had but recently come over

from Germany. His girl friend was a native American of Ukrainian parentage. He spoke some English; he knew a little Ukrainian, which seemed to amuse everybody. A German speaking Ukrainian! He joined in singing the Ukrainian songs, which he said he liked very much; and he made a great hit.

There were other Nazis just like this fellow at every second or third table. Still others worked on the Ukrainian group elsewhere. Theirs was a threefold purpose:

One: to strengthen the Ukrainian movement wherever it could be strengthened for possible use in Hitler's plans to disrupt Russia.

Two: to pick out people of Ukrainian nationality or background who through fanaticism or corruption might serve as saboteurs in American industries when and if necessary.

And *three*: to encourage anti-Semitism and other forms of antagonism against people in the United States who stemmed from countries holding Ukrainian territories.

One needs no elaboration.

Two deserves amplification. I have reason to believe that Nazi agents here anticipate severe public, industrial, and governmental discrimination against German Americans of the first, second and even third generations. In fact the agents work toward that end. Nazis are adept at exploiting negative situations, and their purpose is to keep as many German Americans as possible away from any trend toward national unity. But discrimination would bar German immigrants from jobs facilitating sabotage. The pro-Nazis among them with marked German accents obviously could not successfully adopt the camouflage of non-German names. But people with Ukrainian names and accents might not be suspected by plant managers and foremen.

But *three* was probably the most important. Its success was already clear in '39. Most Ukrainians and Ukrainian Americans with whom I talked at the Newark banquet were anti-Semitic. Or they had it in for the Poles or Hungarians, including those in the United States. For "minority" peoples tend to "against" attitudes. It is the quickest way to acquire a feeling of superiority about oneself. Ukrainian Americans are no more susceptible to this tendency than are most other elements in the population—except insofar as Nazi agents have done more work on them than on any save the German American group.

Since the summer of '39, followers even more than the leaders of the Ukrainian movement have had their emotional ups and downs. First, they couldn't make head nor tail of the Russo-German pact. Did it mean that Hitler, after all, would not disrupt Russia—would not free the Ukraine? That Hitler, to begin with, might have had other plans for the Ukraine than freedom and sovereign independence had probably never occurred to many.

But his conquest of Poland gave them a lift. He treated the Ukrainians there better than the Poles. Consequently some of the Ukrainian element here turned a bit more pro-Nazi.

But all this pro-Hitlerism—except that of the corrupt, Hitler-paid leaders—has been sporadic and wobbly since American policy became definitely anti-Hitler: for it must not be forgotten that in common with other new-stock groups the bulk of Ukrainian immigrants and their children are inevitably, even if sometimes not too clearly, American.

As Americans many have long been uncomfortable, inferiority-ridden. Their experiences as newcomers from non-English-speaking peasant countries or as their "foreign" children, most of whom have never even seen the Ukraine, have not been entirely happy. America at large has looked down on them, made fun of their "foreign" names. So, partly as a negative withdrawal from an unfriendly American atmosphere, partly in keeping with positive "old-country" attachments, and partly in response to the astute work of Nazi agents, some turned fervently to the Ukrainian cause.

But as the United States got caught in all the crosscurrents of the world crisis, confusion deepened in the Ukrainian Americans working for the Hitler-controlled Ukraine movement. As I write, Hitler is actually trying to snatch the Russian hunk of the Ukraine. It is the first part of his promise: to free the Ukraine, and to restore it intact to the Ukrainians. But at the same moment the Britain-aiding, lend-leasing United States Government goes pro-Russia! President Roosevelt sends Harry Hopkins to confer with Stalin! What in heaven's name can a mixed-up anti-Russian American in the Ukrainian movement do—especially when the F.B.I. bends a sharp gaze upon the activities of some of the Ukrainian organizations?

It is a dilemma. His sons and brothers and cousins and nephews are in the United States Army; how can he be pro-Hitler even indirectly? On the other hand, the Ukraine remains "under the Russian heel."

The Ukrainian-language newspapers have been trying to resolve this dilemma without much success even when they are helped by clever Nazi agents. The editorial staffs of most of them, in common with the administrative officers of organizations which publish them, are split along lines redrawn from day to day under the impact of international shifts. One of the most recent attempts to straighten the twisted Ukrainian American position was made in *Svoboda* (Liberty), published in Jersey City, New Jersey, by the financially powerful Ukrainian American Union some of whose leaders *The Hour* has accused as individuals of occasional close collaboration with Hitler's agents. Its English-language section for July 28, 1941 contained this editorial:

OUR STAND

Some people seem to think that the British alliance with the Soviets has placed us, Americans of Ukrainian descent, in a dilemma. They say that our irreconcilable opposition to the Reds may be regarded with disfavor here, and even construed by some as pro-Nazi. They counsel us, therefore, to become less intransigent on this issue, or, at least, to soft-pedal it.

We fail to see their point. The fact that Stalin is fighting Hitler does not change our opinion of him in the least. We still think he is Freedom and Democracy's Public Enemy No. 1—with Hitler, of course, a close second. We give Pal Joey precedence here because his Reds have been far longer in power than the Nazis, their brutalities have been more cruel and on a far greater scale, their persecution of the Church much worse, and, finally, because their predecessor was the rapacious imperialist Tsarist regime which for centuries stood for autocracy in its most anti-democratic and oppressive forms.

Aside from this traditional anti-democratic character of Moscow, however, we also have to consider in this connection the fact that the Reds are fighting the Nazis not for the sake of any principles of freedom and democracy but simply and only because of self-preservation—to preserve Communism with Moscow as its center.

If freedom and democracy had ever meant anything to the Reds, they would have joined forces with the Allies back in the summer of 1939. Instead they betrayed the Allies and tied themselves up with the Nazis. Then when Hitler wolfed Polish and Western Ukrainian territories they acted as his jackals by seizing what he threw to them.

All appeals to them to assume a less ignoble role, to break their sycophantic relations with Hitler, to strike for the cause of freedom and democracy, especially when he was engaged in the West, the Reds cynically ignored, but kept on sending more and more food and supplies to Germany. Meanwhile they engaged in marauding expeditions of their own, occupying the already-mentioned Western Ukraine, as well as parts of Finland, Lithuania, Latvia, Estonia, and finally Bessarabia and Bukovina.

And thus the Soviets would have continued along this torturous course of betrayal, robbery and rule by terror, had not Hitler suddenly become alarmed by the growing dimensions of his jackal, and decided to get rid of it before it tried to become a wolf like him. As a result, we now find that jackal yelping to the four winds that it's fighting for world freedom and democracy, and calling upon the British Lion and the American Eagle to come to its aid.

We think it would be best for us Americans to realize once and for all that our enemy is not only Nazism but Communism as well. In fact, Communism was so active here that we had to jail the head of the communist party here; drive communist agents out of our schools and colleges; and fight against communist agents in the labor unions, especially their attempts to wreck our defense program. To help, therefore, Stalin to win this war between Nazism and Communism, would be to strengthen Communism not only in Europe but even here. If Stalin wins a clear-cut victory it will be he, not our Roosevelt or England's Churchill, who will dictate the peace terms; and they will be just as bad as Hitler's terms.

So the best we can do, is to hope that both these predatory powers, Nazi Germany and Soviet Russia, exhaust themselves in their war, to the extent where neither they nor their anti-democratic systems will menace world progress and civilization. In the meantime, we should continue to strengthen that remaining European bastion of freedom and democracy—England.

Such then are some of the reasons why we refuse to get on the Soviet bandwagon and cheer for a Red victory.

But there is still another big reason why we, Americans of Ukrainian extraction, will never compromise in our antipathy towards Moscow. It is that Moscow represents that abysmal force which for centuries has kept the Ukrainian nation in slavery and chains, which has denied to the Ukrainians even elementary human rights, which has stifled much of their creative urges, which has oppressed and mistreated them barbarously, and which, finally, has killed off millions of them by famines, concentration camps, gallows and firing squads.

So long as Moscow continues to thus brutally enslave and despoil our kinsmen in their native land, Ukraine, so long as it blocks their centuries-old movement to establish a free and independent and democratic Ukraine, so long will we and all other true friends of freedom and democracy keep up our fight against it.

The editorial speaks for itself.

It appeared before Stalin gave Harry Hopkins a personal letter to Roosevelt. Now what? . . . And what if Hitler conquers the Russian Ukraine and establishes a puppet state? And what if at the head of it he puts old General Paul Skoropansky? A former Tsarist general who in 1918 served as Kaiser Wilhelm's puppet ruler of the Ukraine, he is now one of the Fuehrer's main Ukrainian stand-bys. According to *The Hour*, he and his son Danylo are fiercely anti-Semitic; eager to repeat the pogroms of the first Skoropansky regime twenty-three years ago.

The tragedy of such statements is that they issue not from a balanced heart and mind, but from the compulsion of outer events upon an inner confusion rife among people, wherever they may be, who feel insecure.

From a reliable anti-Nazi source within the group, I learn there are about five thousand "Ukrainians in America" who are active in the Ukrainian cause in a pro-Nazi way. One-fourth to one-third of these are native Americans of Ukrainian parentage. Not a large number relatively. But it may be that their propaganda, directed by Hitler's agents for the last half-dozen years, has touched a quarter of a million people who in consequence are not anti-U.S.A. but are certainly anti-British and anti-Russian; and, to that extent, pro-Hitler —although most of them will deny this. In addition to being anti-Semitic, most are anti-Negro, some even refusing to work on the same jobs with colored men.

There is a small pro-Soviet, pro-Stalin group. Some are Communists; those who are not least believe that the Ukraine problem will eventually be solved only by getting all Ukrainians within the Soviet Ukraine. But alongside the Hitler-controlled or -influenced element they are negligible.

It is not surprising that the first court-martial case in the new United States Army which has attracted public attention concerns a draftee with a Ukrainian name—John Habinyak. Early in the summer of '41 he was tried for repeated insubordination; previously, according to press report, he had expressed himself favorably about Hitler.

In mid-August some anti-Nazi Ukrainian Americans in New York formed the Ukrainian Committee to Combat Nazism, issuing this statement: "The Ukrainian community in the United States is appalled by the widespread Nazi propaganda among Ukrainian Americans and by the activities of certain subversive groups subsidized by the Nazi Government. All true Ukrainians feel that the presence of these cliques in their midst tends to create a false impression about Ukrainians regarding such vital matters as their loyalty toward America and their attitude toward the invasion of their original homelands by the Nazi hordes."

The Committee intends to fight the effects of the Nazi propaganda "in various ways," including the calling of mass meetings at which they mean "to register their protest against the Nazi invasion of the Ukraine and the Nazi machinations among Ukrainians in this country." But the probability is they are a little late. They will have a tough time undoing in a hurry the long, patient work of the best subversive propagandists in the world. What good will their "protests" do? Aren't they apt to be merely negative in effect? What is their program for the future of the Ukraine with which they plan to attract the now pro-Nazi Ukrainian Americans, whose "old country" complex is as strong, active and inevitable in them as it is in Czech, old-stock and all other Americans? Have they any notion how to straighten out their people's America-inspired passion for a free Ukraine which Hitler has twisted to his own ends? Or what to do about the personality and character of native Americans like John Habinyak and others I know who have been affected by Nazi propaganda? . . .

The Ukrainian Committee to Combat Nazism does not say. The probability is it does not know.

The Pain of Poland

It is well-nigh impossible to describe the pain which Polish Americans endured when Hitler and Stalin invaded, conquered and partitioned Poland. Pain is the word. It was literally physical with many. They huddled around radios, unable to restrain sudden sharp, agonized cries of hurt outrage, hate. Many suffered more acutely during the bombing of Warsaw than they might have were devastation and falling debris overwhelming their own homes in Chicago, Buffalo or Detroit.

For no country has a stronger hold on the people of its blood than has Poland. It is a prodigiously idealized land. And no group in the United States is more responsive to the "old country" than are Polish Americans. There is no clearer example of the American "old country" complex.

In the Autumn 1940 issue of *Common Ground* magazine, a young immigrant-American writer, Lola Kinel, half Polish and half Polish-Jewish by birth, revealed the anatomy of this complex as it exists in Polish Americans. She lived in Poland a very short time as a little girl and does not know the country well at all. But in her is "a sort of imaginary Poland; an idea, a memory, and a sentiment—an allegiance formed in my childhood and persisting throughout my life." When she was naturalized and the judge in Los Angeles asked

135

her to foreswear her "allegiance to the Republic of Poland," she had "a strange . . . pang of regret, almost of self-reproach." She had no particular interest in the Polish state and government, yet for a moment she felt "as if the judge had asked me to renounce my love for Mickiewicz and Slovacki, for Chopin and Moniuszko, for the Polish language and that romantic and sentimental regard for Polish history which lurks somehow in all Polish hearts. . . .

"[An old-stock] American may perhaps not understand this. An Irish immigrant would. So would a Czech or a Slovak or the native of any country which has been long in subjection. Nationalism in countries like these becomes not only heroic, it becomes an obsession; it colors all life, thought, and art. It becomes a sort of ideal . . . and to renounce an ideal is always harder than mere political allegiance. In Poland nationalism has colored the literature for a century to such an extent that all the great writers and poets have written around that one eternal subject of Poland's downfall and coming rebirth. The result has been a literature of tremendous passion and force, which has kept alive in the Polish people a smoldering fire of never-ending hope, yet has, simultaneously, rendered it too insular for the outside world."

Mrs. Kinel believes that the basis of her "old country" complex is her memory of a few childhood summers on her Polish grandmother's estate, where "we lived in a glorious succession of adventures, explorations, and perpetual delights of the senses as well as of the imagination. For never since those days has anything tasted so well. Nowhere in the world were there such plums and cherries and pears; nowhere were the mushrooms so white and berries so fragrant, hay so sweet and air so pure. . . ."

It was the Hitler-Stalin violation of *this* Poland, dwelling in beatifying memory, which produced in many of the three or four million Polish Americans and unnaturalized American Poles so painful an agony and hatred. The hatred of Hitler was more vehement than that directed at Stalin, and its tendency was to spread beyond the Nazis to the traditional Polish enemy, "the German race."

And so in those early September days in 1939 the "Polish element" the country over swung anew into a movement to collect money, to help the "old country" within the limits of the United States neutrality laws.

Poland, Poland——

The second generation felt a little differently than did their parents. Like the second generation in other groups, they had always been restive because they were "foreigners"—"Polaks" with "difficult" consonantal names; but now that somehow fell away under the impact of events abroad. In fact, since nearly all America was outraged over the invasion, to be "Polish" changed abruptly from a disadvantage into at least a tentative asset. During the siege of Warsaw people spoke to you with a special interest and solicitude.

But their sense of outrage over Poland's fate was made bitter to the second generation. Their improved standing in America; their first experience in unity as

Polish Americans with America at large was gained at the expense of the "old country." It was paid for by this last awful moment in Polish history. Poland had to die to become alive in them.

Third- and fourth-generation Polish Americans, or Americans of three or more generations who are partly "Polish," were often filled with clearer passion and greater pain than the second generation, for unlike the latter they had in most cases no need to work themselves out of new-immigrant inferiority feelings and inhibitions. One young third-generation American who is half Polish, one-fourth German and one-fourth old-stock American, scarcely slept during the first two weeks of September '39. When he did fall asleep, he would wake up weeping.

There was a great letdown to some Polish Americans when Poland's government and army command appeared ineffective and when her resistance so swiftly crumbled. And in some for a time the pendulum swung toward isolation: to hell with Europe. Others—in Chicago on October 15th for instance—vented their anguish by burning Hitler and Stalin in effigy.

Since July 1940, however, especially since the Lend-Lease Act, the overwhelming majority of Polish Americans of all generations has tended toward intervention. Their Polish blood is a factor in this, and their Polish pride is heartened by the knowledge that some of the best fliers in the R.A.F. are Poles.

Poland's fall dissolved the post-Munich antagonism between Polish and Czech Americans and brought them closer together than they had ever been before. Early in 1941, for instance, some "Czech" and "Polish" clubs in Chicago began to hold joint meetings. But the anti-German sentiment of both these groups continues strong. In September 1939 many a marriage engagement was broken between young Slavic and German Americans.

Many Polish Americans—along with many others of Slavic derivations—have suddenly forgiven Stalin and the Soviet for invading Poland in '39, and have found satisfaction in the hammering the Red Army gave Hitler's *Wehrmacht* during the summer of '41. Some are experiencing a resurgence of pan-Slavic feeling.

The anti-Germanism of some Polish-immigrant factions runs extremely high. A Polish-language newspaper in Cleveland attacked me because I had joined as sponsor an organization called The American Friends of German Freedom, of which the anti-Axis German American, Dr. Reinhold Niebuhr, is chairman. I was informed that there was nothing German anywhere under the sun which any decent person in America could afford to befriend; everything German was bestial, predatory, evil— "It may be that decent people live in Germany but they are not the Germans."

But the pain over Poland is all the worse because it is accompanied by a feeling of helplessness. Passion is frustrated. Polish Americans read about the terrible things going on in Poland. Two or three million of their kin are in slavery. Hundreds of thousands have been killed. More are shot or hanged daily. Among these victims of Hitler's terror are what the Polish Americans and unnaturalized Poles in the United States consider the best people of Poland: professors, writers, priests, artists. . . . And they can do nothing.

The Polish-language press in America publishes stories of sabotage and resistance in Poland which give the readers a "lift." But the more thoughtful ones cannot help wondering—with growing dismay—about the future of their old country even should Hitler be decisively defeated. You should see their faces as they sit in the famous Leonard's Café in Chicago or in the restaurant of the Polish National Home on St. Marks Place in New York. They do not criticize General Sikorski and his government in exile in London; in fact some fly to their defense when *The Nation* publishes an article attacking them for their semi-official anti-Semitism . . . but they wonder.

The heart-rending effect on Finnish Americans of the
1939–'40 Russo-Finnish war was partially ameliorated
by a deep pro-Finnish reaction throughout the United
States—already an admirer of the only country which
paid its debts on the dot. For decades previously many
native Americans of Finnish descent had felt uneasy
about their heritage; now in the light of American
sympathy for Finland they wore it like a feather in
their cap. Many blossomed out as people, as Americans
—Finnish Americans.

That Finland was finally compelled to sign a "peace"
with Russia, giving up a relatively big strip of territory,
depressed many Finnish Americans. But Finland's heroic
resistance had been well noted by America, and her
continued sympathy reassured them.

In the summer of '41, however, Finland had to join
the Third Reich in its assault on the Soviet Union. This
confused profoundly most of the four hundred thousand
Finnish Americans. They are passionately anti-Russian
and, in the great majority of cases, almost no less anti-
Hitler. But they are still not fully integrated subjectively
with the population of the United States, and the important question in their minds now is: what will
America think? So far the American people in general
have "understood," even those who want the United

States to start shooting at the Axis right away. But what will be the inner plight of Finnish Americans when and if we do get into a shooting war against Hitler and his allies, one of whom at the moment is reluctant Finland—the country which in 1939–'40 we admired so highly? . . .

In mid-July I wrote to a number of my Finnish American friends asking them how they felt about it. Their replies draw a graph of confusion. The anti-Sovietism of a few is so strong as to toss them clear into the middle of the Nazi camp; but since as Americans and as "Finns" they are essentially anti-Nazi their dismay is greatly deepened. One answer had but a single sentence: "I am ready to weep."

My contact with Finnish Americans during 1938–'41 makes me consider them one of the best new-immigrant elements in the country. Members of no other group think more clearly, less sentimentally. And my wager is that, whatever the United States does in the future, Finnish Americans will be lucid in their attitude and straightforward in their function. This is manifest in a letter dated July 26th from Mr. E. A. Jasberg of Hancock, Michigan, whose name is well known to Finnish Americans:

. . . I deeply decry Finland's position in the conflict, however worthy her aims and purposes may be. Aid given by Germany to Russia during Finland's fight for liberty against the Reds cannot be denied to have been decisive in the ultimate defeat of Finland, and Nazi tyranny may seem to some preferable to Red aggression, but for me as an American it is hard to accept their choice to lead themselves into further conflict with Russia and as it appears also with Britain and, in a large sense, our own United States. We realize as liberty-loving Americans of Finnish origin that Russia's act in annexing Karelia and depriving a small democratic nation of territory hers for innumerable centuries, should deprive Russia of all democratic sympathy (such as that of the U.S.A.), were her enemy any other than Nazi Germany. But Nazism is everything opposed to democratic ideals and purposes. Her move against Russia is an act of equal unfairness, and to have the Finns aiding such aggression is hard to believe (though true). I cannot condone the act although I appreciate the motives actuating it. Finland lost so vitally in the annexation of her eastern territory and feels the loss so acutely that she has momentarily lost her sense of proportion, and is risking the loss of American sympathy which was of vital importance during her struggle with Russia. I can therefore speak freely as an American first, and a "Finn" only after that. Whatever Finland does from now on as an ally of Nazi Germany is more apt to enslave than free Karelia. Hitler cannot be trusted and his promises to Finland can bear no faith. Small nations of greater population than Finland have been made mere puppet states working reluctantly but more or less efficiently for Nazi domination of Europe and the Western Hemisphere. Poland, Czechoslovakia, Rumania, Hungary, Belgium, Holland, Norway and Denmark are too impressive a list of examples to fool any sane and logical person that Germany means to keep any of her promises . . .

We Finnish Americans are in a bitter predicament. But we have only one choice—America: may she be always right, but right or wrong, America first. I *know* the greatest majority of my fellow Americans of Finnish derivation share this view—or will share it ultimately. I hope the non-Finnish Americans will realize this——

What was true of Finnish Americans apropos of the 1939–'40 Russo-Finnish war was true of Greek Americans a year later when Mussolini, Hitler's executive officer in Italy, ordered his reluctant army in Albania to invade Greece.

One of the newest, the Greek American group was among the least integrated and most depressed, although it includes a number of eminently successful individuals. The second generation was particularly weighed down by inferiority feelings; feelings which in some cases were reversed into exaggerated, defensive pride in their background.

But Mussolini fixed all that—or rather the Greek army which bodily shoved the Fascist forces back into Albania and which later fought to the death when overrun by the Nazis. Even those native Americans of Greek parentage who had changed their names and "passed" as "just plain Americans" came out into the open, announced their Greek blood, joined impressive Greek American parades, and went to work for the Greek War Relief, started by that amazingly successful American theatrical tycoon Spyros Skouras, a native of Greece. The organization appealed to *all* the people of the United States, and—as in the case of Finland a year before—they responded with several million dollars.

The money has not yet been of much help to Greece, for very little food and medicine could be sent over in a hurry during the war; now the supplies are being held in Eastern seaports to be shipped to the old country after the Axis is defeated. But the episode—episode in relation to the whole war, tragedy to those who took part—has been of enormous value to hundreds of thousands of Greek Americans. The war has enslaved Greece for the time being, but it has freed many people here of the vague reflex defensiveness and confusion that—to repeat—are the inner problem of millions of new-immigrant people.

But the sudden excitement in this country over the Italo-Greek war also focused the prejudice of many Greek Americans onto Italian Americans. This, in its turn, prompted my friend Constantine Poulos, a native New Englander, to write as follows in the January 1941 issue of his English-language *Hellenic Spectator*, published in Washington, D. C.:

A Greek American parent does not allow his son to play football with an Italian teammate.

A Greek American priest announces to newspapers his desire to clean up all the Italians in the world.

American Greek youths write letters to newspapers condemning the Italian people and sign the letters "Proud Greek" and "Very Proud Greek."

American Greek children pick fights with American Italian children.

All these events multiplied a thousand times are disheartening developments. The successes of the Greek Armies have furnished a natural incitement to the Greek Americans to brag extravagantly, to argue vehemently with Italian Americans, to condemn heatedly all Italian Americans, to speak derogatively of all Italian Americans and to attempt to suppress Italian American opinions and protests.

We are living in a critical period, not unlike such earlier crises as at the close of the Revolutionary War and the Civil War. The present condition of world affairs is producing the unfortunate situation in this country of setting one group against another.

The necessity of teaching and preaching to the Greek Americans and to their children the blind idiocy of fighting the Greco-Italian war over here in America is great and immediate. It must be realized that the Italian Americans share equally in this crisis along with the Greeks, along with all recent-immigrant groups in America.

America is a free country, and we must do our share to keep it free by appreciating the position of the Italian people here.

America is a symbol of that liberty which makes it possible for Greeks and Italians and Germans and Jews and Irish and Swedes to live and work and love, side by side.

America is the heir of the common fund to which Greeks and Italians and Germans and Jews and Irish and Swedes have contributed bountifully.

Relentless persecution and contemptuousness, which disregards the dignity, the pride, the spirit of any one of these groups, by any other one of these groups is a despicable attitude, unworthy . . . of America.

The group which ignores these facts sows the seeds of its own downfall and destruction.

It is wrong for Greek Americans to speak disparagingly of Italians.

It is more important that our people know and understand

these things than that $25,000,000 be raised for Greek War Relief.

It is the duty of the Greek-language press in the United States to stress these points. Pages and pages devoted to the relief-fund-raising activities of every community in the country do not aid our people and our people's children in formulating proper attitudes and ideas for the present and for the future.

The heads of the Greek Church in America who have been so eager "to get the credit" for raising relief funds here in America have not yet given even a moment's thought to the pressing need of guiding the people's minds in the proper direction toward good will—a fundamental American tradition and principle.

Unthinkingly, thousands of Greek American parents talk bitterly in the presence of their children about "those macaroni-eating wops."

In this way, these parents are unconsciously creating in their children a racial prejudice as insidious as an opium habit. And, in the larger sense, they are betraying the America which offered them faith, haven, freedom, and opportunity.

This editorial received considerable attention in Greek American circles and exerted an influence. . . . But I should like to add that such an outburst of prejudice as Mr. Poulos condemned was not a manifestation of something peculiarly "Greek." During the Italo-Ethiopian war, school children born in Harlem of Italian immigrants began suddenly to throw things at Negro children. The idea was that they were fighting the "niggers" the way the Italians were fighting them in Ethiopia. I would not be surprised, however, if things like this were deliberately stimulated by Fascist agents in the United States who, like Nazi agents among German Americans, are busy in the innumerable Little Italys.

Hitler's swift conquest of Greece after overrunning Yugoslavia lowered the new high spirits of Greek Americans as earlier the Nazi-Soviet successes had depressed Polish Americans in September '39 and Finnish Americans in March '40.

Now one of the Greek Americans' chief aspirations is to defeat Hitler, somehow—to free Greece and send to her hard-pressed people the supplies accumulated by the Greek War Relief organization. In most cases their thoughts go no further. In common with many Americans of other stocks, most are still escapists, conscious or unconscious isolationists. If they believe in a shooting war, they are afraid to come out for it openly: they fear the America Firsters will call them "foreigners" and accuse them of wanting to involve the United States in the actual hostilities in order to help Greece. If they venture beyond the work of Greek relief, their minds plunge into confusion. They have not yet answered the question: *What sort of world will Greece be a part of?* . . .

In one of the larger Eastern cities, in mid–December '40, the fifteen-year-old American-born son of a naturalized Italian immigrant attempted suicide while alone in the house after school. Fortunately his father came home early that day, in time to turn off the gas, carry the almost-unconscious boy to the porch, open the windows, and run for the Italian American doctor whose office is in the same block.

Revived, the boy explained he had wanted to die because so many people were so happy over Italian defeats in Africa and Albania, and got such a kick out of kidding the dejected inhabitants of the Little Italy neighborhood about the Italians' poor fighting qualities.

"Drives me crazy," he said. "It's terrible to be Italian. . . . When I was out of the room at school today one of the kids stuck a newspaper article on my desk. It was by that guy Westbrook Pegler, razzing the Italians, and somebody wrote 'Ha-ha-ha!' on it in big letters. Because my name's Italian! But *I'm* not, Dad; I'm *American*! . . . I wanted to hit him, but didn't know who it was. I didn't look around, because I thought maybe he was watching how I took it; I didn't wanna give him the satisfaction, whoever he was. I read part of the article, then crumpled it up and threw it under my desk, like it didn't matter. But when I got home, I just couldn't stand it any more. . . . I'm sorry, Dad; I know it's not your fault you were born in Italy."

The boy's mother had died two years before. His sisters, both older than he, were on a visit and would not be home till the next day; now he begged his father not to tell them what he had done. Nor anyone else. His father and the doctor promised to keep it a secret, and they agreed on a story to explain his illness should he not sufficiently recover from the gas by the time the sisters returned.

His father came to America at thirteen with his parents. In 1917–'18 he served in the United States Army. Now he is an insurance agent in Little Italy where he owns a house and transacts most of his business, although both he and his children would like to move: "a living is a living." He considers himself Americanized, reads English-language magazines, borrows books from the public library . . . and in '39, after getting hold of my "broadside," he started to correspond with me.

"About Mussolini," he wrote in an early letter, "I don't care one way or another. He may be O.K. for Italy; I am an American, and it's none of my business what they do over there, although I think the invasion of Ethiopia is terrible. . . . I think the United States ought to steer clear of the whole mess." Later he mentioned the Fascist propaganda in Little Italy which seemed to be financed and directed from Rome, and which disturbed him; but he was determined, he said, chiefly for business reasons, to keep out of the arguments raging in the neighborhood.

In the summer of '40, I met him. We talked. Mussolini's declaration of war on France and England had upset him, and he thought America's "stab in the back" reaction to it was bad for Italian Americans. "It makes them feel they're on the spot."

Now he wired me: could he come to see me immediately on an urgent personal matter? . . . He came with his boy who stayed with my wife in the living-room while he and I went to my study.

"Johnnie doesn't know why I want to see you," said the worried father. "I told him you were thinking of taking out a policy. . . . He's a good kid with a fine school record, but maybe a little too sensitive. Lately he's been very quiet. But so is everybody else in the neighborhood, and I wasn't specially worried. Also I've been busy outside collecting insurance and haven't seen the boy a great deal. I knew, though, he was bothered about something. One evening after the Greeks took Koritsa he snapped at me as I turned on the radio for a news broadcast. He said he was studying and didn't want to hear 'that war stuff anyhow.' . . . Now—suicide! Whose fault is it? Mine? I don't think he'll try it again, but he needs to straighten himself out. How can I help him? . . . Johnnie knows you're a writer; can you say something to him, without letting on you know that he tried to kill himself—something that'll help him?"

What could I say to the boy? The assignment was

something new and made me a little uncomfortable. . . . But after a while the father and I agreed on a procedure which I didn't quite like; it put me in the role of an adviser; nonetheless it worked.

When we sat down to lunch I turned the radio to a news broadcast full of more Italian retreats. After I switched it off the boy's father and I exchanged a few remarks about Mussolini and the Italian soldiers. The youngster was tense and all ears.

"These defeats," I said, "don't prove the Italians are poor soldiers, as some people claim. They were great fighters under Garibaldi when they were fighting for liberty—for a good cause. But their present cause is a bad one; and they know it. They see that Mussolini has tricked them into this war. They know he's really just Hitler's tool in Italy. And if Italians don't feel like fighting for Hitler, it looks to me like a sign of intelligence, not cowardice. ——"

"It would help a lot if *we* could see things that way," played up the father. "Some of us are pretty miserable at times."

"One reason for that," I said, "is because Mussolini's agents have doused Italian neighborhoods all over America with propaganda. And incidentally it's partly your fault. You Italian Americans didn't fight that propaganda hard enough. You were afraid it would hurt your business, or you were indifferent, or maybe a little bit ignorant. Maybe you didn't realize it was actually Hitler's propaganda. Hitler wants to stir up trouble over here so he can ultimately break up this country. Well, that propaganda persuaded some Italian Americans to think their lives are tied up with Mussolini's fortunes. They are wrong. They haven't thought things out. They are all mixed up inside. Of course they can't forget the 'old country'; besides why should they? Italy's a swell place; I've been there. Mussolini isn't Italy. He is only a two-legged mistake that happened in Italy. He won't last forever. . . . The fact that you are *Italian* Americans has nothing to do with Mussolini. The fact that you are Americans of Italian descent is much more likely to mean that your ideals are those of Garibaldi and Mazzini ——"

"Oh, yes," put in the boy, "I know about Garibaldi."

"Swell!" I said. "Garibaldi and Mazzini were patriots—heroes like Washington and Jefferson. They fought and worked for freedom and democracy just as a lot of people all over the world have fought for it. And of course there was Mazzei . . ."

"Who's he?" asked Johnnie.

"An Italian too, and a darned good one. He came to America by way of England before our Revolution. He settled in Virginia and became a close friend of Jefferson's. In 1774 he wrote some essays in the Italian language on liberty and democracy. Jefferson translated them, and the phrase about all of us being 'created equal' seems to have been originally Mazzei's—it came from one of his essays and found its way into the Declaration of Independence."

"Gee, I never heard of him, Dad!" said Johnnie.

"Where can we learn more about him?" asked the father.

"Your librarian will dig up a couple of books for you about him," I answered. "Mazzei is part of the highest American tradition, and I think Italian Americans ought to know about him. It would make it easier for them to become more completely integrated with America—they would see that they are part of American history. Also part of the world progress toward a better civilization. If they knew about Mazzei, I don't think Mussolini's ups and downs and his propaganda would make any real difference to them.

"Of course this goes for Americans of other strains too. It would be good for Polish Americans if they knew that Poles helped Captain Smith to save the Jamestown Colony at the very beginning of the America we know today. They ought to know about General Pulaski and General Kosciuszko, who fought side by side with George Washington in the Revolution . . . And it would help Jewish Americans if they knew about Haym Salomon, who lent Washington a huge sum of money to tide him over a crisis in the Revolution. The money, incidentally, was never repaid. . . . And it would help German Americans if they knew about General von Steuben and Carl Schurz ——

"And it would be simply great if old-stock Americans also knew about Mazzei, Pulaski, Haym Salomon, von Steuben, Schurz and other such 'foreigners.' It would free many of prejudice and intolerance toward their fellow Americans.

"It would help this fellow Westbrook Pegler who's been writing a lot of dumb stuff lately. . . . Of course maybe the trouble with Pegler is that he is himself the son of a 'foreigner,' an immigrant, and feels a little uneasy about it, has doubts about his being a full-fledged American; so he sounds off at the expense of others, to convince himself that as an American, by God, he's as good as they come. . . ."

Awhile later the boy's father wrote to me:

". . . Johnnie has read up on Mazzei. So have the rest of us. I think he'll be O.K. now and I guess we're all proud to be Italian *Americans.*"

We have been corresponding ever since. A letter from him reaches me as I write this book. ". . . I've been thinking of Italy lately. I can't help myself. A lot of people in our neighborhood are bothered. What will happen? Mussolini will go down with Hitler; what then? . . . Maybe revolution; Italy is a very poor country, you know . . . People over there are going to be terribly mixed up. I wish I knew how we in America could help them. Somebody will have to. I was talking about this with the kid last night. Then all of a sudden, about an hour later, he said, "Gee whiz, Dad, we ought to get a Mazzei to send back to 'em! . . ."

Denmark— Norway— Belgium and Holland— France
. . . they went one after another like a row of ten-pins.

Led by the President, the reaction of the United
States to the great *blitz* of 1940 is well known.

Its most obvious result was "Defense."

But the *blitz* evoked special sentiments in different
elements of the population.

Before the *blitz* many Scandinavian Americans were
disposed to be pro-German in a vague, general way,
which occasionally made them appear pro-Hitler. To a
less extent, this was true also of recent-Dutch Americans.

There were several closely connected roots of this
pro-German disposition of North-European immigrant
groups. One was proximity, and the long ties of their
old countries with Germany. Another was a feeling of
distant "racial" (Nordic) kinship with the German
people whom they admired in many ways. A third element was the importation of a tendency toward resent-
ing the British. All this helped over a long period of
time to bring Scandinavian and Dutch groups in this
country into close contact with Germans and German
Americans, and probably many were exposed to Nazi
propaganda; it took seriously only with some, who

rather approved of Hitler's Jewish policy. Many rather looked down on Poland, Bohemia and other East European countries, and were not too upset when Hitler took Czechoslovakia and Poland.

His aggression in 1940, however, altered the picture.

Take the fall of Denmark and William Knudsen, for example. Prior to April 1940 this Danish immigrant who made good in the American automobile industry couldn't make up his mind to dislike Hitlerism; in fact, when he returned from a trip to Germany in the late '30s, he seemed to admire or tolerate certain phases of it. But when Hitler grabbed his native land, he found himself definitely anti-Nazi . . . thus completing his qualifications for the most prominent position on the President's Defense Commission, created soon after.

This rapid anti-Hitler crystallization occurred in many other Danish Americans all over the country.

In Brooklyn, New York, large "Norwegian" and "German" settlements exist side by side. At many points they interpenetrate. And for decades the relations between German and Norwegian Americans were the best. They traded in each other's stores, went to each other's picnics. They intermarried. They worked in the same shops. They kiddingly called one another "Dutchmen" and "squareheads."

But, when Hitler bagged Norway, this occurred.

A Norwegian American walked with a large empty sack into the German delicatessen store where he and his wife had been shopping for years. He filled the sack with the goods displayed on the counter, and carried it out. The proprietor—an American citizen—ran after him, shouting protests. "I am doing to you," explained the Norwegian American, "what your goddamned Hitler is doing to Norway!" and turned the corner with the sack on his back. The store-owner yelled for the policeman on the opposite side of the street who was watching the incident, but the cop, also of Norwegian stock, only laughed at him.

Similar things happened in the Northwest where German and Norwegian Americans had lived together as good neighbors for years.

The future of Norway is now a lively concern of perhaps a majority of Norwegian Americans. They too have collected considerable sums of relief money.

They are most numerous in Minnesota. So on April 10, 1941 the Norwegian minister to the United States, Wilhelm Munthe Morgenstierne, appeared by invitation before the State Legislature to give an address on Norway's aims and hopes. And on April 21st Minnesota's Senator Joseph H. Ball asked and received the unanimous consent of the United States Senate to have the address printed in the *Congressional Record*.

Pella, Iowa, is a town founded by Dutch immigrants in 1847. Some of the "Hollanders" living there are fourth-generation Americans.

May 10, 1940 was the day of Pella's annual *Tulpen Feest* (Tulip Festival). In the morning, according to one of my correspondents, no one quite believed the headlines about Hitler's invasion of Holland, Belgium and

Luxembourg. "It was like a faint rumble of something far-off. . . .

"In the afternoon, however, some of the people became terribly upset, especially those who have relatives in Holland. Some cried. Many could not sing the songs they had rehearsed for the *Feest*.

"At three o'clock the crowd gathered before the *Tulp Toren* (Tulip Tower) in the town square and bowed their heads while the organ played the Dutch anthem, *Wien Neerlandsbloed*. I glanced up and saw tears running down many faces. A deep seriousness held the assembly as one of the local ministers read a cablegram which had just been sent to Queen Wilhelmina: 'TULIP TIME FESTIVITIES OF PEOPLE OF PELLA COMMEMORATING THEIR HOLLAND ANCESTRY PROFOUNDLY SADDENED BY CRISIS IN OUR MOTHER COUNTRY. YOU HAVE OUR DEEPEST SYMPATHY AND OUR PRAYERS FOR DIVINE GUIDANCE IN THIS TRIAL.'

The scene was poignant.

"Last winter we in Pella prided ourselves on the fact that the war had not become an issue in the conversation of the people. We were neutral. This was America. The European war was none of our business. That is all gone now.

". . . I asked a laborer who has sisters and brothers in Holland if he thought the United States should try to rescue the fallen countries in Europe. He said no; he had come to America to get away from war and had no desire to go back. . . . Another man dislikes 'the British economic dictatorship over the Continent and the colonial world' so much that he is tempted to try German domination for a while, although he has no love for the Nazis and their methods. . . . England has few friends in Pella. . . . Any number of young men, however, say they would volunteer to further democracy. . . ."

In the town of Holland, Michigan, also founded by the Dutch in the 1840s, a similar mood prevailed.

During their onslaught on Rotterdam, Nazi dive bombers destroyed the birthplace of Hendrik Van Loon, the well-known American writer. Ever since he has been devoting himself to the cause of his native Holland, and he has become one of the leading interventionists.

And President Roosevelt's Dutch ancestry seemed to inject a special note of pained sympathy into the message he sent to Queen Wilhelmina on May 11th.

The fall of Belgium had a drastic, bewildering effect on the few Belgian immigrants and their American-born children.

The collapse of France caused a rather special confusion among French Americans. A small anti-British, pro-Nazi element appeared; most of the rest have floundered ever since between pro-Vichy and Free French sentiments, shot through with sharp, profound worry about the future.

But Dunkirk and the ensuing Battle of Britain evoked the most widespread "old country" sentiments.

I have already referred to old-stock Americans'

natural feeling about the "Mother Country" in times of crisis. It began to produce interesting scenes even before Hitler directed his *blitz* at western Europe. On Sunday, October 22, 1939, sitting with the congregation of St. James Episcopal Church at Hyde Park, New York, President Roosevelt heard with "his head bowed" and "amid a deep hush"—according to a front-page story in the New York *Times*—the following prayer by the Reverend Frank R. Wilson, "[his] pastor, from Campobello Island, N. B.":

"O Lord, most heartily we beseech Thee with Thy favor to behold Thy gracious sovereign, lord, King George; and so replenish him with the grace of Thy holy spirit, that he may always incline to Thy will, and walk in Thy way; endow him plenteously with heavenly gifts; grant him in health and wealth long to live; strengthen him that he may vanquish and overcome all his enemies, and finally after this life he may attain everlasting joy and felicity, through Jesus Christ our Lord. *Amen.*"

In the Washington Cathedral on Sunday, September 29, 1940, when London and other English cities were under severest attack and no one could say when Hitler might invade Britain, a congregation of fifteen hundred United States Government officials, diplomats and private citizens knelt in prayer for the British people. In a front-row aisle seat was the late British Ambassador, Lord Lothian; and Bishop James E. Freeman prayed:

"In this hour of their need, do Thou strengthen and sustain them. Guard and save them from the violence of their enemies. Ease their burdens, heal their wounds, calm their fears . . . and preserve to future generations the gifts and virtues of the British Empire."

After the prayer as the congregation rose, the organ thundered: "God Save the King" . . . whose score is of course also that of "My Country, 'Tis of Thee."

Traveling about the country in 1939–'41, I came to know men and women of all backgrounds who in many ways were superb human beings. Finding friends was one of the most rewarding phases of the project.

But then all of a sudden, as we talked about America the Gentiles among them were as apt as not to say, "But what about the Jews? They are a different problem, you know."

Things like this would happen:

One day I was walking on Michigan Boulevard in Chicago with a Czech-immigrant businessman who is an American citizen and in most respects a fine, intelligent man. He was interested in my "Plymouth Rock and Ellis Island" ideas and agreed with most of them.

"But—" he abruptly stopped in the shadow of the Tribune Building—"*what* are you going to do about the Jews?"

"What do you mean?" I said.

"Well, they have all the money."

"They haven't either," I said, reaching into my pocket; "I've got a few dollars myself."

"I mean they have all the business."

"They haven't either; you're in business and, so far as I know, you're not on the verge of bankruptcy."

163

"I mean they control everything."

"What—for instance?"

"Everything!"

I said, "The *Tribune* here is one of the biggest things in Chicago; do the Jews control it?"

"No, but——"

"But what?"

"Nothing; you're too damn precise."

Some time before I had read an excellent article in *Fortune* magazine showing that the Jews in the United States own and control only their proportion of the national wealth. I knew firsthand that most Jewish Americans were factory and white-collar workers. . . . and I told him so. I said I knew Jews whom I disliked very much as individuals just as I disliked some Catholics and some Protestants, a certain Mormon, a number of Slovenian and old-stock and Irish and Lithuanian Americans. And I wound up by saying there was no Jewish problem in America; there was no Negro problem, or Czech, Polish, Irish, Armenian . . . or German problem; there was only the American problem—the human problem, the same here as elsewhere.

An hour before my Czech American friend had almost wept over Hitler's seizure of Czechoslovakia. But now, paying no attention to what I had said, he suggested a plan for what "we," the non-Jews, ought to do with the Jews: round them all up and exile them to the Dakotas! "Let them do what they like there, but nowhere else in this country."

"You mean a kind of concentration camp," I said.

"Call it what you like," he said. "They get the best of you."

"That's exactly what Hitler is doing in Europe," I said, "and what he hopes will happen here. You're helping him. Where did you get this idea anyhow?"

"Several people I know believe in it."

"Who are they?"

He told me about them. They were average-run people, business and professional men. One was a Slovak priest, a Coughlinite. One was a German American; one a Polish immigrant; one a man whose name begins with "Mc."

A half hour earlier my friend had seemed very intelligent. Now suddenly, on the subject of Jews, he bordered on insanity.

What was this I was running into everywhere?

Of course it was partly the profound, intricate, age-old, self-generating Gentile-Jewish psychosis; but why should it be popping up so forcefully here and now? I knew the usual explanations: the Depression . . . the crisis . . . the need of a scapegoat . . . propaganda. They were all true.

There could be no doubt that the exile-to-the-Dakotas idea was of Nazi origin, spread by Nazi agents. I came upon it again in Cleveland, Philadelphia and Newark, chiefly among new-stock people.

Why should anti-Semitism be specially flourishing in new-stock groups? Some had brought latent or active forms of it in their immigrant baggage. Now it was stirred up intentionally by Goebbels' propaganda, and it soothed their troubled innards. The "pleasures of prejudice"! This applies to almost all "anti" -isms. They give one an illusory sense of balance in a screwy world, alleviating feelings of insecurity. They smooth out inner conflicts, including that between "escape to America" and the "old country." They conceal the evidence of one's inadequacy or impotence. Also "Let's deport the Jews to the Dakotas!" seems to take one off the defensive and out of vacuity, offering a deceptively definite program of action.

"But don't you see," I said to my acquaintance in Chicago, "if you exile the Jews to Dakota, someone else is apt to say why not deport other 'foreigners,' the 'Hunkies' or 'Wops'—or all the 'Czechs'—to Alaska?"

"Oh, they'll never do that with us Czechs," he said.

"Who's 'they'?"

"The Americans," he answered.

"You're a citizen, you're an American, aren't you?" I said.

"Yes, of course; I mean ——"

He meant the old-line Americans; people like Colonel Knox of the *News* and Colonel McCormick of the *Tribune* and General Dawes; big people who run things. He unwittingly revealed his immigrant inferiority; his fear; his lack of integration with America; his *need* for prejudice.

"But why do you think 'they' won't ever exile the Czechs to Alaska?" I asked.

"Why should they?" he said. "We're all right. They're all for us. All America sympathizes with

Czechoslovakia. Who gives a damn about Palestine or what Hitler does to the Jews? . . . You're crazy: they'll never try to segregate us. But Jews are different."

His anti-Semitism defined him to himself. He was a Czech, therefore he was all right; America was strong for Czechoslovakia, that got him "in" with America; and so he was safe. But he needed a contrast to affirm his security; the Jew.

I wondered about this man. As a Czech, how did it happen he wasn't anti-German? I tried to get an answer to this question, and I think I succeeded. He had a number of German American business connections; he could not "afford" to be anti-German. . . .

Anti-Semitism among Polish Americans is something special. At least every other person of Polish blood is anti-Semitic, even though he is likely to have a Jewish friend or to regard highly some outstanding Jewish American.

Why is this?

I may be wrong, but here is a notion of mine: Polish immigrants brought their anti-Semitism from Poland; a country in perennial difficulty through no direct fault of her own. Her people therefore always needed a scapegoat to help them attain definition and an illusion of security within the chaos of their endless predicament.

Anti-Semitism produced the extremely concrete evil of the Polish-Jewish ghettos; with the average Pole, however, anti-Semitism was usually in the abstract, seldom personalized. He hated Jews collectively and railed against them a mile a minute (for he could not criticize the Czar or the Kaiser and his imperial officials), but he did not dislike individual Jews; in fact he rather liked those with whom he came in contact. "Every Pole has his Jew" runs a Polish saying. . . . And when he emigrated, his anti-Semitism emigrated with him.

In an Eastern city in January 1941 I ran into a fellow immigrant from Slovenia. He loves America. He is a fine man. Churning in him are sound ideals.

He was worried about Slovenia, about Yugoslavia; Hitler was bound to take "our old country." What were we going to do? He told me he couldn't sleep nights for thinking about it.

Then . . . abruptly . . . he began to tell me that within a very few months there were going to be pogroms in New York City. Blood would flow.

Talking of Slovenia and Yugoslavia, he looked haggard. Now there was a flash in his eyes.

"What have you got against the Jews?" I asked.

He stopped short and looked at me blankly. Then he was ashamed. He knew no Jews himself; he realized he had nothing against them. He had merely heard a lot of talk by some people who belonged to a movement called the Christian Front. ——

And what about the great, widely exposed target of anti-Semitism in America—the four million Jewish Americans derived from Old World lands, principally from Germany, and old Austria-Hungary to which once belonged Poland and Bohemia, and from Rumania and Russia?

They are on the defensive of course.

As Jews, harking back to many "old countries," all the way back to ancient Egypt, they have always been on the defensive. Their great religion sprang up in the face of oppression and mass exile in the ancient world. And the interworking of their religion and their defensiveness has produced within them, along with many faults, terrific positive passions—passions for freedom, justice, the right of a man to be what he is.

Jews, including Jewish Americans, are intense, extreme people. They have been so for thousands of years, producing the noblest of men and others unutterably vile. Like all the rest of humanity, they are molded by the relations between them and the world at large; by their experience, their history.

Woodrow Wilson once said: "America lives in the heart of every man everywhere who wishes to find a region where he will be free to work out his destiny as he chooses." I believe this is more true of the Jewish than of any other migration. They were the keenest anti-Europeans; the frankest escapists, the most conscious seekers for a new world. And a great many of them were among the best Americans, among those most devoted to the principles and propulsions of the American process. But with some, their very devotion was extreme, leading them off on wild compensatory tangents: for overdevotion—extremity of devotion—even to something good, is often nearly as destructive or perverting as apathy; its root is as unhealthy; and it leads many of us, Jew and Gentile alike, down the river. . . .

Again extreme: Jewish immigrants fearful of being

overtaken by Europe, the hotbed of anti-Semitism, were violently isolationist—witness the people in Albert Halper's novel *Sons of the Fathers*, which is partly autobiographical.

At the same time, also through extremity, Jewish Americans were—are—the great victims of something akin to the "old country" complex of other groups. Their continuity springs from Judaism, from being a Jew, rather than from a geographical land. They had left the ghettos of Poland and Rumania and the Ukraine and White Russia, and the discriminatory atmosphere of Hungary, Austria and Bohemia; but they had suffered there and had caught glimpses of human beauty; and they had left relatives and friends there . . . still in the ghettos, still under attack.

So when Hitler's persecutions began their awful crescendo, Jewish Americans reacted fiercely. Their anti-Hitlerism and their eagerness to help the Nazis' victim knew no bounds. There is passion in the Jews. It erupts.

Insofar as it is too extreme, and insofar as it is still only defensive, it is part of the Jewish end of the Gentile-Jewish psychosis; and it evokes reactions in the Gentile which are part of their end of the psychosis. So anti-Semitism, historically present, occasionally latent, began to spread—carefully helped along by cunning Nazi propaganda.

The paradoxical human impulse to homogeneity and diversity is strongest in the Jews. My correspondence and personal contact with them shows that no strain in the American population is split into more factions. The hasty-minded among the Gentiles have been wont to observe that "the Jews are the most anti-Semitic people in the world." It is true there are great differences among them which have given rise to various intra-group antagonisms; but at the same time no American strain is capable of greater unity in time of stress.

This was demonstrated in the late 1930s. But in part it was a negative (intra-Jewish) unity forced by anti-Semitism.

In the 1920s many Jews were drifting away from Judaism, becoming "just Americans." Hitler's rise swung them back again—and with typical passion. The membership of their organizations doubled, trebled. They gave millions to fight anti-Semitism here and help its victims abroad. Some of this money was spent none too wisely; it went merely to combat anti-Semitism. Lately, however, the organizations have gone beyond that, to the wider work of developing democracy in themselves and in the United States—positive work rising above their defensive position.

The Zionists have redoubled their work for Palestine, and their cause is not unlike the Polish, Czech, Greek and Ukrainian causes; only it is even more difficult, less substantial, when your mind seeks to penetrate the screen that hangs between you and the future.

And Jews want to go further. Their isolationism is disappearing. They are surmounting escapism. They want to help clean up Hitler. Many are behind the Committee to Defend America and the Fight for Freedom Committee; some think we should start shooting . . . but they are usually afraid to say so within the hearing of Gentiles. Among them are hush-hushers who advise

discretion; for the "America Firsters" are already talking of "the Jew warmongers."

The predicament of Jewish Americans is not unlike
that of some of the other "foreigners" I have mentioned;
only it is worse. It has fewer compensations. Danish
Americans are proud of William S. Knudsen, whom
leading Americans of other strains regard as an American patriot and a great production man; while many
Jewish Americans, proud of Sidney Hillman who is
Knudsen's co-worker, are not sure that his high position
in "Defense" is good for them, since to many Gentiles
he is not a patriot like Knudsen but a Jew.

So the great passion in them is blocked . . . by a
stepped-up, war-crisis anti-Semitism and by the fear of
still worse anti-Semitism if they give vent to their
passion.

The tragic waste!

Most Jewish Americans are afraid. Both as Jews and
as Americans, many function with caution. Before me is
a copy of a letter from a native American to his Jewish
immigrant father, and the theme of it is: "We Jews
should lie low. We should put up with anti-Semitism,
adjust ourselves to it." He believes the American
Jewish Congress, probably the most outspoken body on
the subject of anti-Semitism, "should be dissolved, and
the sooner the better."

Not that this young man represents a majority of
Jewish Americans. But he does speak for a number of
them. And he is opposed to admitting more Jewish
refugees; for, in his narrow view, he blames them for a

good part of the anti-Semitism to which he wants to reconcile himself.

The September '41 *Harpers* contains a distressing article on "The Jewish Question After the War." The author—Benjamin Akzin, a specialist in foreign affairs and international law on the staff of the Library of Congress, formerly of Harvard and the Portia Law School in Boston, now also on the faculty of the College of the City of New York—gives an objective account of the results of Hitler's drive against the Jews. He has dispossessed them in Germany and in the conquered countries where they now hang suspended between death and the next scrap of food, or serve in forced-labor units, or are in concentration camps. Gentiles now own their property, and will no doubt be reluctant to return it after Hitler's defeat. Consequently, even such relatively liberal governments in exile as those of Czechoslovakia and The Netherlands have displayed a tendency to wash their hands of the "Jewish problem" in their countries. They—including, it seems, such men as Eduard Benes and Jan Masaryk—implicitly favor the emigration of all Jews from Europe: and "emigration" is but a euphemism for "expulsion" of several million people. Hitler has tricked them into this position which, in the case of Benes and Masaryk at least, goes against the grain; but they are helpless. They know that when and if they return to their countries they will have greater problems to deal with. That of keeping themselves in power, for instance; in which any decent approach to the "Jewish problem" will be no help at all.

So, Dr. Akzin points out, as things stand now, the

expulsion of European Jews who will have survived the Hitler terror is a certainty. Where will they be sent? Dr. Akzin does not say; he merely poses the problem. He is a Zionist leader; but surely he does not assume that Palestine could take them all. They cannot presumably go to the United States; President Roosevelt's policy in respect to the "Jewish question" is concerned with finding an uninhabited place where they might settle. Britain, also conscious of the immense post-war problems of her own Gentile populations, has likewise implicitly washed her hands of any real responsibility for the European Jews; she is unfriendly to the suggestion that she open certain of her African territories to them. Her Government's implicit excuse is fear of local anti-Semitism, which might extend even to England.

Within the frame of the current thinking about the world crisis, the problem of European Jewry is *insoluble*. This is the most oppressive fact gradually entering the consciousness of American Jews whose "old country" is Europe as a whole. It will become the central factor in their increasing confusion, in the further frustration of their great passion, in their growing ineffectiveness as people who are fiercely interested in a better world.

The only way this can be prevented is to change our present thinking about the crisis and the post-war world. This is *not* a "Jewish problem." It is a human one—worldwide.

Hungary—Rumania—Bulgaria ——

Hitler swallowed them one after another while he let the Greeks pound Mussolini in order to remove any possible doubt as to which of the two was master.

It was early in 1941; Yugoslavia's turn was bound to come any day now.

All at once the whole war situation—Hitler's hammering at Britain; Vichy's helpless senility and active evil; the enormous British shipping losses; the maelstrom in Washington; the problems in Latin America; but chiefly the interventionist-isolationist debate in the United States—became nearly intolerable to me; so I escaped into my project, my American job. I must be practical: to the devil with the damned war: there was nothing I could do about it: things would just have to take their course.

So in mid-February '41—like the American I am—I decided also to escape physically from the East where I live, and where all the war and anti-war palaver was concentrated into an immense, nonsensical tumult. I drove off—to the Southwest where there were several people who had written me about "Plymouth Rock and Ellis Island."

But there was no escape. I didn't have sufficient character to take the radio out of my car or to keep it turned off. Also I am a sucker for newspapers and magazines; I get my hands on everything in print wherever I go; and even in places smaller and more remote than El Paso and Tucson, six or seven thousand miles away from the scene of events, eight-column headlines read "HITLER PUTS SCREWS ON YUGOSLAVIA." A boiler-plate cartoon in a Texas small-town weekly represented a great dragon with a small mustache under his nose licking his chops in anticipation of gulping down the little animal before him, half sheep and half goat, which was labeled "Yugoslavia."

In Tucson I picked up my forwarded mail, and there were several letters from strangers who, remembering *The Native's Return*, wrote me sympathetic words about the plight of my old country. A Vermont correspondent said: "I know how dismayed you must be seeing your native land on the verge of being swallowed by Hitler."

How *could* I concentrate on my American job?

I kept turning on the radio as I drove, sometimes to hear again the news items of an hour before, or to listen to Raymond Gram Swing, Elmer Davis and John Gunther who—objective as they try to be—kept implying when they did not say outright that Yugoslavia's days were numbered. The insatiable maw was about to engulf another country—the country *I* was born in.

I was getting radio stations in Mexico; their broadcasters too were talking about the plight of Yugoslavia.

I tried to think.

The cumulative effect of headlines, cartoons, news

items and radio comments was not quite accurate. Strictly speaking, Hitler, in order to swallow Yugoslavia, was "putting the screws" on the Belgrade government which had virtually no mandate from the peoples constituting the country's population.

The nominal ruler of the country was seventeen-year-old King Peter II, son of the assassinated Alexander. The actual ruler was the Chief Regent, Prince Paul Karageorgevitch, a native of Czarist Russia educated at Oxford, a weak man. He was a dilettante in art and something of a cynic and fatalist in statesmanship. He held his position because he was a prince, a cousin of the murdered king. He really belonged on the Riviera.

For the last two or three years I had not been paying any particular attention to political developments in Yugoslavia, except in an occasional conversation with one or another of my friends—Stoyan Pribichevich of *Fortune* magazine; Don Niko Grskovich, a former Croatian-language newspaper editor in New York; and Jurica Bjankini, a Yugoslav journalist in Chicago—who did follow events; but I knew almost as well as I knew anything, that the majority of the ministers in Prince Paul's government were, to put it mildly, inadequate.

The majority were the kind of men dictatorship or near-dictatorship inevitably brings to the top in a small country: schemers, opportunists, bootlickers, shysters motivated principally by personal ambition; innately incapable of rising greatly to any critical occasion.

But, I was saying to myself, they were perhaps essentially no worse than the great majority of European "statesmen" since the early 1930s. Behind them were

several years of a policy furthered by men exactly like
themselves. It had not been specially their own. It had
been organic—as cancer may be called organic—with
developments in Europe immediately preceding and following Munich; organic, that is, with the whole process
of European defensiveness, degeneration, "madness"
and collapse which became apparent even to the blind
in the summer of 1940.

Yugoslavia had been entangled in that process from
the beginning. Just like Czechoslovakia, Poland, Scandinavia, the Low Countries and France; just like England; just as the United States is now ——

I imagined glumly that the Yugoslav Army, sup-
posedly a rather formidable defensive force under King
Alexander back in 1933 or '34, had almost certainly de-
clined under the Regency and its successive governments, most of which had included ministers amenable
to the Nazis. Benes, when I talked to him, had referred
to Stoyadinovitch, premier of the Belgrade government
for a considerable period in the late '30s. Prior to that
he had been a flunkey of French, German, Swedish and
British business interests in Yugoslavia which had added
the finishing polish to his education in deviousness and
corruption. When the inept Regency raised him to power
in the period of Nazi ascendancy, he turned—at first
secretly, then openly—pro-Nazi and became a personal
friend of Goering's. . . . Now, confronted with the
news about Yugoslavia's supreme crisis, I couldn't help
fearing that during his regime, under the direction of
his Nazi pals and with the tacit approbation of the Chief
Regent, whose extreme anti-Bolshevism veered him to-

ward Nazism, Stoyadinovitch and his Belgrade side-
kicks had missed no opportunity to reduce the Army to
impotence. They had made no effort to replace obsolete
and worn-out *matériel* with up-to-date armaments. They
retained in command old-dodo generals. They kept Croatian and Slovenian troops on the malarial frontiers of
South Serbia, and Serbian soldiers on the Italian and
Austrian borders, as far away from home as possible;
thus affecting their morale. . . . In effect, they were
virtually traitors.

Now in February and March 1941 the news was of
Prince Paul and his premier and foreign minister shut-
tling back and forth between Belgrade, where the German minister behaved like the deputy ruler of a province
inhabited by an inferior breed, and Berchtesgaden, where
Hitler doubtless yelled and raged at them as he had
yelled and raged at Schuschnigg and Hacha. Not that I
blamed them for running to Berchtesgaden. They had
no choice. It was the inevitable result of the Belgrade
policy for years back, which, to repeat, was in its detail
and entirety part and parcel of the European process of
the 1930s. But since I happen to be native to a country
within Yugoslavia, their trips to Berchtesgaden were
humiliating and upsetting to me, almost as humiliating
and upsetting as I was sure they must be to many people
I knew in Yugoslavia.

In a way, I was sorry for Paul and his ministers. When
he went to Berchtesgaden, His Highness wore his slick
army uniform; perhaps he had his valet see that it was
specially slick that day. Perhaps he took an extra look

in the mirror before he set out on the last lap up toward
Berghof.

When Hitler yelled for the Belgrade ministers, they
wore long black coats, striped trousers, shiny high hats,
and gold stickpins in their silken neckties, as European
diplomatists must on important occasions. But they and
their Prince were less inspiring creatures than the grass-
hoppers and caterpillar worms that were being crushed
by the wheels of my car on the highways that stretched
like lovely ribbons through the open spaces of Texas
and Arizona.

All the news that reached me, most of it in the form
of rumors emanating from Nazi sources, was to the effect
that Belgrade was "yielding to Hitler." The implication
was: what else could it do? Yugoslavia was not going to
resist. How could she? She was going the way of Austria, Bohemia, Slovakia, Hungary, Denmark, Rumania
and Bulgaria; the way of all the countries Hitler had
lately brought under his thumb and heel without sacri-
ficing a single German soldier.

I remember the weary tone of Elmer Davis' voice as
one evening at the end of his five-minute broadcast he
referred to Yugoslavia in a single sentence. To him it
was just another country going under.

To me it was Yugoslavia going under without a
fight.

Somehow I couldn't quite believe it.

Driving in the American Southwest, nearly as far
away as I could get from my old country, I was almost
painfully conscious that I was a native of Slovenia. My

family was there. They were part of this country called Yugoslavia. My father had died some time before in his mid-eighties, but my mother, four brothers and five sisters were in the land Hitler was about to take over as a month or two before he had taken over Bulgaria.

Perhaps my family would not necessarily be severely affected. My mother and several of my brothers and sisters based their lives almost entirely on the old farm they owned, and they might manage to exist even under Hitler. In fact, so far as my family was concerned, at least for the present, it might be better if Yugoslavia folded up under the Nazi pressure, quietly and simply, without a struggle. For all four of my brothers were soldiers in the reserves, and should it come to war they would be required to fight. They might be wounded, killed ——

But no, I *knew* I was wrong.

In its very nature as a small European country, Yugoslavia was a defensive state, fourteen million people on the spot; but Yugoslavia ought to fight now, even if it looked futile, even if she was foredoomed. She ought to fight ——

One day late in February or early in March, in a hotel lobby in Tucson, I ran into William Allen White of Emporia, Kansas, long a good friend of mine. He and his wife were in Tucson for the winter. The previous spring he had started the Committee to Defend America by Aiding the Allies ("the White Committee") and I had joined it at once. He had lately resigned as chairman because the majority of people at or near the head of it

wanted to go beyond mere Aid-to-the-Allies, which now
meant Britain and Greece, and he was against the United
States' entry into a shooting war if it could at all be
avoided.

It was the same stand he had taken in '40. I had shared
it then; now I was close to disagreeing with him. I did
not want to argue about it in a hotel lobby full of people
who were all excited by the annual rodeo to begin that
afternoon. But somehow I became *sure* then and there
that mere *"Defense"*—mere "Lend-Lease," which was
certain to pass Congress—would not be enough. It was
getting at the problem of American security from the
grim old isolationist angle. It was going to put us officially in the war—by the back door.

What then?

How ——?

We would have to go *out*, all-out, and fight—fight on
the production line, fight with planes and bombs perhaps, and with ideas—*certainly and especially with ideas*.
We were probably weakest in ideas. Our isolationism,
our escapism, our ex-Europeanism, kept us from origi-
nating them. It was our great national lack.

I joined the Fight for Freedom Committee.

How much had the "old country" to do with this
newly reached conclusion of mine? I tell the truth about
it; let the reader judge.

The "old country" . . . there it was . . . right where
X would mark the spot . . .

I clarified my thought about it too. It must fight, if
only as a token. It must not just fold up. . . . This was

the sentiment also of other immigrants from Slovenia, Croatia and Serbia whose letters and telegrams reached me during the next few days, urging me to "do something" about it.

What *could* anyone do six or seven thousand miles away from the scene?

From Nogales on March 13th I sent a cablegram to the only member of the government of Yugoslavia with whom I was on speaking terms. He was the leader of the Croatian Peasant party, with a democratic mandate from a considerable section of the people, Vice-Premier Vladko Machek:

"THIS MESSAGE GOES TO YOU OVER MY SIGNATURE ON THE URGING OF NUMEROUS AMERICANS OF YUGOSLAV BIRTH AND DESCENT WHO CANNOT BE INDIFFERENT TO THE COURSE YUGOSLAVIA WILL ELECT TO TAKE IN THE PRESENT CRISIS. WE EARNESTLY HOPE YOU AND OTHERS NOW IN CHARGE OF YUGOSLAVIA'S DESTINY WILL BEAR IN MIND THE COUNTRY'S TRADITION OF NEVER SUBMITTING TO TYRANNY AND FORCE NO MATTER HOW SUPERIOR WITHOUT BATTLE. PERSONALLY I HAVE FOUR BROTHERS IN THE YUGOSLAV ARMY AND SHOULD YOUR DECISION BE TO RESIST HITLER WE IN AMERICA WILL GRIEVE OVER THE SHEDDING OF YUGOSLAV BLOOD, BUT WHILE WE REALIZE IT IS EASIER FOR US TO SEND YOU THIS CABLE THAN IT IS FOR YOU TO DECIDE IN THIS MOMENT, WE ALSO FEEL THE HEROIC ACTION OF GREECE IS VASTLY PREFERABLE TO THE IGNOBLE AND MELAN-

CHOLY FATE OF RUMANIA AND BULGARIA. IN THIS WE REPRESENT THE OVERWHELMING MAJORITY OF AMERICANS OF YUGOSLAV BIRTH AND DESCENT. . . ."

Copies of the message were wired to the principal newspapers in Yugoslavia. I also cabled Ivan Mestrovich, the world-famous sculptor, and several other people who are not known in the United States. And, as I learned subsequently, other South Slavic Americans flooded the "old country" with similar cables. I don't know whether any were published; the terror-stricken Belgrade regime probably forbade it; but I don't doubt that, *via* the grapevine, our cables became part of the consciousness of the South Slavic peoples; the consciousness which, beginning about March 18th, began to generate the revolutionary mass mood that made possible General Simovich's sensational *coup*—one of the most dramatic, tragic and important episodes of the Second World War.

The rest is history.

On April 6th Hitler invaded Yugoslavia, crushed her in a week, then dismembered her. Now over a quarter of a million Serbians and Slovenians are in Nazi and Fascist concentration camps. Thousands are being executed. Many outstanding people of Croatia, Serbia and Slovenia either have been killed or are in special prisons. (Oh, if we in America had only been able to get together and bring them over early in '39!) But, according to report, the peoples of the one-time Yugoslav regions are not defeated. They are waging a consistent guerrilla warfare.

And what about us Serbian and Croatian and Slovenian Americans?

Pain and confusion ——

The backwash of the Belgrade regime from 1928 to '41 had tended to split us here. Croatian Americans were prejudiced against Serbian Americans who more or less approved Belgrade. Now some of us are farther apart than ever. The Axis created the puppet state of Croatia, and there are pro-Axis Croatian agents in the United States who bedevil Croatian Americans so that many don't know what they feel.

But some of us Serbian, Croatian and Slovenian Americans are getting closer together than we have ever been before. Some are collecting money among our fellow immigrants for relief when and if Hitler and Mussolini are defeated: as I write this in the summer of '41, some of us are not sure they will be. There is as yet no *idea* beyond hatred of Hitler with which to challenge his "New Order."

There is a tremendous passion in us, inhibited by our own limitations; by misgivings; by what we remember of the pre-'41 Yugoslavia; by what we know of Europe since 1920. . . . Should Britain win, can we trust her with the reorganization of Europe? We are not sure. We like what we know of Churchill, Bevin and Morrison; but how long after the war is over will they last? We cannot forget that post-Versailles Europe was in great part a British scheme.

Do we want to see Yugoslavia "restored" as it existed in March '41? Some of us are not sure. We hardly think so. What would mere restoration amount to? *What sort of Europe will a restored Yugoslavia be a part of?* . . .

How far will America go? Ah, America! She is in the war but wants to think she isn't. Who will say to her: *Listen, America!* . . . We are Americans, and there is a passion in us, a surge of feeling for a free America, a free Europe; a free world; a free Slovenia, Croatia and Serbia; a free Bulgaria, a free Italy, a free Hungary, and a free every-other-land; but, because we are immigrants or "foreigners," and because we are inferiority-ridden and on the defensive, on the spot, and because in us are leftovers of our escapism, anti-Europeanism and American isolationism . . . because of all this and for other reasons suggested in this book, we South Slavic Americans—like our fellow Americans of Polish, Czech, Slovak, Greek, Jewish, Norwegian, Danish, Dutch and other strains—are not really doing anything. Our brothers and sons and neighbors are in the United States Army, at Fort Dix and Camp Bragg; what for? *Where is the passage to the future?* But we are silent. We are afraid to speak out boldly with such notions as we have . . . and thus we add immeasurably to the Great American Indecision of 1941.

Instead, to ease the discomfort of our special, separate indecisions, we are anti-Semitic, anti-German, anti-Hungarian, anti-Bulgarian, anti-Italian; and thus in reality pro-Hitler, anti-American, anti-ourselves, anti-future.

In some of us there is a sharp pain; suddenly we

wince . . . then try to figure out how Bulgaria and Hungary ought to be punished for taking part in the destruction of Yugoslavia.

We hear that for every Nazi killed in Serbia by the guerrilla-*chetnitsi* one hundred Serb men and women are immediately executed . . . and we have difficulty in retaining our sanity.

We wonder about the Yugoslav government in exile in London.

Some of us write letters to the New York *Times* arguing with Count Sforza, erstwhile Italian foreign minister, now in the United States, and other aspirants to power in post-Mussolini Italy. The polemic swings around Trieste: is it to remain Italian or be made part of a new Yugoslavia? . . . Who is going to have what when Europe is reorganized? But then, to begin with: *who is going to reorganize it? What will be the formula, the principles? Who will put them into effect? How?*

No one knows; in all the world no one knows. If he thinks he knows, he doesn't say.

So we meet, some of us; we meet and talk. "We must do something." So we compose "tentative" plans and statements about the future of our "old country."

Or we read over and over again a letter from a woman in Slovenia which somehow reached the United States and the desk of the editor of *Glas Naroda* in New York, who published it under the title of "Big Friday in Slovenia":

". . . Then came the Germans. . . . They closed the schools. They rounded up the priests and locked them up. They gathered up the golden chalices in the churches, and confiscated them. They removed all the mayors. . . . They burned most of the monasteries; the monks and nuns they dispersed far and wide, and they seized their belongings. . . . There is a rumor they are going to uproot us and send us elsewhere; all of us, our whole nation. Where to? Nobody knows. Up around Maribor they have already moved the populations of whole villages. . . . Be thankful to God you are in America. Here we can feel no longer that our homeland is our home."

Or in our pain we give vent to cries such as Janko Rogelj, the Slovenian immigrant in Cleveland whom I mentioned, emitted in the Slovenian-language papers late in July:

"I am thinking of my native land. I am thinking of my mother; I remember my father, and my brothers and sisters are moving in my memory. I am thinking of my friends and acquaintances, many of them; and of those I have never met or seen but who are my kin by blood, by native speech and laughter, by the songs they used to sing, and because they have suffered.

"My homeland is a tragic place. Woe has come upon her from the east and west, from north and south. Never before has Father Triglav witnessed anything so dreadful. The rivers Socha, Sava and Drava are long tears today. It is terrible to think of the immense bitterness that has engulfed the Slovenian earth and the people who have sprung from her, but I can't help thinking of her and them.

"There is the bayonet now, the gallows; there is hunger. There are women without men. People suddenly vanish. . . . Guns bark. . . . Priests, teachers, writers are being exterminated. . . ."

With other Americans of various strains—in the same intricate plight, concerned about America and the "old country"—we want to join our passion and have it used, not merely to "defeat Hitler," not merely to "restore" something, but to create something infinitely better.

The poet Archibald MacLeish, son of an immigrant from the British Isles, has said, "It is a strange thing—to be an American." It is even stranger perhaps than he realized when he wrote this line. It is extremely bewildering to be an American in this period of the greatest crisis in the world's history.

Whether one admits it or not, and even against one's will, one now becomes definitely, passionately an Anglo-Saxon American, a Czech, Slovak, Ukrainian, Polish, Finnish, Greek, Italian, South Slavic, Lithuanian, Norwegian, Danish, German, Dutch, Belgian or French American; so much so, in fact, that one is apt to find that he refers to himself simply as a "Czech," a "Pole," a "Hollander,"—or weeps at the mention of a river or mountain in Slovenia or Finland, or when he hears "God Save the King."

I have indicated the discomfort, pain and confusion accompanying this sudden wrenching backward, and how their combination, imperfectly mixed with our strong loyalty to America and to everything basic that she represents, short-circuits our functions as American citizens. It short-circuits us too as people derived from the "old country," as members of the human race, and as workers on the side of freedom and universal welfare in the general forward process of the world. I have told how some of us work furiously or fumblingly for our separate causes which, we feel hesitantly, ought to be connected. But they aren't; and we haven't yet discovered a formula for merging them. I have told how the great crisis-stirred passion in us is frustrated by things within and outside ourselves. We long for unity, unity-within-diversity, but, separated from each other, we don't know how to achieve it. So, stabbed by the double-edged blade of inferiority and impotence, hemmed in by our isolation, some of us resort to aggressive prejudice in order to wrest an illusion of definiteness and reality from the spiritual chaos in which we feel we are caught. Thus, unconsciously but effectively, we come to be working for Hitler, against whom our national policy and the major part of our national sentiment is directed. Instead of approaching an integrated unity, we achieve but the homogeneity of confusion ——

However, if it is a strange thing nowadays to be an American for those of us who derive, no matter at what remove, from the British Isles or from the conquered anti-Axis countries, or from Finland, Lithuania, Esthonia or Latvia, or from the equally conquered Axis satellites like Italy, Hungary and Rumania, or from Switzerland, Sweden, Portugal, Spain or the Near Eastern lands which are in danger from Hitler . . . if it is strange and confusing for us, it is infinitely stranger and more confusing to be German Americans. And it should be borne in mind that next to the Anglo-Saxon they are the most numerous element in the country.

In the United States of today there is more of Germany than of any other "old country" except England.

The "German element" got an early start, playing a large role in the American Revolution. It has made enormous contributions to American civilization and culture. And as human material German Americans are, actually and potentially, among the most constructive people in the country.

But they are too the most directly on the spot.

Not that they are flawless as a group or as individuals. This chapter does not pretend to defend them; German Americans do not need a special whitewashing job. They are afflicted with most of the shortcomings of the other new-immigrant strains; and, in common with them, they have some special faults of their own. But these are not due to their "German blood," as fanatic anti-Germanists would have it. They are a consequence of a largely justified pride in their "old country" background and in their history in America. And this is coupled with the extreme degree of defensiveness forced upon them by the unintelligent but natural by-products of our foreign policy in 1914–'19 and today.

Sometime in 1938, apropos of the one hundred fiftieth anniversary of the State of Ohio, in whose development German immigrants played a great part, Dr. Fritz Konrad Krueger, professor of political science at Wittenberg College, Springfield, Ohio, delivered an address which the Cleveland German-language paper *Waechter und Anzeiger* published in its issue of June 20th. Most of the speech was devoted to a resume of the "German element's" history in the United States and in Ohio, leading logically to its conclusion:

". . . while we German Americans desire to be nothing else but Americans, we must refuse to serve as cultural or political fertilizer for Anglo-Saxon ideas. We do not listen to the voice which calls to us: 'England expects every American to do his duty!' We are suspicious of those who suggest to America an Anglo-Saxon community of political interests. We German Americans desire a purely American foreign policy on the basis of the wise ideas of the father of the country, George Washington, which he expressed in his immortal farewell address. Our experience in the past has taught us that interference in European affairs has usually been desired by those who wish to further the interests of those countries which have legalized and thus want to perpetuate an unjust situation created by them in previous years. We German Americans heartily applaud our Under-Secretary of State, Sumner Welles, when on May 24th he told Americans: 'The cause of world peace, and the fundamental objective in our foreign policy, of keeping our own country at peace, are not furthered by our participation in international polemics and recriminations over internal policies of other nations regarding which we have no rightful concern. What we must avoid as a people,' he said, 'is confusion between what is an attack upon our own institution and the purely internal policy of a foreign government.'

"Culturally we German Americans reserve for ourselves the privilege to perpetuate in America the values which we have inherited from our ancestors, a Luther, a Kant, a Bach, a Mozart, a Beethoven, a Wagner, a Goethe, a Schiller, a Bismarck, the great German scientists, all those who, in a word, represent the 'eternal Germany.' By cherishing these cultural values and by embodying them in the life of the United States we believe that we render it infinitely more intelligent and greater service than if we exchange Kantian idealism for James' Pragmatism, our German folk songs for jazz, Beethoven's Fifth Symphony for the Symphony in Blue, German piety, ever struggling to find its way, for the exposition of Christianity by Sally Rand, the Fan Dancer. We German Americans do not in any way consider our culture superior to that of the English or the French mode of living and thinking, but it is *our* way and we want to retain our approach and attitude towards life, convinced, not that it is a better way than is the way of others, but that it is a *good* way and that it is the best and most natural way for *us*.

"Thus we retain a bridgehead in the beloved land of our fathers, while having another bridgehead in our equally beloved new home; two bridgeheads which we desire from the bottom of our hearts to unite by a bridge of good will and understanding a work upon whose accomplishment we call the blessing of Heaven for the happiness of Germany, America and humanity as a whole."

There are openly Nazi or pro-Nazi factions of German aliens and naturalized and native German Americans under extremist, anti-assimilationist leadership who regard the "German element" in the United States as a section of what they call "Germandom," which, rooted in Hitler's Germany, has a vast, long-range purpose, and is world-wide. They are well known to the F.B.I. They are relatively small factions, but not negligible in the aggregate. They include some very energetic, able individuals. Most of their adherents are foreign-born, but some are second- and third-generation Americans. (The latter compare with some third-generation English Americans who, still regarding themselves as English, honor the pictures of British royalty on their walls.) Some members of pro-Nazi factions are paid Hitler-Goebbels agents; others volunteer, hoping to get in on the ground floor of a world movement which, if successful, and they think it is almost bound to be, will make them top dog in America. Before the German Consulates were closed, in July '41, these agents, paid and unpaid, were the "front" for Hitler's diplomatic officials in the United States. Always obedient servants, they are still working for Hitler. The ablest undoubtedly took over some of the responsibilities of the expelled consuls.

Their chief function has been propaganda—verbal terrorism aimed at German Americans. It is linked to the work performed by humbler Nazi agents—such as I described in Cleveland in 1938. And this terrorism has not been unsuccessful.

This does not mean that any considerable number of German Americans are 100 per cent Hitlerites. They are not. But many have been impressed by the propaganda in conjunction with Hitler's enormous successes in Europe. Some have become Nazi-inclined.

The core of the Nazi precept as addressed to German Americans is this: Hitler and "Germandom" will rule the world. The United States, a mismanaged, confused, degenerate, graft-, Jew-, Slav-, and Greek-ridden so-called Anglo-Saxon country, will be taken over by "Germans," that is to say, German Americans, who will run it and really make something of it.

This theme song finds an echo in the secret recesses of thousands of German Americans who are on the spot, on the defensive against practically all other elements in the population; they remember their own or their fellow German Americans' experiences in 1917–'18, or have been carefully reminded of them by Nazi agents who, delivering their bread or selling brushes, stop to talk to them.

The song finds an echo in people who have been hurt and who want revenge. Ach, it *would* be nice to be top dog in this great country! Then they could show these English Americans and the others—the Jews and the Poles! And they really could run things better than those hypocritical grafters now in office! . . . Of course the idea is a little fantastic; but then—look at the headlines! Hitler really seems to be conquering the world. Nobody can stand up against his *Wehrmacht*. It *may* be a good idea to get in on this. In fact it may be the only thing to do. Remember what Dr. Walter H. Silge, of the German American National Alliance, said in a speech over station WHIP in Chicago in '39: "those [German Americans] who join [the Einheitsfront—united front] in good time *may discard all fear. Apprehension of the future impends only for those who stubbornly remain on the side lines.*"

This has been repeated over and over again for the ears of German Americans throughout the country, always in connection with the flat statement: "Nothing can stop us!"—or words to that effect. And you must come clean now, you American Germans, get on the Nazi bandwagon now; if you don't, you are going to get it doubly in the neck—you and your relations "at home"—because you are "Germans" and you held back when a Nazi America was still only a gleam in Der Fuehrer's eye. . . .

Verbal terrorism. "Propaganda" is no word for it. And it went on for years while America as a whole was developing a hostile attitude toward Germany, Germans and German Americans.

It has touched a large proportion of German Americans who are still on the side lines. How many? Impossible to say, but I don't doubt their number goes into the millions.

Others it has given something to think about; and while they are thinking, they too are "on the side lines," not only from the long-range Nazi angle, but also in relation to the issues of the Second World War. In effect, most German Americans remain escapists, isolationists, anti-British. For the reasons already suggested of other groups, they are also anti-Semitic, or tend that way. They back the America First Committee; they are one of its mainstays. They go to Lindbergh rallies. And thus adding their share to the wide confusion and hesitancy of the American mind and energy, they help Hitler —even if that is not their intention. How many like him? Most of them don't. Or, rather, they don't like him in some ways. Others think he has done pretty well by Germany, which hit bottom back in the 1920s and early '30s. And look at it now! "You've got to give him credit."

The "old country"—the "fatherland"—is as important to the thoughts and feelings of German Americans as it is to all other Americans; perhaps sometimes a little more important, to make up for its present unjust disrepute among so many other Americans. It is so strong it sometimes does almost incredible things. I know of a Jewish refugee from Germany who escaped concentration camp and likely death by the skin of his teeth, but who amazed his friends and himself by suddenly bursting with pride in Germany when the Nazis tramped into Czechoslovakia!

Back in the 1920s the tendency to forget the "old country" was the same in the "German" group as in the "Czech" and other groups. Immigrants and their native-American children wanted to be "just Americans": let Germany take care of herself. They intermarried; mostly with Scandinavian and Hollander and old-stock Americans, but also with Slavic, Lithuanian, Hungarian and Jewish Americans. . . .

Then—Hitler!

Then—the success of his aggressive diplomacy, and his excesses against the Jews; which promptly reverberated in this country.

Then—the anti-Hitler boycott of German goods in the United States!

This was serious. It was not at all unreasonable from the anti-Nazi angle. But it set off as nothing else could have done the German Americans' latent "old country" complex, their *Heimweh*, along with their fears and hates harking back to 1917–'18: for at the same time up cropped talk about the "next war." This brought into his own again the type of immigrant who exists, with slight variations, in all groups; who is here only in the flesh, and whose motto is: *"Amerika verpflichtet, Deutschland verbunden*—indebted to America but bound to Germany." . . .

To many German American eyes, which began to see red, the boycott looked not so much against Hitler as against Germany. People told salesgirls they would not buy anything "made in Germany." Stores advertised that they refused to handle not "Hitler's goods," but— *"German* goods." Many stores were Jewish-owned; so by-and-by the boycott seemed to be instigated by Jews. Anti-Semitism! Many German Americans began to approve of Hitler's Jewish policy—even if he was a little too drastic.

In 1930, with the help of Prohibition, most German American organizations were evaporating. Even in St. Louis, Cincinnati and Chicago "German clubs" were closing up. The German-language press had a hard time making ends meet. But now, in '35 or '36, German American organizational life surged again. Germany! The "fatherland" . . . *"das Vaterland!"* The old clubs revived; new ones were started. Repeal helped. The Germania Club in Chicago, once the oldest and strongest and wealthiest in the Middle West, was about to go into receivership; now it rallied once more, with almost a thousand new members in 1938.

Soon after I began my project I received a letter from

a young third-generation German American named Smith (changed from Schmidt in 1917 under the whip of war hysteria). It was an autobiographical, subjective response to my questionnaire:

"I am of pure German descent; blond, with blue-gray eyes; five-feet-eleven inches tall. My grandparents came to the Middle West about one hundred years ago. Both my parents were born in Missouri. So was I.

"I am thirty. . . . Five years ago I watched with indifference, almost satisfaction, the disappearance of the so-called 'German American' life. . . . Now I feel differently. Now I am a member of two German clubs. . . . How can we Americans of German blood help ourselves? We find ourselves in a part-alien atmosphere. . . . Germany was one of the United States' best customers; then the Jews began to boycott, while the Anglo-American big-money groups in Wall Street, through Roosevelt, started to meddle in European affairs . . . and now there is talk of our being pulled into another war to help England and France. Why should *we* let that happen if we can help it? . . .

"We German Americans are being driven to approve of Hitler and the Nazis. Frankly, I see a lot of good in their ideas and methods. I think England *is* corrupt (I was over there), and I know that the English stock here, sitting beside its money-bags, is morally bankrupt. The Anglo-Saxon Americans were not bad before the Civil War. What have they done since? Look at Pendergast; remember Hanna, Platt, Taggart, and a score of others. Compare British and American political graft, corruption, waste, with the honest governments in Holland,

Denmark, Sweden. . . . I believe we 'foreigners' ought to kick the old-stock-holders into oblivion and *make something of this country!* But maybe they sense that is coming; so, with the Jews who always side with the master group, they are plotting another war on the side of England . . . the old hands-across-the-sea stuff . . . in order to emphasize once more the fallacy that this is an Anglo-Saxon country, and thus prolong their tenure. . . ."

Later I met this young man. If he was not a Nazi, neither was Hess. But, from his point of view, he was entirely logical. And I am not startled when I read in the papers of August 28, '41, that the F.B.I. arrested one Kurt Frederick Ludwig, an American-born son of German parents, on charges of "sending abroad information concerning the strength of the United States Army."

In March '41, I encountered another young third-generation German American, the scion of one of the Middle Western brewing families worth millions. He knew almost no German, yet he was a Nazi, although one of his grandfathers had been a Forty-Eighter. I talked with him a long time. It was clear that, like the blond, blue-gray-eyed Mr. Smith, he had become a Nazi not out of thin air but in conjunction with the whole complex situation in Europe and in the United States as he interpreted it. He hated F. D. R. on all scores. He hated "the Anglo-Americans" because they had put over Prohibition and thus "perverted the country." He favored "something newer" than the New Deal, which was nothing but a pro-British, Jewish trick to get the

United States to save the British Empire and "the Jewish Internationalism" in Europe. ——

The fellow made my head reel. . . . But I am sure he and Mr. Smith and Kurt Frederick Ludwig are not typical of any large body of German Americans of whatever generation. The great majority are not so bold in their minds and actions. They are afraid.

Many refused to discuss "Plymouth Rock and Ellis Island" problems. "You're a Slav" they said to me; "you'll misunderstand whatever I say!" They do not talk much of their problem even among themselves. How can you articulate spotlighted fear and confusion?

But if some are for Hitler, hundreds of thousands of German Americans, millions of them if you go beyond the third generation, are anti-Nazi. Their sentiment has different degrees. Some are much more strongly anti-Nazi than many Anglo-Saxon Americans, and of these a few have come out for intervention. Tens of thousands are in the United States Army and Navy. But the majority are ungrouped, inarticulate, unconnected with the "German element," which is organized in its defensive, sometimes obstreperous clubs and societies.

The organized "German element" and the people on its fringes do not wish to give an opinion on the issues of the Second World War. Only a few German American organizations, mostly labor groups and old Austro- and Sudeten-German societies, have officially and unmistakably declared themselves anti-Nazi. And out of one hundred seventy-eight German-language newspapers, only about a half-dozen have taken a clear anti-Nazi stand. Two of these are new journals started by small anti-Nazi factions. About a dozen dailies, over a hundred weeklies, and more than a score of monthly publications appearing all over the United States are pro-Nazi and anti-British in their news coverage, but on the whole—some almost strenuously—pro-United States and guardedly pro-"old country" editorially.

Here are translations of excerpts from editorials which appeared in the Cleveland *Waechter und Anzeiger* during the spring and summer of 1941:

May 27: Now that our nation is building modern war machinery there is bound to be a shortage of certain products. The government, realizing that an emergency exists plans a systematic collection of old aluminum utensils and other articles of light metal. It is doubtful whether it will gain much from this experiment; but it will be worth while, because it will bring to every citizen the realization that it is his duty to contribute to the defense of his nation.

June 11: In almost every branch of industry national defense orders receive priority. The OPM has already curtailed automobile production for the coming year, and Detroit auto plants have been converted into armament industries. This naturally will not only increase prices but will result in a shortage of cars. The increased purchasing power of the working masses shows especially in an increased demand for automobiles. Logical though it may be to raise the standard of living, under the present circumstances our private interests should be sacrificed to the interests of the defense program.

July 11: England's request to America, "Give us the tools, and we'll do the job," does not seem to stand up any more, as Gen. Wavell and Sir Claude Auchinleck both frankly admit the necessity of an American expeditionary force. Gen.

Auchinleck says: "The war must be won completely, not half. It must be brought to a decision on German soil, and, therefore, I am of the opinion that we are just as much in need of American soldiers as in the first World War. How we are to get to Germany is a different problem, but we will find ways and means."

The general obviously expects to find American boys on the European battle fields within the next year or two, ready to live and die for Great Britain. With the channel coast occupied by Germany, it may cost hundreds of thousands of American lives to invade the continent. They may break through France, the Netherlands, and possibly Norway and Denmark in order to save England from her worst adversary. After their job is done, the Yankees—provided there are any left—may return home, and England will reap the fruits of peace.

That's what the general thinks, but the American populace may be of a different opinion.

This is probably a fair indication of the inner state of several million German Americans. Small factions are anti-American; the great majority are not. The majority are for America in their own potentially valuable German American way. The "old country" works strongly in them, but "America First" (Committee and slogan) appeals to them too. They are right now at odds with the rest of the country. So they are glad that Charles Lindbergh and the Chicago *Tribune* and Father Coughlin and Norman Thomas and Kathleen Norris are on their side. It demonstrates that their attitude is not exclusively "German"; it is American. They themselves are afraid to speak out. "Whatever we say will be misunderstood." They are right. For what they have to say is extremely complicated and would be presented to a temporarily unsympathetic ear. The more or less organized "German element" has become one of the most exclusive groups in the American population. If at all possible, many avoid having any contact with non-"Germans." They are uneasy, even fearful.

There is a great passion in many German Americans —for America, for the "old country," for the Right Thing—but it is stultified by their inner conflicts. Also by things that happen to them at the hands of us non-German Americans. They are being pushed around. We discriminate against them. Since the Fifth Column scare in June 1940 we have refused them new jobs and turned them out of old ones. . . . American-born young people just out of high school or college apply for work. There is a question on the application blank: "Where were your parents born?" They answer: "Germany." When the employment manager or agent sees this, he tears up the form in their face. . . . No wonder they whisper together. We are driving them into themselves —and into isolation. . . .

The "old country" complex is as strong, as inevitable, and as human in German Americans as in the rest of us. But some of us act toward them as though it is not or ought not to be.

In the summer of '41, Judge Walter L. Hetfield of the Union County Naturalization Court in Elizabeth, New Jersey, denied the application for citizenship of Henry Horst Heide, an editor of the *New Yorker Staats-Zeitung* on the grounds that, according to the Federal naturalization examiner who had questioned him, he had "expressed partial approval of the Nazi regime in Germany." The man insisted he had made no pro-Hitler statements, and said it was "all a misunderstanding." I don't know the people concerned, but I would not be surprised if Mr. Heide were right. As quoted in the New York *Herald Tribune*, he explained himself as follows:

"I don't know why I was rejected. I am here since 1921 and I am always loyal. I have been only once over there, in 1926, and never since. I am married to an American citizen and my daughter is living here. . . . I have certain cultural connections with Germany, inasmuch as my father and mother are living there, and of course I can't cut those. But I have never had anything to do with the Nazi regime. I am not and have never been a member of the Bund or any other German American society influenced from over there. . . . I never had anything to do with politics. I'm not interested in politics at all. All my work is of a literary nature."

Nor would I be surprised if Mr. Heide had moments "of partial approval of the Nazi regime in Germany." That is to say, he may be anti-Semitic, but so are millions of native American citizens; he may like the Nazi economy or industrial methods, but so do or did Phil La Follette of Wisconsin and Bill Knudsen of the OPM; he may be an isolationist, but so are Burton Wheeler, Gerald Nye, Henry Ford, Kathleen Norris and Norman Thomas, to say nothing of millions of other Americans; he may be impressed by Hitler's genius and prowess, and by the fact that he has conquered all of Europe, but who isn't? I am myself.

The core of this episode is that the "old country" is strong in Mr. Heide and—with millions of other "Germans" in the United States—he can't help it.

Should Hitler win? Most German Americans hope he won't. But they do hope that before he cracks up he will destroy the British Empire and Russia. It is certain that the overwhelming majority do not want him to gain any sort of dominance over America. Some do speculate about the idea. But they hope America won't have to go into a shooting war against Hitler; that would be "hell for us—like 1917-'18."

A people on the spot ——

Should America enter the military war, the great majority as in 1917-'18 would support her loyally, although unhappily. For they would be fighting against their "old country." They are so caught up in the immense drama of Hitler's rise that it is hard for them to isolate him from Germany.

They do not want Hitler to win. They do not want Britain to win. For if she wins, *what will she do with Germany?* Will she dismember her? Will she chop up the "old country"—now so painfully alive in their very bones?

They are afraid of the Union Now idea, gaining headway in England, the United States, Canada, South Africa and Australia. It sounds to them too much like an "Anglo-Saxon" coalition against Europe—especially against Germany; against them, here. It is apt to mean a new and worse Versailles.

They listen to what the voices of authority are saying, and what do they hear?

On August 4, '41, Senator Josh Lee of Oklahoma spoke in the United States Senate: "I should like to say that in my opinion the only thing that was the matter with the Versailles Treaty was that it was too ladylike. If we made a mistake then it was because we did not go far enough. If we made a mistake then it was because we did not follow the advice of General Jack Pershing and take the war into the country . . . of the enemy. Germany has always been able to fight her wars on the other fellow's territory; and I say to the Members of the Senate that whenever this war is over if the spawning ground of war, Germany, is left intact, there will be a recurrence sometime in the future. If Germany, the very incubator of war, is left intact, there will be another war later; because somehow or other the Germans—the Nazis—have a congenital feeling that they are born to dominate."

Two days later Senator Claude Pepper of Florida spoke: "The World War is just beginning, if there is any hope for human liberty. Imagine how long it is going to take to shackle Hitler, to bind his arms and his legs with the chains of society's retribution, to throw him back into the impotency of the Teutonic forest, where he may find companionship with the pagan gods of an earlier day, before whom he kneels!"

Similar views appear daily in both important English-language newspapers and obscure immigrant journals.

For instance, the Cleveland Rumanian-language weekly *America* editorialized on July 19, '41: "If the world only listened to the advice of its wise men, it would be saved much suffering and misery. By wise men we mean leaders such as Thomas G. Masaryk, president-liberator of Czecho-Slovakia, who belong to all free people. After the World War the allied statesmen decided not to follow up their victory by occupying Germany. To do so, they argued, would cost 100,000 lives. Masaryk said: 'The omission will cost you more than 100,000 lives.' The shambles of enslaved Europe stands today as grim testimony to Masaryk's warning. Had the democracies consolidated the peace, had they turned a deaf ear to the propaganda of 'organized sympathy' which the hollow German republic carried on and which Hitler exploited to the limit, Europe would still be secure and unthreatened. Statements of Allied war and peace aims by British Foreign Secretary Anthony Eden and others give reasons to believe that this error will not be repeated."

German Americans hear such voices and read such articles, and they are afraid, and the passion within them is twisted, thrown back upon itself.

If only someone could say to them: Hitler and Nazism will be destroyed root and branch—but not Germany! If only someone could still the voices, in England and America, which are saying "this time—*this time*—we'll do what we should have done in 1918."

They would like to have a clear feeling about the Eight Principles given out by Churchill and Roosevelt in the summer of '41, but ——

Near the end of June 1940, in the wake of the sweeping events in western Europe initiated by the one-time Austrian-German housepainter, a rather amazing thing occurred in the United States. Assembled in one of the most unusual conventions in its history—"open," unbossed—the Republican party nominated for President a man named Wendell L. Willkie, the Indiana-born son of an immigrant from Germany who had come to America as a child.

A major party had nominated a second-generation American once before—Al Smith in 1928; but Al was "Irish"; he had also been long prominent in the American political scene and was one of the most astute politicians in the country. But here was a rank amateur, boasting about it; a former Democrat who six weeks before had not even been in the political picture—and who was a "German."

However, in June and July no one thought of Willkie as "German." Obviously and in subtle details, he was deeply American; far more representative of "the American citizen," in mood, manner and speech, than had been any major-party candidate for a long time back.

Willkie made no secret of being a second-generation American of German-immigrant parentage; the press did not ignore it, neither did it emphasize it.

210

But as the *blitz* continued to backwash on the United States like a tidal wave, the "Defense" hysteria increased along with xenophobia . . . and Willkie saw fit to include in his greatly awaited Acceptance Speech in mid-August at Elwood a longish passage about his background. Listening on the radio, I sensed an uneasiness in his delivery when he came to it. He told only facts, all of them perfectly all right from any American angle; yet there was a note, not of apology to be sure, but of explanation.

It was part of the "Plymouth Rock and Ellis Island" problem. Even a man like Willkie, a major-party candidate for the Presidency, could not get clear of it; it would color the campaign.

I was not on the famous Willkie campaign train, and I have not discussed this with anyone who was, but I don't doubt that the Republican candidate's German-immigrant status had—together with endless other factors—a subtle effect on his campaign manner. I listened to most of his speeches and read column after column of newspaper reports from the train, and I am sure that from mid-August to Election Day Willkie's personality and mind were somewhat different from those of the Willkie of June . . . or the Willkie I talked with (not on this subject) in New York toward the end of March 1941, when he impressed me as a big man.

One can give many explanations of his campaign manner. He is not naturally a good speaker. He was inexperienced. The whole thing happened too quickly; he had no time to familiarize himself with his new role. Some of his managers and advisers were not the best.

He was under a great strain . . . Yes; but I think the "German" issue was not an unimportant part of the strain.

By the middle of the campaign the "German" issue became very clear. It was whispered about the country probably with the knowledge of the local Democratic leaders. Finally, early in October, it burst into the open with the publication of the following memorandum of instructions issued by the Colored Division of the Speakers Bureau of the National Democratic Headquarters in New York to Negro campaigners for President Roosevelt:

Wendell Willkie's father was born in Germany. Willkie's grandfather was born in Germany. Willkie's mother's parents were born in Germany. Willkie's wife was born in Kentucky of German parentage. His whole background is German.

Hitler in his book "Mein Kampf" states that "NEGROES ARE LOWER THAN APES." HE SAYS THAT FRANCE MUST BE DESTROYED BECAUSE IT IS POLLUTED WITH NEGRO BLOOD. No Negroes are allowed now to entertain in that part of France occupied by Germany.

Willkie was never a candidate for public office until the present international situation arose. He had no ambition for public office. He had no desire to devote himself to Public Service. He was too busy squeezing a large personal fortune from the pocket books of the poor.

Willkie was nominated in Philadelphia by the Hitler formula, otherwise known as the blitzkrieg method. Hitler grabbed power and control of Germany in this manner. (Fifth columns, bribery, trickery and false propaganda.) Senator

Vandenberg was the only presidential candidate at the Republican Convention to release his delegates to Willkie or to any other candidate. Vandenberg is the leading obstructionist to preparedness in the Senate. He leads the interference to all things that would prepare us against the invasion of Hitler.

Willkie was nominated by Congressman Halleck of Indiana. Halleck leads the opposition to the New Deal in the lower branch of Congress. He, too, leads the interference against all things which would prepare us against invasion. The Floor Leader and spokesman for Willkie at the Republican National Convention was Governor Stasson, the Governor of the "German" State of the Union—Minnesota.

Unsigned, unidentified anti-Willkie leaflets appeared all over the country. One in Birmingham, Alabama, for instance, declared that Willkie "has a sister who is married to a German naval officer in Berlin . . . Are we going to stand idly by and permit a German to become President of our country?" Actually, the sister referred to is Mrs. Paul E. Pihl, whose husband, a Commander in the United States Navy (who graduated No. 13 from the Naval Academy in 1920) was then on duty as assistant naval attaché with the American Embassy in Berlin.

So on October 8th, in a speech in New York City, Willkie said: "I have been shocked in this campaign where the opposition has conducted a whispering campaign and they have been able to induce certain groups, economic, social, racial or religious, to be opposed to me on the basis of my presumed ancestry. . . . Let me say this to you also, and I say this with the utmost sincerity, when anybody comes to you in a whispering campaign in an attempt to prejudice you, remember that you can teach a dog to fetch and you can teach a dog to carry. The very person who will attempt to stir up prejudice about another will stir up prejudice about you and about other people in America. All men should stop that, not only because that is their duty as American citizens but because if we once start that in American life, then we are torn to pieces."

He made several more such statements. In fact they popped out of him in most of his more important impromptu speeches. He was not at his best in making them. I think his difficulty may be stated as follows: He had to establish what he had always taken for granted —his American self, which, in typical American fashion, he had never stopped to examine. He had to dispel the suspicion that he was a "German," a potential Nazi in Hoosier disguise, a dark horse who might be Trojan. This was a tough task; tougher than anything he had ever encountered. There was nothing he could hit back at in his outright Willkie style. His opponent never accused him; only once did F. D. R. refer to the method by which Willkie had won the nomination as a *blitz-krieg*. There were only tenuous suspicions. There was the sea of worried American eyes, faces waiting for his words. What were they thinking? What did they want to know? Hearts and minds had to be reached—could be reached only through the sincerity his voice and manner could convey. To many, he conveyed it all right; but he couldn't be sure, so he overweighed his utterances, repeated himself. He became self-conscious; self-assurance went through uneasiness to distortion.

Looking back on the 1940 campaign, I think Willkie was then a greatly misunderstood man. This was partly due to himself, to his apparent inability to keep the forces whirling about him from distorting him; partly to the whole quality of the campaign, which touched an all-time low, but largely to the mad period in which it occurred.

Willkie received support from many groups with which, as it turns out, he had nothing in common. Some he repudiated. Others he knew nothing about, although local Republican leaders and managers did; and they perpetrated or encouraged politics which were at least as dirty as those on the Democratic side.

For instance, anti-Semitic tendencies were appealed to by whispers and leaflets hinting that F. D. R. was part Jewish and saying outright that he was the candidate of the Jews, who were for him almost in a body.

But much of this propaganda was spread by Nazi agents whose job it was to defeat F. D. R. on the erroneous theory that Willkie as President might be less likely to take the United States into war against Germany, less eager to give effective aid to Britain.

Nazi and Fascist agents and their volunteer assistants knew they could swing many "German" and "Italian" votes to Willkie, and they did—it was an integral part of their main work for the Axis. It was not difficult, for F. D. R.'s foreign policy, as it bumped against the "old country" complex, had got him in bad with millions of German and Italian Americans.

But those interested in defeating Roosevelt either through Nazism-Fascism or from a wider pro-German or pro-Italian standpoint were not going to miss a trick. The sun shone for them and they proposed to make hay, not only as a temporary expedient but for their long-range purpose. So lots of very interesting verbiage cropped up all over the country. Such for instance as the following editorial—entitled "The German American Wendell L. Willkie"—in the November second issue of the Cleveland *Waechter und Anzeiger*:

At a time when the sentiment in our country toward the Germans cannot exactly be called friendly, one of the two major political parties has selected a man of German blood as its candidate for the highest office in the land.

It is now up to the voters of German descent to see that Wendell L. Willkie is elected. Would it not be tragic if the votes of German Americans prevented a man of German blood from becoming President?

Willkie possesses all the traits which have gained the Germans the respect of the whole world. He is sincere and straightforward, loves work and hates hypocrisy. He has risen from the people and understands their problems. And since he has worked himself up to a high position he also understands the problems of our great industries. We may therefore assume that he will be equal to the demands of the office.

If Willkie becomes President it can be expected that German-baiting will diminish. Perhaps we shall again be considered equal with the other nationality groups.

Because of their pioneer work in building up this country the German Americans really deserve to have one of their own in the highest office of the land.

Or such as the following "straight-American" rationalization of the above—in the same number of the same paper—by an officer of "Stadtverband Cleveland" (the Cleveland Federation of German Societies), an American citizen and attorney for the German Consulate:

Elect Willkie! The fifth of November will be a fateful day for our nation. On that day it will be decided whether our workers will continue to receive alms from the WPA for an indefinite period, or whether work shall be found for them in private industry; whether trickery, fraud, hypocrisy, and hatred, or honesty shall be the rule; whether faked crises and hysteria, or calm reasoning shall guide the internal affairs of our nation; whether civil rights and liberty, or tyranny and slavery shall be our fate; whether our sons shall be slaughtered on the battlefields of Europe for British imperialism, or whether they shall remain in this country for the defense of the United States; whether our country can be put into a state of war by arbitrary decision of one man, or, in accordance with our Constitution, only by Congress; whether we shall solve our own problems, or the problems of the whole world; whether our form of government shall be democracy or dictatorship; whether the United States shall continue to exist as such, or whether she shall become a part of the British empire; whether we Americans of German blood shall become subject to persecutions, or whether we shall remain a free group of the American nation.

All this is in the balance for us. For Americans of German blood, for the welfare and continuation of our nation, there can be only one choice: The choice of free labor in private industry; honesty in the administration of our country; calm action in our internal life; security of civil rights and liberty; the maintenance of constitutional government; the solution of our own problems; democracy in the administration of our country; the continuation of an independent and free United States; keeping our sons at home for the defense of our own country; no meddling in the affairs of other nations; and an existence without persecution of our nationality in the United States.

In the coming election it is not a question of choice between two parties but between two systems. The preservation of our democracy can be guaranteed only by the election of Wendell L. Willkie. By all that is sacred to us, let us elect Willkie.

Stadtverband Cleveland—per Otto Fricke.

Willkie knew nothing of such propaganda; he may not know of it even yet. But it was immensely influential . . . and still is.

I was sure after a swing around the country early in November that Willkie was going to get between eight and ten million votes solely because he was "German." And I was fairly sure which states would give him their electoral votes. In fact I collected a few small bets on this point. The decisive factor in those states was the "German" vote.

Roosevelt's Charlottesville "stab in the back" speech in June was the greased chute through which no end of "Italian" votes slid away from him; his Columbus Day address at Columbus, Ohio, in which he praised Italian Americans, did not repair the damage. Roosevelt's loss to Willkie of much of the normally Democratic "Italian" vote in the large eastern and western centers was over-balanced, however, so far as results were concerned, by other forces motivating other voters; just as the huge blocks of "German" votes for Willkie in states like Ohio and Illinois, and the "Irish" votes he drew because the President was considered "pro-British," were swamped by votes from other groups.

In fact the line-up of the so-called "racial-block" vote was all in favor of F. D. R. Although two Italian girls threw a lemon and an onion at him in Brooklyn, he was cheered there and everywhere else in the country by Jewish and Slavic Americans and by those of other strains whose "old country" complex responded to his anti-Axis foreign policy.

Not that Willkie—as is now clear as daylight—was any less anti-Axis than Roosevelt; but it was feared that if he were elected he would be a captive of his support-ers. Millions of people suspected him of secret pro-Nazi tendencies—a suspicion which persisted until his return from England in 1941, after which there could be no lingering doubt about where he stood. Some of these people worked fanatically against him during the last three weeks of the campaign. I met a great many of them early in November . . . and my impression (which I can't document) was that between ten and fifteen million votes (most of them in such important states as New York, Pennsylvania, Illinois and Ohio) would go to

Roosevelt either wholly or in part out of the "old country" complex.

The importance of the "old country" complex in American politics is of course nothing new. It has not been called this before, but it was established a long time ago. It was a great factor as recently as the 1928 election when the issue was Catholicism. It has long played an active role in every state and every community of any size which contains considerable numbers of new-immigrant voters. Sometimes of course candidates without qualifications are nominated and elected simply because they are "Polish" or "Italian." But it also works the other way. It brings up a La Guardia in New York, a Frank Lausche in Cleveland; political leaders who get started within their group and then develop into first-rate public servants supported by people of all backgrounds.

It plays a part in old-stock American political careers; in that of F. D. R. obviously. It was important with two or three New England governors in the 1930s who formed alliances with "Polish," "Jewish," "Italian" and "French Canadian" blocks in order to oust the "Irish" bosses and officeholders who had been in too long and grown corrupt. It has had a hand in the political rise of Harold Burton, twice-elected Mayor of Cleveland who became the United States Senator from Ohio in 1940 partly because of his genuine, intelligent interest in new-immigrant groups and in the principle of unity within diversity.

It is a considerable factor in the senatorial life of

Pennsylvania's "Puddler Jim" Davis, himself foreign-
born. His state includes numerous Ukrainian, Slovak and
Polish Americans; so in 1940 he delivered carefully prepared addresses before the Congress of Ukrainian Organizations and the Conference of Americans of Slovak
Descent sponsored by the Slovak League of America.
Both speeches contain much accurate if selected information about these groups, much understanding of their
"old country" attachment, and no little intuition about
what will appeal to them. And one day also in 1940, he
delivered a half-hour talk about Poland and Polish
Americans in the United States Senate. . . .

In principle, I have no quarrel with this sort of politics. In practice, at its best, it has an educational and
long-range cultural value. Speeches such as Senator
Davis', or those which Senator Burton used to make in
Cleveland, do much to reveal the make-up of the numerous groups composing our population. It is through
recognition, familiarity, comprehension and acceptance
of resemblances and differences that we will draw nearer
to each other in our common search for unity.

It is another kettle of fish, however, if the idiosyn-
crasies of any group are discussed with an eye to detach-
ing it from the rest of us, or with an intent to stir up
antagonisms. It all depends upon the motive and the
method. When senators and representatives speak at
Bund dinners (as did the late Senator Lundeen of Minnesota) or deliver speeches in Congress calculated to
ignite prejudice on behalf of groups palpably organized
to further the designs of Hitler, or stage "investiga-
tions" of the film industry because it is headed by Jews

and is anti-Nazi, they are not working toward unity but toward disintegration.

It is something to think about. How long can the United States afford to allow the "old country" complex and its twin, the escapist or isolationist quirk, to create and distort issues in American political campaigns?

Roosevelt would have been elected anyhow in 1940 on the basis of his New Deal record, which the majority of working people liked. The point is that the issues created by this two-in-one complex affect American political thinking and American life as a whole. In times of international crisis they are generally detrimental, both immediately and long after.

THE PASSAGE BACK

"America can write her own ticket on war material after 1943 and this ticket can, as far as I am concerned, be twice anybody else's ticket."—WILLIAM S. KNUDSEN, speaking at Hotel Astor before the New York City Defense Production Clinic, August 13, 1941.

"Defense" . . . Is America Dislocated?

John Smith
talking to himself
in mid-August, '41:

"Defense" is the big thing now. It got really going good, and what I mean *going*, a few months back; back in April and May 1941. Now it's August.

Now it's *big*.

Work—there's lots of it, all of a sudden. We can hardly believe it. We rub our eyes; we pinch our hides. Some of us were unemployed for years. Relief almost got to be normal with us. Some of us never worked before at all. Now we've got jobs, and can you beat it? we're asked to work overtime and faster, faster . . . as fast as we possibly can.

"Defense"——

Billions and billions of dollars and most of the basic materials are going into armaments. "Get them rolling, men!" Time is what counts. But what's it all about? Don't ask questions; hurry up! Here's an order stamped "RUSH" in red ink and capital letters. That means *rush*. Savvy? Time is what counts.

Man, there's lots of work. We were pulled away from our old jobs, if we had them, and we were pushed into something new. "Keep them rolling, men!" And we roll 'em. Wages are good; we are making money, by God.

But—hell, it's all a joke. We stand on our heads and we hear the tinkle of the money we make as it falls out of our pockets for new taxes and a higher cost of living . . . and the word goes around, "This is just a beginning." The wages we make; the money the boss makes—it's a joke. We laugh about it.

Everything's cockeyed.

Everybody's been stood on his head.

Of course things got dislocated during the Depression. And how! Now and then things were pretty bad. But that was one kind of thing. It came on slow-like, if we remember right. Then came F. D. R. Then we got used to it.

But *this* is different though. The end of *this* dislocation is nowhere in sight.

It came like a storm out of nowhere. It storms on.

"Defense"——

Word goes around that this thing is li'ble to last for years: two, three, four years. Maybe longer. Nobody knows. Those who talk are careful as hell they don't put themselves out on a limb. They hem and haw: *maybe, perhaps, possibly, if*—That's how they talk. They don't know the first thing, all these big-shot dopesters.

There's talk of inflation. Money won't be worth what it's supposed to be.

And we are starting to roll them out: planes, tanks, guns, bombs.

Now Mr. William Knudsen says, "America can write her own ticket—" That's what he said; it was in the papers this morning. "America can write her own ticket ——"

Where to, Mr. Knudsen? Where'll we go? Where do we want to go? Take ourselves for a ride? What do you mean, Mr. Knudsen? He doesn't say. Nobody has anything to say about anything that makes sense. Just "Keep them rolling, boys!" That makes sense if you don't think about it.

Does anybody know anything?

Not that we mind it. It's all right. What the hell! We grumble of course. We strike once in a while, and that gets us into the headlines. But we really like it. We have a funny feeling we don't talk about: maybe something really *is* happening. Maybe we really are doing something. But who knows? Sometimes we doubt it. So we strike. Why not? A guy gets nervous; no? A guy wants to know. He wants more than words; he's got to know in his fingers, that do things.

But, God, we *must* be doing something; we're working like hell. We roll 'em out. All this can't be for nothing.

Here's a thought. Maybe Britain is still there on that island because we rolled 'em and we sent 'em to her. In fact there's no maybe about it. Is that something or isn't it? We're not asking; we're telling the world. We saved Britain from being pushed over.

But to hell with Britain. We're helping her only to save America. This guy Hitler!

Now it's: "God Bless America!" May be O.K., but sounds a little phony to me.

This guy Hitler! He was a nobody; now look at 'im! He's got the whole world by the tail. Jeez, Napoleon was a soda-jerk alongside this baby.

Now along comes a fellow named Douglas Miller
who spent fifteen years in Germany, looking out for
Uncle Sam's business there. A smart fellow, this Miller.
Now he writes a book called *You Can't Do Business
with Hitler*. Everybody's reading it; everybody's saying
you ought to read it; and that's O.K. by me. *Of course*
you can't do business with Hitler. Who said you could?
Never mind Lindbergh and his pals; far as I'm concerned, they don't count. You *can't* do business with
Hitler; he's proved it himself, and that's that.

But, Mr. Miller, what *can* you do?

What *are* we doing?

Me, I haven't got time to read books. Mr. Miller,
just *tell* me what it's all about. Give it to me in a nutshell. I want to know. Tell me what we *can* do, so it'll
mean something to me. I'm not any too bright, and I
got to be told plain. I'm an American, and before I know
anything I got to *feel* it. I got to *see* what's doing. I got
to know why.

"Defense" ——

Yeah ——

"Keep 'em rolling, men!" I get *this*, all right; who
wouldn't. But I don't savvy. Who does? Nobody.

I go to the post office; I go to the bank; I go to my
lodge hall . . . and there are the placards: "Buy a
Defense Bond." I drive to work in the morning, and I
see a billboard: "Buy a Defense Bond." Uncle Sam
needs the dough. Needs it bad. Sure he does. This thing
costs a lot of money. There'll be a ten, fifteen, twenty

billion dollar deficit this year, whatever that means. Maybe Henry Morgenthau knows.

"Buy a Share in Your Country."

That's what some fellow printed on one of the placards. It's a good line; it gets me right away. O.K., O.K., I'll buy a bond; I'll buy as many shares in my country as I can. But what kind of country will this be after a while? Will I want to have a share in it? How do I know I won't get gypped? Don't misunderstand me; I'd just like to know.

How long will this thing last? My name's John Smith; I'm an American, trying to be a good one; but I'm dumb, so all I can do is ask questions. It's a free country; or ain't it?

I want to see it stay free. Goddamn my hide, I can be an American only if it stays free. *So it better!* I mean this; I'm serious now.

This "Defense" thing is big now. Look at it. Everything going full blast. There are jobs. Jeez, it's wonderful. After the long Depression, it looks like a boom—almost.

But it's no boom. This is something else. No real money in this thing for anybody. It's pulling the pants off a lot of guys. Lot of the big guys too.

Those who are supposed to see ahead say big unemployment is just around the corner again. It'll get going in October or November.

There is rationing of raw materials now.

Priorities.

"Defense" comes first. All right now; everybody out

of the way. Gangway for "Defense." . . . No, not now; not yet; no can do—wait awhile, maybe later. . . .

Priorities.

This is the big idea now. It's got to be, though nobody knows why. Time is what counts.

So what'll happen? Thousands of small industries and businesses will fold up. What else can they do? No business! There'll be nothing else for them to do but close down and turn out the workers.

Dislocation— That's "Defense" for you. Cuss all you want, gnash your teeth; that's "Defense" for you. "God bless America!"

Of course the government isn't asleep this time. Some of the dislocations will be taken care of; so the rumor goes. Some will last "for the duration." But hundreds, thousands of firms will never open again.

So it goes.

Unemployment ——

I bought a share in the U.S.A.; but what the hell kind of country is it that can't keep people working?

Funny thing, "Defense"—a big thing, biggest ever; and it'll absorb, they say, many of the new jobless. But they'll have to move away from where they now own their homes. They'll have to get the hell away from where they send their children to school, go to church, belong to clubs and lodges, and see their friends. They'll have to move where "Defense" is going on.

That's how it is. Talk about dislocation.

What'll it mean? Well, families will be split up; some communities will not be the same. Everything will change. What can you expect? This "Defense" thing is big. So big you can't figure out what the hell it's all about. And there's nothing in it for any of us.

You make money, but where is it? Now you see the dollar you earn, now you don't.

That's how it goes. . . . Faster, faster, everybody. "Keep them rolling!" Listen, all you fellows down the line: overtime tonight. Nobody quits when the whistle blows; you work till nine.

Time is what counts; time and materials—and guys that can work.

Shortages ——

Dislocations ——

Ghost towns here, boom towns there. That's how it goes. And there's no time to figure things out so they'll make sense.

You drive a car? You make your living by hauling stuff in the truck you "own" on installment plan? Do you live in the East? You will get just so many gallons of gas a week, and no more. That's how *you'll* be dislocated, and you'll like it and lump it! Or you'll hear from Harold Ickes, and you know how he talks.

Will you need an alarm clock so you'll get up in time to be at the plant at seven? Are you thinking of buying a typewriter, a new car, a pencil sharpener in November or December? You're li'ble to have a tough time getting them for love or money. Things like that will be scarce by November, say those who claim to see ahead. Metals of all kinds are needed for "Defense" and there are priorities. There aren't enough metals.

"Defense" ——

You may be in the Army. Or you're about to get called. Ha-ha-ha! That's one on you. How do you like the extension of your service from one to two and a half years? Not much? O.K. But you'll stick it out of course. What else can you do? You won't go over the hill. And in a way you really like it, only you aren't telling. You're a goddamn American, Corporal Czulik. You're part of something big, Private Bakjian and Sergeant Jones and Lieutenant Chesarek, even if you don't know what it is, any of you.

How does your girl like it, Dick Lockley, you being at Fort Knox, Kentucky, and she back in Flemington, New Jersey? Never mind about her. There are girls in Ol' Kentuc and there are other guys in Jersey. But no kidding: in a way she likes it too. She's in on this "Defense" thing because she's nuts about you; have I got it figured out right?

Hi there, John Habinyak! So you're on the way to Leavenworth, eh? Too bad.

You were born here, but your people came from the Ukraine; so Nazi agents got to work on you, and now you think Hitler is all right because he's against Stalin, who has the Ukraine. So you don't want to soldier for Uncle Sam, because now, all of a sudden, F. D. R. is working with Stalin. . . .

There's something to what you say, John Habinyak, but I don't agree with you. I don't like your attitude.

You're supposed to be an American. You were drafted under a law passed by Congress.

So to the pen with you for a couple of years. Think it over. You'll see: this is something big.

This is something *big*.

"Defense" ——

In a way we're all in it, even if we don't know it so we could talk about it like Dorothy Thompson can or F. D. R. or Raymond Gram Swing on the radio.

Well, no matter. We roll 'em out, and we feel we're doing something. Christ, we *must* be.

"Defense" ——

Somebody called it a furious futility, which sounds kinda clever to a mug like me when I first hear it. Then I think about it, and I say to myself: it can't all be just for nothing. It *must* be for something. We can *make* it count for something—somehow.

This is something *big*.

Hi there, soldier; they send you all the way to Iceland? What the hell for? Let's see the map: where *is* Iceland? Who ever heard of it? . . . How do you like it there, First Sergeant Anderson? Say, did you learn to pronounce Reykjavik yet? What kind of town is it anyhow? Know anybody there yet? What kind of people are the Icelanders? We hear there are some of them in the Dakotas. I guess they went there because it's nice and cool in winter. Of course they're Americans now, those Icelanders in Dakota. And they say this Arctic discoverer, what's his name—Vilhjamur Stefansson—

comes from Iceland too; just an immigrant from Iceland. . . . How do you like midnight at noon, Corporal Schapiro—or is it noon at midnight? Or is it now one, then the other? Must be a funny place. Of course you growl, but it must be fun in a way.

Is it cold in Iceland like they say? I guess you all wear fur coats, like the Finn soldiers when they tackled the Russkys. Don't you feel like hell about the Finns, now they are on Hitler's side? Jeez, what a shame, this god-damn war!

How long will they keep you in Iceland, Sergeant Schlimmer? You don't know. Nobody does. Nobody knows anything. Except that in '43 we'll be able to write our own ticket. That's what William S. Knudsen says.

Where *to*, Mr. Knudsen? Tell us if you know. Maybe you don't know. You're just an immigrant like a lot of us. We're all a little dumb, one way or another.

You came from Denmark. Hitler has it now. Does it worry you, Mr. Knudsen? The "old country" worries most of us. You say, "Keep them rolling, men!" and we roll 'em—you're the boss, we work for you, but we're all the same. Americans—goddamn our hides! You made good in Detroit, most of the rest of us didn't make so good in Scranton, Pee-ay, or Cleveland, Ohio. Now we're working for you. But what's the diff! We're all in the same boat. We all worry about the "old country." And we're in "Defense," whatever it is. It's got us stepping.

Where are we going? Where do we want to go?

Say—if we can write our ticket anywhere or any kind we like, why not write it *Denmark*—and *Germany* —and *Italy*—*Norway*—and *Croatia*—and *Lithuania*— and *Hungary*—and *Serbia*—and the *Ukraine* . . . or just *The Old Country* in big letters so there'll be no mistake. . . .

Say, here's an idea, Mr. Knudsen. Let's think about it. To hell with inflation! To hell with dislocation! Maybe this thing we're mixed up in isn't only "Defense."

Gee whiz, Bill Knudsen, this may be something else! This may be even bigger than it looked a minute ago.

This may be an idea; something *big*—like air-conditioning Hell or making a park out of the Brazilian Jungle.

Maybe this isn't only to aid Britain. Britain is all right, but—hell, maybe this isn't only to finish Hitler. To hell with Hitler, he's as good as gone; it'll just take a little time. And maybe there's something to what he did. Maybe some things Over There had to be knocked over. They were no good. Of course just knocking them over doesn't make him any good either. He's knocking over things that are O.K. too. He's like a bull in a china shop. He's got to be put out of business.

But never mind him. We're thinking. The guy next to me in the shop is thinking. The damndest questions he asks me! . . .

Say, I just thought of something—something I tried to forget. My name is John Smith now, but it didn't always used to be. When I came over from Germany in 1848, it was Johann Schmidt. When I came over from

Slovenia and Croatia, it was Janko or Ivané Kovač—
with a little hook over the *c*, which made it *kovach*,
meaning "smith." Now, ain't that something? . . .

Gee whiz, Bill, something is going on; how do I
want to put what we mean? We think we have an idea.
We all came Here from Somewhere Over There. You
came from Denmark. That was the Passage Here.
We've been here for quite a while now, both you and
us. You still have the Danish accent; and even I know
your grammar ain't perfect; but it's all right; to hell
with it; we understand you. "Keep 'em rolling, men!"
Who wouldn't get that?

Well, anyhow, we got away from Over There because we didn't like it. But we really got to thinking
about the "old country" *after* we got Here. Isn't that a
funny thing for you?

Now they're in a mess Over There, those we left
behind. Something is rotten in Denmark, Bill. Who
said that? Never mind who. They're in a mess in Denmark; Hitler's got 'em. And we're in the mess with
them here. So we got to roll 'em and you got to tell
us how, Bill. . . .

It's a helluva situation, if you think of it. Can't we
get at it somehow? Maybe *we* could straighten it out
for them Over There, and straighten ourselves out too,
at the same time. There's lots cockeyed with us. Half
the guys in this shop are a little screwy. Or am I?

Well, don't let's argue. Somebody'll have to straighten
out this world. Maybe we'll only need to help them
Over There. And they'll show *us* a thing or two. We're

pretty smart, we Americans; we're not as screwy as we act; but we don't know it all. I bet Ole Yurrup's got a thing or two on us even yet.

Denmark, for instance. I heard somewhere Denmark is one of the most civilized countries in the world.

Say, Bill, listen here, we're talking to you; don't be just a mechanic all your life. We got to dope out something. We've got an idea. Why don't you just write "THE PASSAGE BACK" on the ticket? Put it in great big letters so there'll be no mistake about it. Now *there's* an idea for you. That'll cover us all.

Let's talk it over, all of us; what do you say?

And, Bill, did you say that we can write this ticket *after* '43? Do we have to wait that long?

Can't we get at this whole thing sooner? Can't we finish Hitler, this crazy war, and all the rest of it, say by summer 1942? Don't say we can't. We can do anything if we mean business.

Now don't misunderstand me; we know you're the boss and we got a job to do, we got to roll 'em. We don't mind this "Defense" business . . . but why call it "Defense" when it's something else? And why can't we get at this new idea of ours *right now*?

Don't let's hem and haw; let's hit straight from the shoulder. Time is what counts; it sure counts.

Keep 'em rolling sure. O.K. But let's get the old noodle working too . . . overtime. "God bless America!" O.K. But hell, God helps those who . . .

Say, Bill—maybe this isn't a dislocation after all! Or we can make it something else. Maybe this is *all right*!

Write the ticket. Get F. D. R. to write it. You see him every couple of days, don't you? He's your boss, ain't he?

This may be the chance of a lifetime. The chance of America's lifetime. Maybe this is what we meant when we talked about the Land of Opportunity.

Maybe this is the biggest opportunity yet and we oughtn't to miss it.

Say, Bill—say, F. D. R.—that 'Italian' kid Johnnie who tried to commit suicide: what did he say to his old man who was worried about Italy? "Gee whiz, Dad, we ought to get a Mazzei to send back to 'em! . . ."

Say, have we got a Mazzei?

Why, we've got thousands of 'em! We've been making them hand over fist for a hundred and fifty years.

It is no purpose of mine to enter the bailiwick of military experts. But it is necessary for my purpose to record —as of late summer '41—some facts and basic assumptions relating to the course of the Second World War.

After two years of war, Hitler is the actual or virtual master of all Europe except Britain and the Irish Free State. He can have Sweden, Switzerland, Spain and Portugal any time in the near future he wants them. Possibly also Gibraltar.

In all probability Britain will not be invaded in '41. Hitler is in a predicament in Russia; and even should his campaign there "succeed" before winter begins in earnest, he will be unable to organize his newly gained Russian resources so as to be immediately useful to him. But if he does invade Britain, the chances are—more and more—against him.

British morale seems high; the island is in no immediate danger of starvation. The United States, with its "patrol," which since September 12th is out to eliminate Nazi submarines and raiders in the Western Hemisphere's "defense zone," has swung the Battle of the Atlantic against the Axis; most of the Lend-Lease material appears to be reaching Britain, in increasing volume and variety.

The effectiveness of "the few to whom so many owe so much" is steadily growing, partly because of American planes. At the moment the R.A.F.—which includes American fliers—is master of the air, day and night, over Britain, the English Channel and a considerable way eastward into Europe; and it is not likely to lose this advantage during '41.

For all practical purposes, the United States is in a shooting war in the Atlantic. From the viewpoint of this book, it may not be very important if we formally declare war on Hitler and Mussolini or not. The point is that *we are in the war*. But I hope that if we do go through the formality, the declaration will be made to read that we are warring against Hitler and Mussolini, not against the German and Italian peoples.

It is possible that America will suddenly have a big job in the Pacific which may take time but is sure to result in our victory . . . and it will not seriously hamper us in the Atlantic.

Our armament production must go on full tilt. It will rise; the stuff will be delivered.

We will probably take over the Azores and other tiny but important places in the Atlantic, with or without shooting; also the Vichy possessions in the Western Hemisphere. If Hitler gets to Dakar, which is probable, the Latin American situation may become acute, forcing upon us extremely unpleasant but necessary steps.

After the Russian campaign, *if* he wins it, Hitler may get busy in the Near East and/or the northern and northwestern parts of Africa. The latter appears more likely. But, to repeat, even if "successful" his Russian campaign will affect Hitler's punching power seriously.

So far the Soviet has made a much better showing than military experts expected back in June and July. In fact the performance of the Red Army has been superb. When Hitler suddenly attacked Russia, he roused "Mother Russia" in Stalin's people, most of whom have since been fighting not for his brand of communism, certainly not for his dictatorship, but for something that has been their deep and private passion for centuries. This probably more than anything else delayed the schedule of the *Wehrmacht* and made it much less of a *Macht* than it was in the spring of '41.

But the great war on the Eastern front has doubtless also sapped the strength of Russia, and she probably cannot be a dominating power when peace finally breaks out after Hitler's collapse.

There is only a remote possibility that the Russians will push the Nazis back into Poland, Slovakia, Hungary and Rumania.

After Hitler has done his worst in Russia, and counted his dead and wounded whose number may reach as high as two million, he will try to make peace with Britain and the United States—on his own terms of course. He will fail. For meanwhile, with American production increasing by leaps and bounds, the British-American coalition will have attained great strength. Why should it consider Hitler's "peace," which would be but a trick of a perplexed war lord?

The war will go on.

There remains the possibility of greatly intensified warfare in Africa and the Near East which—in conjunc-

tion with the possible war in the Pacific—might spread
as far as Afghanistan and India. Or there might conceiv-
ably be a long lull in large-scale land maneuvers, and
there will be instead a combination of the old *sitzkrieg*
and air attacks, possibly with the introduction of poison
gas by both sides. It would be a war of attrition, of augmented power *versus* growing desperation, of *fait ac-
compli* confronting the British-American ability to develop ideas.

There seems—during '41 or even '42—no likelihood
of an invasion of the Continent by land forces from
Britain except for experimental raids, unless the
American-British side unexpectedly produces a type of
machine and strategy not now in sight. Even a much
more depleted Nazi army than it is likely to be after the
Russian campaign could probably thwart any effort to
land a substantial force anywhere in Europe.

It is important to bear in mind the probable ability
of the Nazi army to prevent invasion. It constitutes a
central factor in the mentality of the Nazi-occupied countries. It weighs on their spirit. It is a great weapon for
Hitler.

As I write, the Petain-Darlan combine has entered
into "full collaboration" with him in establishing his
"New Order." In Croatia he has Pavelich; Quisling in
Norway; others in Hungary, Slovakia, Rumania and
Bulgaria; and still others will probably appear in other
conquered and captive countries. And, in spite of the
success of such excellent propaganda stunts as the V-
campaign, there will be—especially should the Nazis
appear to have "won" in Russia—a certain tendency on

the part of the people of Europe to reconcile themselves to Hitler and make the best of a bad situation.

At the same time subversive resistance to Hitler will continue, but weaken—unless the anti-Nazi forces outside the Continent *produce an idea and plan so dramatic and unique, so sound and feasible, that it will seize the imagination of the European peoples and set their souls afire; not only of the conquered and captive nations, but of the German people as well.* For it is probable that no one else can destroy Hitler and Nazism more quickly than they.

It is almost certain they can destroy Hitler in no time if they want to—and they will want to if they get hold of an idea which will be more advantageous to their future than what Hitler dangles before them. Large sections of the German nation are discontented with him, but there is as yet no other *idea*—no other force in the world which offers them a better alternative. That fact is Hitler's chief source of power. This is the opinion of such reliable observers and reporters as William L. Shirer (*Berlin Diary*) and Joseph C. Harsch (*Pattern of Conquest*).

And the chances are that if Britain and America go into a long war of attrition—say two, three, four more years of war—their eventual destruction of Hitler and Nazism will not be of great benefit to the world. In two or three or four more years of war (which, let me emphasize, many experts predict as likely *on the basis of purely military considerations*) the human world is apt to be so far gone that there will be very little left of it to care about any sort of future even remotely related to liberty, democracy and decency.

And, to my mind, it is only we Americans—we ex-Europeans, with our American experience, our American problem inside us—who can produce such an idea with its consequent plan.

Before me are two piles of books, magazine articles, newspaper columns and editorials, and speeches published in the United States and England during the summer of 1941 on the nature, issues and prospects of the Second World War and the question of the future beyond it.

On the small pile are extreme expressions of anti-Germanists like Senators Pepper and Lee whom I have quoted. Most of them are precise. They know exactly what ought to be done—what will be done if they have anything to say about it. Their idea is simplicity itself: conquest and dismemberment of Germany. In the event of an Anglo-American victory, if we don't care about the inevitable consequences five, ten or twenty years later, it can be carried out with no difficulty whatever. Conquerors have had lots of experience in that sort of thing. If we are a little green, we can brush up on the correct procedure by recalling what Hitler did in Czechoslovakia, France and Yugoslavia. One extreme anti-Germanist goes so far as to urge that all German males between eighteen and forty-five be declared slaves of the victors for five to fifteen years, depending on how long it would take them—under the direction of an international commission—to repair all damage done by the Nazis in every occupied country and in Britain

245

from September 1, 1939 to the close of the war. The theory is that the German nation—each individual member of it—is wholly responsible for Hitler and the Nazi movement, and that all Germans must be made to pay. They must be taught a lesson once and for all. Underlying this theory is the premise, regarded as a historical fact by those who hold it, that the "German race" is a people apart, intrinsically and inevitably predatory, barbaric, and forever dangerous from the viewpoint of civilized nations.

The much larger pile includes a variety of material. Nearly all the writers and speakers are fairly reasonable and desirous of exerting every effort to put human society upon a firmer basis of decency, peace, prosperity, freedom, democracy, Christianity and related ideals and principles. But some are pessimists while others incline to optimism or even achieve a full measure of it. And the majority have no inkling how to go about the task.

Several churchmen tend to the belief that Hitler is essentially but a tool in the hand of God Who is wroth at humanity. With Dr. Charles Clayton Morrison, editor of the *Christian Century*, who first expounded it in June 1940, they cite the phrase "rod of my anger, and staff of my fury!" in Isaiah 10:5. They are optimists, and their feeling about the future rests also on Isaiah. "O people of mine, be not afraid of Assyria [Germany: Nazism: Hitler] . . . for in a very little while my fury shall cease and my anger shall come to an end." So, led by Dr. Morrison, most of them are pacifists, anti-interventionists, isolationists; some are even anti-Defense. To them, in effect, Hitler is not "that bad man," as Churchill understates his feeling about him, but one who is doing a necessary job, destroying—says the editor of the influential *Christian Century*—"our nationalistic civilization, undergirded by empire capitalism . . . [through] cataclysm and tragedy [in order that] the evils so deeply entrenched in it could be seen for what they are, and before a new order could be created." Their tendency is to stand aside while the wrecking job is done and urge faith in God's anger which "is clearing old things away" and in "the wand of His creative mercy . . . making all things new."

I agree that Hitler has destroyed much that needed to be destroyed, but he has also wrecked many good things and will ruin still more if he is not stopped. I side with Dr. Reinhold Niebuhr, the well-known German American theologian, who leads the opposition to the isolationist clergy. Mysticism has its place and time, but not Here and Now.

Yet it attracts non-theologians. Here comes Hendrik Willem Van Loon with a letter to the New York *Herald Tribune* of August 13th, the theme of which is "When God tires of him, Hitler will disappear," a paraphrase of a remark by Victor Hugo about Napoleon. Van Loon is quite sure God is already tired of Hitler. This idea comes from his "historical instinct . . . from a general philosophical angle." He may be right; but his prediction, joined to Dr. Morrison's Isaianic one, bewilders me. I suspect Van Loon of wishful thinking, and I am for action to end Hitler, to save the good he hasn't yet wrecked, then to remove as much of the evil he has fostered as possible—not through nihilistic destruction, but by starting up positive, creative forces. My guess is if we even try to do this it would be pleasing to God.

Nor am I prepared—as is Gáret Garrett, the isolationist *Saturday Evening Post's* chief editorial writer, in its August 9, '41 issue—to count on Hitler's destruction by the accumulation of his own blunders. Let me repeat: the military situation appears in his favor for the rest of 1941 and possibly a good part of '42, while the psychology of the German people—the only nation in Europe which can topple him over in a hurry—will not be fatal to him as long as they can see no alternative preferable to what Hitler offers them. As for the morale of the German soldier, the following from one of his letters from Poland (July '41 *The Living Age*) is interesting:

"You will remember that when I was thirteen, I had to wait in line for bread. You know that I was alone, lost, without support from any human being or institution in Germany. The same fate was shared by thousands of others. We longed to get away from that disorder. We wanted to know where we stood, what we had to do.

"But in building an orderly society, we Germans have succeeded only in the army and in our military organizations. I know hundreds among us here who prefer this life at the front to our existence at home, for at least now we know where we belong and we have some sense of values."

There are other gropers in the maze.

A most eloquent anti-Hitler statement of the war-victory-peace problem appears in the August '41 *For-*

tune. It is by Russell W. Davenport, the magazine's managing editor who was one of Wendell Willkie's lieutenants in the 1940 campaign. It is entitled *"This Would be Victory"* and subtitled: "Whose revolution is it—Hitler's or ours? In the answer lies a great new vision of democracy."

He points out—what should be as obvious as daylight, but isn't—that the United States is in a *de facto* state of war against the Axis; that we are "blundering" lamentably; that some of us talk of *"total* war" and *"total* victory," but the country does not yet "know what we are fighting for," nor apparently do most of our leaders. "And until we do know we cannot win."

Mr. Davenport asks: "For instance, can it be that we are fighting to re-establish the *past?* If so, how should we go about it? Should we send an expeditionary force to Europe, land it on the bloody beaches of Dunkirk, fight our way through northern France and Belgium, capture Berlin and all its tributary capitals? Even allowing for the results of the conquered peoples eager to help us, the notion is fantastic. But supposing it could somehow be done. What next? a peace conference? To determine what? Shall we—or anybody else—undertake to judge the German people; to control their industries and meddle (once more) with their finances? Shall we undertake to write the boundaries of a new map of Europe? Scarcely an American breathes who would risk his life for that."

There follows a concise, exact statement of the American predicament and problem: ". . . Americans . . . do not want Hitler's world. They do not want their old world back again. They do not as yet see any other world. And yet they are in the fight. It is a situation without parallel in American history. And it is a situation that cannot last long. *Either it will demoralize us utterly, or else we shall think and fight our way through to a solution.*" (My italics.)

The fight is for the future whose "possibilities . . . already are dimly visible. They rise up like mountains across the Colorado plains in the early morning: in the darkness you can see that there is something big and formidable ahead. We could probably discern the shape of this future thing, if we dared to look. But we do not dare. We are afraid because we sense that we are living in the midst of a gigantic revolution and that this revolution must be our revolution or Hitler's revolution—one or the other. If any future lies ahead for us, for our way, then we know it must be a radical future. It must be revolutionary. It must be to our time what the American Declaration of Independence was to the eighteenth century—a breaking up of the past, an opening of a new world so vast and so little explored as to frighten off the imagination.

"The nature of this revolution, like our modern world itself, is infinitely complicated."

Russell Davenport sketches the kind of revolution he thinks is needed; a very radical revolution indeed; but he falls, it seems to me, into the serious error continuously common to both "capitalistic" *Fortune* and "communistic" *New Masses* writers—the error of basing his thesis almost exclusively upon the European and world *economic* problem. The problem is a terrific one, and Mr.

Davenport's ideas are interesting and sound, but his failure to consider seriously the endless other factors which will face us when the "next peace" breaks out leaves him floundering at the end of his article. Every important point he makes is true and deftly handled. Aside from a few broad suggestions, however (all impressive as ideas), he gives no hint of *how* Europe and the world could proceed in a *practical, immediate sense* from the point where we will find ourselves on the day the war ends following the Nazi collapse.

Mr. Davenport says some pertinent things about freedom and democracy, but all are touched by his extreme emphasis of the economic problem. The article is available in libraries, and I recommend a careful reading. I shall not examine it in detail; I shall only suggest that perhaps Mr. Davenport's difficulty lies in his abstract rather than concrete approach. He works almost entirely with ideas, concepts, and other intellectual tools instead of thinking of people as *people*—not nations but individuals—as men and women with all their diverse backgrounds, impulses, relations, hangovers, lags, problems and sentiments. Intellectual paraphernalia are exceedingly useful instruments if one doesn't forget that he is dealing with an endlessly intricate human condition, which, because human, is essentially also simple *if* approached by human beings in terms of human beings. We cannot reach down to it from above. Not with mere manifestoes, nor in theory. We can touch it horizontally only, from the same level of common experience.

Near the beginning of his article, Russell Davenport writes a beautiful sentence: "Within us there is a light," meaning us Americans. It follows this statement: "There exists within our concept of society a potential leadership so strong that, if we will but give it expression, men will follow it into the future as they have followed it in the past." Terribly true. Then: "The time has come when we must turn up that light and let it shine out across the world. . . . For in that light Hitler will appear upon the stage of history in his true character— a bloody villain exploiting the fears and the desires of helpless people."

Here he points at the living heart of the situation, for he has more than an average share of the light that is within us. Then, in his eagerness which is almost desperation, he looks about for ways and means to determine America's role in the world; but instead of seeing them in the very light of which he speaks—*in the very existence of the American people*—he goes off on another intellectual tangent. He says that what the world needs is an International party—a revolutionary party made up of people from all corners of the earth who have certain passions and characteristics. It doesn't occur to him that such an *international and revolutionary party* already exists. It has in fact one hundred thirty million members trained by a long experience in doing exactly what Mr. Davenport says needs to be done in the world. But they have temporarily forgotten their long experience, or are confused about it, because within them rages a conflict between themselves as escaped Europeans and as Americans devoted to the "old country"; a conflict whose resolving needs people with Mr. Davenport's talent.

This is all the more amazing because the same issue

of *Fortune* contains another excellent article, written but
not signed by John Chamberlain, dealing with the *international* derivation of the American people and their
great diversity whose centripetal path is toward unity.

As I write—on August 14th—announcement comes
that Franklin Roosevelt and Winston Churchill have
met in the misty North Atlantic, and agreed on Eight
Principles "for a better future world" after the "final
destruction of the Nazi tyranny":

1. No aggrandizement.
2. No territorial changes imposed by force.
3. Restoration of sovereign rights to those who
   have been deprived of them by force.
4. Equal enjoyment by all nations of world trade
   and raw materials needed for prosperity.
5. Improved labor standards, economic advancement and social security for all.
6. A peace assuring safety and tranquillity the
   world over.
7. Freedom of the seas to all.
8. Abandonment by all nations of the use of force
   and disarmament of aggressive nations pending
   the establishment of general security.

Press reaction is very favorable. My own feeling is
that the Principles are better than nothing, which was
what we had hitherto; and that in all probability they
represent neither the private thoughts nor the content
of the conversation between the two men. What do they
really mean? Aren't they just decent words? . . . Assum-

ing that both statesmen will still be in office when the war ends, and that the world's mentality and feeling will not be in a much worse state fundamentally than it is now, *how will they go about implementing the Principles?* They don't say; perhaps they know, but the rest of us don't know that they do. They are both great men, but we cannot be too certain that they have it all figured out. Also one is free to suspect that some of the Eight are phrased for American, domestic British and governments-in-exile consumption. And, too, one reluctantly remembers the Fourteen Points.

How can the German people feel sufficiently sure of the Second Principle to burn their bridges and overthrow Hitler? *Who* will replace him the moment war ends? I think the German people will have to know and to approve before we can expect them to act. And that question will have to be answered satisfactorily before we non-German Americans can expect German Americans to unite with us wholeheartedly in the job which the double logic of our American experience and problem impel us to tackle.

How can Number Eight, as stated, possibly appeal to the people of Germany and to German Americans afflicted with the "old country" complex? It means an Allied army of occupation, perhaps for years. As the isolationist mimeographed sheet *Uncensored* (August 16) puts it, "It would again make Germany a pariah among nations and an easy prey for Hitler-like demagogues."

Number Three is ambiguous. Are we committing ourselves to "re-establish the past"? Will the governments in exile be put in charge of the states whose sovereignties President Roosevelt and Prime Minister Churchill have obligated themselves to restore? *Who* are the people in these governments in exile? Will they or their successors be capable of co-operating on Principles 4, 5, 6 and 8.

I very much doubt it.

Ideas are beings, creatures. The life stories of important and unimportant ideas have always interested me. Some are exciting. So when—in the middle of July '41—the idea which I hope is beginning to take shape here first occurred to me, I thought at once I might present it as a story, rather than a formal statement.

A story of an idea-as-experience.

Ideas are strange creatures. They originate in different ways. In Europe most of them used to originate— before Hitler, that is—in the heads of professional thinkers, philosophers, who knew a lot—too much, in most cases; and much that wasn't so. The professionals put the ideas into fat tomes: Hegel, Spencer, Nietzsche, Marx, Huxley, Spengler, and so on. Then, in time, life in the countries where these big books were taken seriously began to be regulated or disturbed or affected somehow by their contents. I don't know; but there may be a piece of an explanation of Europe in this notion.

Europe is the parent of Philosophy, and its victim. The post-Renaissance Europe has speculated too much in the abstract, but done very little practical thinking to resolve its differences. On the contrary it has hugged the illusion of abstraction—pure reason!—and permitted its fires to turn into conflagrations: its periodic wars are the result, in part, of the "philosophical detachment" of its intellectuals. Difficulties have been permitted to reach such critical stages that only wars could result. . . .

Since Hitler there haven't been any new ideas in Europe worth mentioning. His own seems to be a kind of anti-idea.

In America ideas mostly pop out of experience. Few can be claimed by individuals.

In fact American ideas can scarcely be called ideas in the European sense. They are not so much intellectual productions as feelings. Hunches. Procedures. Ways of doing things. They are instinctive, intuitive, rather than cerebral. We "hit on them" first and only later put them into intellectual terms.

This may not be the best way of getting ideas, but at any rate it's the American way.

America is Experience.

So if one tells about an American idea he may as well do it in the form of a story, as the record of an experience.

I can't claim the idea in this book. It comes, it seems to me, out of a lot of American experience; some of it my own; some of it other people's. It just happened to click in my head one day, after I had been knocking about America a good while . . . after I had got into the "Plymouth Rock and Ellis Island" project. I suppose pieces of it had been converging and tossing around in me for some time. This piece had come from here, that from there.

Ideas are strange creatures; in America, at any rate. Most of them pop up in several places at the same time, clicking in a lot of different heads.

Take this idea.

I started writing the book about five days after it had rolled itself together: July twentieth, to be exact. Four days later I received the letter from the Italian American whose young son had tried to commit suicide, telling me that Johnnie had said we ought to send a Mazzei back to Italy to help the people there get straightened out after the war.

The boy's remark startled me. But it also gave me a good feeling. My idea was also his. It clicked in his head out of his experience and environment. It was reassuring.

Then on July twenty-eighth I read Samuel Grafton's "I'd Rather Be Right" column in the New York *Post*. I almost hit the ceiling. There was a good chunk of "my" idea. I was very pleased and a little annoyed—pleased by this new assurance; annoyed (professionally) because Grafton had beaten me into print with an important part of the idea.

By his leave, here is his column in full:

I doubt whether any of the diplomats now in office in England are emotionally capable of conducting a revolution against Hitler in Europe. Nor are the exiled governments of Poland, Norway, Holland, Belgium, etc., the most inspiring sights in the world. These are, in every case, governments of failure, failure in almost a biological sense: they could not keep their countries alive.

They are the governments of military defeat, traditionally overturned when war ends. The only circumstance which permits them to remain nominally in office is that they are in London and that their people are denied—by Hitler—the

right to vote them out of office. If Hitler had merely taken a
bite out of Poland, instead of (now) all Poland, the Poles
would have risen against their government after the event
and punished it for its inadequacy.

We must never forget that revolution in Europe means
revolution against the misleaders of the past, who made Hitler's road easy, as well as revolution against Hitler. The
revolutionary energy of Europe will be directed against the
Polish colonels, the Belgian "neutrality" master-minds, the
Norwegian do-nothings, no less than against the Nazis.
"Bring us back so that we can make the same mistakes for
you again," is no revolutionary rallying-cry.

So there is going to be no return of the natives in this
sense; history never takes up where she left off, nothing is
ever the same twice. This is a somewhat acid fact, but it has
the merit of being fact.

The people of Europe will withhold their revolution,
therefore, instinctively, until the right leadership comes
along. Revolution is the only way of voting that remains to
them, and every revolution is a vote of confidence, cast by
the enslaved for new leaders.

Who can, in good faith, ask the wretched of this world for
that vote of confidence today? England, whom we have still
not armed adequately? We, who still have formal diplomatic
relations with Hitler? With quite a pietistic air, we call upon
the two hundred millions of Europe to revolt, reminding
them smugly: "Hitler is no good; you had better rise against
him," forgetting that they are real people, who have seen
many suns go down, and are waiting to observe whether a
new one is really rising over our shoulders.

We are for European revolution because it would be
mighty nice. But we have to earn this revolution; we have to
deserve it; we have to win it in our own souls first. We have
to realize, deep in our bones, that this is our revolution

against dictatorship, as well as Europe's; that Europe cannot win it without us, but also, and most humbly, that we cannot win it without the people of Europe.

The obligation upon America is great and historic. The hour is striking for Lafayette's return, and Kosciusko's too. We need to develop, among our own tumbling millions of "foreign" origin, the new leaders for whom Europe waits. We need to make contact for them, by whatever miracles of intelligence work, with the new leaders within Europe who must (or history is a liar) be coming forward slowly in every village and town. We must learn to smuggle men out of Europe and to bring them back again. We must have conferences, at which they can plan their futures. We must devise new techniques; every revolution is an invention of a new way of downing tyrants who are in power precisely because they have overcome all the old ways. We must give the people in Europe an earnest that the future they will rise for will be their own, not something devised for them by the relics of their extinct governments in London. We must supply money to the new revolutionary committees, arms, propaganda, military assistance and a hospitality rather different from that bleak unwelcoming consular glare with which we greet refugees today.

Are we up to it? Who knows? We are still in the V-stage, which catches a glimpse of only a corner of the vision. It would be pleasant to say definitely that we are up to it. But just as England is closer to it now than she was a year ago, there must probably be more blood and sweat and toil and tears before the West realizes that revolution in Europe is more serious than cheering for a remote football team; than screaming advice to a contest heard by radio.

There is something in the American air at present

which is apt to catch on—fragments of an idea which may coalesce into an inner compulsion to meet the world crisis head on and deal with it imaginatively and greatly.

While writing the preceding chapters, I did not look at my mail. Now I open the piled-up letters at random.

Here is one from my friend Vaso Trivanovich: ". . . You know, as I think of what is going on in Serbia and elsewhere in former Yugoslavia, it seems to me that a lot of us immigrants will have to return to the old country after the war and try to help the people there get going again in a civilized way. . . ."

Here is a communication dated August 8 from a Mr. Kendal Weisiger, of Atlanta, Georgia. I should have heard of him before but, so far as I know, I haven't. I look him up in *Who's Who*, and he turns out to be a Virginian, an educator, who has been active in various New Deal projects. He sends me a mimeographed piece entitled "Some Ideas on Planning for the New World Which Is to Follow the Cessation of Hostilities," in which he asks a number of questions:

"Who will organize the Expeditionary Force to direct the immediate rehabilitation of destroyed ports, cities, and industries so that men may go back to work, that commerce may again move, and to forestall famine?

"Which human geographers can logically realign and regroup the small European states for geographic, racial and economic solidarity.

"Who will assume the unpleasant, but necessary task of promptly eliminating the leading Nazis, not in vindictiveness, but to clear the stage for the reappearance of leadership, now submerged and cowed, both in Germany and in the conquered countries?

"Are there enough Italians in America who could return to their native land to assist in its political, economic and social reorganization?

"How can Russia be tied in with the New World Order?

"How can the disorder of Poland and the Balkans be replaced by confidence and hope?

"What sort of a political organization can be devised and offered to the countries in chains, so they can be reborn and can order their lives anew under firmer control?"

Mr. Weisiger believes the United States cannot evade assuming world leadership, and he says: "Our next American Expeditionary Force should consist of an organized army of city planners, architects, engineers, builders, public health doctors and nurses, expert dispensers of food and comfort, and courageous souls of many other types; who will answer the Macedonian cry, which we are destined to receive from the devastated peoples of the world. For we shall undoubtedly be called upon to feed, clothe, and rehabilitate large groups of distressed and disheartened people, to rebuild public health and to restore self-confidence."

I reach for another envelope in my three weeks' mail, and find a clipping from the English section of the Japanese-language paper *Rafu Shimpo*, published in Los Angeles. There is a quotation from a speech delivered by the California congressman Jerry Voorhis sometime in late July or early August. My eye catches a sentence: "We can successfully oppose Hitler's 'new order in Europe' only if we have an 'American New World' to offer as an alternative to it."

A letter from a stranger, Mrs. H. F. Bushang of South Bend, Indiana, says: ". . . Why do not the twenty-five hundred well-educated, cultured and financially able immigrants (listed in *Who's Who*) organize themselves into a movement whereby they could induce all the immigrants who have entered the United States during the past fifty years to return to their respective fatherlands, taking with them all their cultural, educational and financial attributes and possessions, to transplant them among their people in all walks of life and watch the great transformation which will take place in those lands. . . ."

Mrs. Bushang is an old-stock American with a slight case of xenophobia; she would like to get rid of all "foreigners"; nonetheless her idea—with a shift in her interpretation—is partly sound.

On August 30th, President Roosevelt read a letter to his neighbors at Hyde Park. He did not name the writer but described her as "an exceedingly good observer" who has been "all over the world." Here are her concluding paragraphs:

"Finally, I want to say to you that . . . there is not a nation of those who have suffered abuse whose people are not aware of what America stands for. They believe in America, despite all the propaganda that is fed to them.

"They know they will never be exploited by America. They pray daily that America will save itself by helping greatly to defeat Hitlerism. They pray for this because it seems to them the only way in which people everywhere can attain peace and live in peace."

And, reading the final proofs of this book, I notice an article by Demaree Bess in the anti-interventionist *Saturday Evening Post* for September 13, '41, entitled "And After Hitler . . .?" The gist of it is that "Europe looks to us to police the peace if the Nazis are destroyed."

But now to go back to Samuel Grafton's column, which comes closest to "my" idea.

Perhaps his being the son of an immigrant evoked the idea concentrated in: "The hour is striking for Lafayette's return and Kosciusko's too." And Mazzei's, and Pulaski's, and von Steuben's. I hope Grafton's sentence becomes a classic.

As a matter of fact, it is the *only* way to ignite the necessary European revolution—and it may be a very quick way, provided the Administration and Congress, and above all the American people, decide upon it in time.

We must do something big, unique—something that will set off our own imagination and Europe's, something that will click with Germany, especially Germany, including some elements of the German army.

It must be no half-backed trick. We Americans are on the verge of a great historic function. And perhaps Europe already senses it. Why was the 1941 Fourth of July celebrated in several parts of Europe before the Nazis realized what it was all about?

I share Samuel Grafton's main point, but I am inclined to be rather less sweeping about the governments in exile. Granted, the majority—or some of them, or some of their members—are by their very nature hopeless from the point of view of any effort toward a better future. They are people of the past, failures in themselves, symbols of European Failure. This may go for de Gaulle too. They are like the Souls in Dante's Inferno: pushed ahead by forces they cannot resist, they turn their faces back. . . . It is probable, however, that some are not totally hopeless. Perhaps quite a few people in the governments in exile still have something in them that can be used. They may have been thinking since Hitlerism hit them. Certainly we shall need all the help we can get!

Edward Benes is head of the Czechoslovak government in exile. I have referred to him with some misgivings as of 1939; but this does not mean he cannot be used.

What little I hear about General Simovich, premier of the Yugoslav government in exile, is all right. Not that he is the answer to the future of Yugoslavia or a South Slavic Federation; but he did pull the *coup* of March 27. He may be useful.

But this part of the problem will solve itself. If we, the people of the United States, decide to ignite a democratic American revolution in Europe, then the useless people in the governments in exile will drop away insofar as they are essentially impotent and inorganic to the creation of a future worth having.

I must repeat: we will need all the help that can be obtained.

Grafton speaks of "the new leaders within Europe who must (or history is a liar) be coming forward slowly in every village and town."

But—how are these new leaders to function? Unless America steps in to offer real—*revolutionary*—help, they will again follow the dreary course of rising in a vacuum and functioning in frustration. It will not be a scarcity of potential leadership in Europe that will confront us, but the bitterness, the hatred, and the vengeance which, without our help, will inevitably subvert that leadership into the desperate, defensive, corrupt, scheming war-bound politics that for centuries have gutted Europe . . . and for decades have interrupted and sharply distorted American civilization.

And this is the unique function of the United States: to ignite, in our own way, an American revolution in Europe.

The United States would not seek to impose democracy upon Europe from without; her function should be to cut loose the vicious tentacles of hate, narrow nationalism, oppression and frustration that keep the *inherent democracy* that exists within the hearts of European peoples from coming to full flower. Inherent democracy! For the European emigrants found in this country a place where they were free to build whatever kind of society they pleased. *And these European immigrants founded a democracy here in America.* The answer is obvious: The people of Europe would also establish complete democracy within all Europe—if they had the chance, if there were no barriers in their way, if they could cut loose from the intricacies of their intra-European system; in a word, *if they were free.* All they need is a historic moment. We can give it to them.

When the war ends with Hitler's defeat, Germany will be the core of the European problem. Who can take hold there? The chief aspirant to power in post-war Germany is probably Otto Strasser, head of the anti-Hitler "Black Front," an underground organization; now, I believe, in Canada. Can he re-create Germany? I don't know Herr Strasser; but if he is not spiritual kin to "Mueller," the superb, desperate, hopeless, broken and afraid underground worker in Lillian Hellman's play *The Watch on the Rhine*, it is a miracle. . . . Personally, I believe that only Americans will be able to help Germany get on her feet immediately after the Nazi collapse.

And the other countries? . . . In the spring of '41 a group of people in New York City, mostly European refugee politicians, formed an organization called The International Free World (8 West 40th Street). There is another group in New York which exists around an interesting magazine, *New Europe* (151 East 67th Street). Their best effort, sincere and intellectually impressive at first glance, are little else than motions in a vacuum. The question: *But how are you going to begin and proceed?* is an unkindness to their manifestoes and programs. . . . Again: I think only Americans can give the European countries a start toward an integrated future. Only America can organize the historic moment they need. They will trust only us.

By what right could the United States assume this function?

First, by the right of simple necessity; the European problem simply must be settled. We Americans know, by now, that we shall not realize a full measure of democracy in America until it has been realized in much of the rest of the world.

Secondly, by virtue of the special relation of the United States to the rest of humanity, we are the only conceivable intercessor in this situation. Being a nation made up of all the peoples of all the world, with common interests in a national unity, we, alone have no axes to grind. We do not hate any nation. The United States has never wished the destruction of Germany, as have France and Britain. We like some countries a little better than others, but *we do not hate any*. We have accepted emigrants from all of them. We alone have the qualifications, accidental or otherwise, to fulfill this duty to history. We can evade it—and perish; undertake it—and live.

This needs to be considered too: a majority of Europeans outside Britain and Germany (Hitler feeds his people with loot and *ersatz*) *are not eating as they should be*. This includes the potential leaders of the necessary European revolution. In an earlier chapter I mentioned the scientific fact that an active adult male needs from three to four thousand calories a day to sustain his physical and mental health, and a sedentary female twenty-five hundred. Malnutrition, starvation is the background for a horrible picture if it is true, as *Time* magazine (July 21, 1941; page 12) reports, that the majority of people in Poland are getting less than eight hundred calories a day; in Belgium only about nine hundred. The list extends.

Anthony Eden will be proved too right. His picture of postwar Europe should be repeated over and over again till it is engraved in every American mind. The old continent will be in *"a state of exhaustion, short of materials, torn by hatreds, confused and doubtful."*

The United States Government is piling up food supplies for Europe's underfed . . . but the ravages of years of inadequate eating or starvation are not instantly repaired.

"We need to develop among our own tumbling millions of 'foreign' origin, the new leaders for whom Europe waits."

Sam Grafton has something here—something to think about at once.

Mazzei, Lafayette, Kosciusko, von Steuben, Pulaski— here we come!

It won't be anything new. Remember, the Creel Committee in 1917–'18 helped Thomas Masaryk and Eduard Benes to organize their setup for the future Czechoslovakia. An agency of the United States Government did that during the last war as part of its strategy to defeat the Central Powers . . . and also because

America believes in freedom for small nations and big.

That worked in a way in 1918. The trouble was that it was done *only* for Czechoslovakia.

Now we've got to do the same job for all Europe . . . in order to destroy Hitlerism (a detail) . . . to hasten the end of the war (important) . . . to save our own national character and morale (very important) . . . and to open the passage to the future for all the world.

Only we've got to do it much better than we did it for Czechoslovakia in 1918. What we did then was a trick, which happened to work—for a while.

We can't go into this thing in a haphazard, half-hearted way. That would be worse than nothing. We can't go in for mere tricks—such as Douglas Miller suggests in the New York *Times Magazine* for August 24, '41: to send money and letters to Nazis in Germany which will get them in trouble with other Nazis, causing them to murder each other. I do not object to this particular stratagem; I only say it is not anything to rely upon.

We must go into this thing with all the passion and vision, with all the strength and *humility* we've got, knowing we're in it up to the hilt; knowing we've got to do it not as a favor to Europe but for our own sake—we can't escape from it any longer. We must go into it with a dead certainty of the logic and historic compulsion behind it.

Sam Grafton: you and I and people like us will have to touch off the fuse, to sell this idea of ours to our fellow citizens.

It isn't a phony bill of goods. They want it—we all want it—terribly, much more than we don't want it. Only as a country we don't know it yet. We only know we're miserable inside, torn, split. We can't eat. . . . I met a man the other day, a Polish American. He won't let his wife prepare his food in the Polish way any more. "I don't want to be reminded," he said. "To hell with the old country." Actually, he is going crazy. . . . We can't sleep. We don't know what's happening to our brothers and sisters. We haven't heard. Personally I don't know if my native village of Blato, in Slovenia, where my family lives (I hope), is part of Germany or Italy. I don't know. We don't know. We haven't heard. Are they hungry? Are they in concentration camps? Are they dead? . . . "To hell with Europe," we cry, "we've got our own lives to think about, our own jobs!" Only we can't think, we can't stop thinking. So we burst into rage, mere rage. "That son-of-a-bitch!"

We're eating ourselves up with anxiety and hate—if we don't stop we'll be washed up. So we've got to make things clear, we've got to understand. We must—or we are licked, you and I . . . and America and our "old country," whether it be England or Bohemia or Germany, or Scotland or Ireland, or Italy, Holland, Belgium or Sweden, or Denmark, France, Spain or Portugal, or Switzerland, Poland, Slovakia, Hungary or Rumania, or Finland, Greece, Lithuania, Latvia or Esthonia, or Russia, the Ukraine, Bulgaria or Serbia, or Albania, Montenegro, Croatia or my own little Slovenia——

We've got to look inside ourselves; dissect the anatomy of our impotence and confusion; realize who and what we are.

We all come from somewhere; from many lands. We escaped from the Old World to make the New. We made a revolution here. That is an accomplished fact. America is a revolution. Democracy is a revolutionary process. Freedom is a revolutionary condition. It allows for dynamic change; it makes the future. It is future. The only future worth a breath.

But starting it here is one thing. We did it because we escaped from Europe, millions of us between the early 1600's and the other day. That was the Passage Here.

Now it's another thing—or so it will look for a while. It really is the same. Now we've got to extend *our* revolution to the Old World. Partly to save Europe, partly to save ourselves, our own revolution here: for if we don't spread it to the "old country," the counter-revolution—ignoble, cruel, barbarous, inhumanly cunning—now rampant in Europe will overwhelm us. There is no doubt about this. We can't escape any more. There was foresight in our calling the Atlantic Ocean "the big pond" for a hundred years now. That's all it is.

Now we've got to go back. In order eventually to feel at home in America, all of us, we've got to take "back home" our revolution here . . . our American idea of democracy or "an open society," our Four Freedoms, our unity within diversity . . . our accumulated American Experience.

We've got to return with our American Experience so that Europe *will see it at a glance* . . . and transform its hatreds, shed its exhaustion and gather strength.

We can do this.

We won't have an easy time agreeing on it; but once we agree, once we combine and focus our separate passions, we can do it. And we'll make history. And we'll save what we've done here.

We call this period a crisis. It is in a way if we look at it that way. But it's something else too. This crisis is an opportunity.

Now it's the Passage Back.

Now it's the Passage Back so we can stay Here.

Bill Knudsen, the immigrant, says we can write our own ticket. . . . O.K. . . . Round trip. . . .

THE SUGGESTION

A Midsummer's Day Dream: I

———————————————————

CHARACTERS: Uncle Sam
John Bull

PLACE: On the *Potomac*, the President's
Yacht, anchored in the fog
off the coast of Iceland

TIME: Early November 1941

Uncle Sam: Well howdy, John!

John Bull: How do you do, Samuel.

Sam: Sit down, John; we'll have some brandy in a minute. It'll chase the chill out of you. . . . Of course, in a way, this is a helluva place to ask you to come to meet me this time of the year, in this fog, but I thought I'd like to get together with you here, about where Winston and Frank met last summer.

John: I thought it a bit odd when I received your invitation. You Americans!

Sam: Just an idea of mine, John. Hands halfway across the sea; that sort of thing. Hope you didn't mind coming.

John: Oh, no, not at all.

Sam: Well, here's the brandy now. . . . To you, John!

John: To you, Sam!

Sam: Well, John, I'm no diplomat . . . and I'm in a hurry to get at what I want to talk to you about. Trouble is I don't know where to begin. . . . I wanted to come up here on the *Potomac*, because that's how F.D.R. came up here to see Churchill when they gave out those Eight Principles. Lots of us have been thinking about them ever since. Things have happened since then. . . . We in America are hitting on an idea. It's crazy as they come—but maybe this is the time for a crazy idea. It's been popping up all over the country.

We're very mixed up in America. In fact this is what's in my mind: This idea I mentioned and our being mixed up. It's really all of a piece. We're a funny country, John. A mixture if there ever was one, and if I do say so, we're a great country—because of that.

We have just about everything—white and black, Gentile and Jew, people who came or whose parents or grandparents came from Poland and Iceland, from Germany and Bohemia, from Italy and Lithuania, and so on. No end to the list. Chinese and Japanese. We all got together from all over the world, all in the last three hundred years. A third or more of us came just recently, the last seventy years or so. . . . It's a wonderful thing, this mixture, when you come to think of it. But lots of trouble too sometimes. Off and on we forget what our country is all about. Some of us don't know who or what we are, where we're going or why, whether we are Americans or what-in-hell? Sometimes we don't get along. Take out on the Coast, for example

—there we have the *nisei*, native Americans of Japanese parentage. They have Japanese faces; what kind of faces would anybody expect them to have? Now there's this mess between us and Japan, and these *nisei* who want to be and are good Americans are up against it, because the rest of us are human and busy and in a hurry, trying to help you beat Hitler, and we're full of troubles, and we don't think because most of us can't do more than one thing at a time, and thinking is not easy even if you do nothing else but.

Things like that.

We have anti-Semitism and anti-alienism, and we're all bothered about the "old country." So there's Bundles for Britain (you know about that); there's Greek War Relief; there's American Friends of Yugoslavia— Hundreds of such outfits. And what does it all add up to? Don't ask me, John; I don't know. Nobody knows. Fact is, I hardly know what I'm talking about, with you sitting there calm as a clam while at this very moment air alarm sirens may be shrieking in London or Dover.

We Americans are different from you English. We're Anglo-Saxon, sure, but we're everything else too, and we're hot and bothered inside. Not so you could see it any time of day. But this war has messed us up, and how. Hitler! My God, Czechoslovakia! Then, my God, Poland! . . . Finland! . . . Denmark! . . . Norway! . . . Holland! . . . Belgium! . . . France! . . . Dunkirk! . . . England! . . . Greece! . . . the Ukraine! . . . Yugoslavia! Do you get the drift, John?

John: The drift?

Sam: Do you understand what I'm trying to say?

John: Rather! You have many races and nationalities. We have them too, all over the Empire.

Sam: Yes, John, I know; that's not the point. We have them *all in the same country.* . . . Maybe I'd better just talk on. . . .

Well, sir . . . this war. We didn't know we were in it for a long time; as a matter of fact, not till after F.D.R. and Churchill met somewhere up here and gave out those Eight Principles. Some of us are still in a fog about it. What's it all about?

That's the question we're asking while we work like blazes on "Defense" jobs. *What's it all about?*

To a lot of us things are as clear as the creek after a cloudburst.

War—Hitler—V for *victory*—the "next peace"——

What *kind* of victory? What kind of peace? We're asking, we in America. What about Europe? Our "old country": what sort of place will it be? Your Anthony Eden made it sound pretty awful. So we're worried, John; we ex-Europeans who ran away from Slovakia and Norway and Italy to make a new life for ourselves.

So we hit on this idea I want to tell you about. It's something we Americans think we'd like to do after the war. In Europe. And we'd like to begin to get ready to do it. We're li'ble to get into it just as we got into the war, without realizing it. And I thought, John, maybe you ought to know about it right now, since we're all in on this together.

I thought you and I ought to come to an understanding about it. I suspect Winston and Franklin have already touched on it in their talks; only I'm afraid they

probably used words which I don't quite like. Rumors
in Washington say that after the war you and I will
"police" the world. Now, John, I have no use for that
word. It implies that we are superior and it's up to us
to "police" the other countries. Fact is, you and I are
just lucky. Your luck is that island of yours, and the
channel; while I've got oceans on two sides of me. Not
that you and I haven't used our heads sometimes; we
have—but, in a way, it's only because we had a chance,
because we are not part and parcel of all the stewing
and suffering of continental Europe. Anyhow, our
"Anglo-Saxon superiority" is out. I'm dead against
our "policing" anybody.

Now about this idea of ours—

John: Yes; I want to hear about it.

Sam: It's that—maybe—*we* could take charge of
Europe after the war. It's a tentative idea, you understand, not worked out yet; we're pretty balled up and
we don't seem to be able to make up our minds about
anything; but then again, just because we are all balled
up, it's li'ble to sweep us off our feet. All of a sudden
we'll be in it, then there'll be no stopping us . . . and
we'll want no interference. That's the point, John.
It'll be a big job and we won't want it to be any harder
for us than it has to be. We've got to do it our own
way, the American way. See what I mean, John?

John: I am not certain, Sam. You say you want to
"take *charge* of Europe"—the whole of the continent?

Sam: Nothing is settled yet, nothing decided on.
But *if* we do get going, we'll want a free hand.

John: But I say, Samuel, I don't understand—why

are you saying this to me? After all, there's Marianne
of France; what will she say? And our good—er—"ally"
now, Russia; what will she say? And the governments
in exile?

Sam: You're asking for it, Johnny! So here goes.
In the first place, I'm not telling Marianne just now
because she's in prison and can't be reached. In the
second place, as soon as you and I get through talking,
I'm off to see Mother Russia and also her boy, Ivan
Ivanovich.

I want to talk with both of them. I want them to
understand the whole thing from the start, so there'll
be no unnecessary trouble later. Mother Russia will
have to realize that she's never been an effective power
in Europe. She'll have to see too that Europe's been bad
for her so far. She's been affected by European politics
for at least a century; maybe longer; I'm not very well
up on history. So she better understand that Europe's
got to be set in order. *She* can't do it. She'll have her
hands full at home; even if she gives Hitler the licking
of his life, she's going to be all bruised and maybe a
little punch-drunk, in no shape to help Europe. Besides,
if she keeps Stalin, Europe'll object to being taken over
by her. Also the Pope will object; and we *mustn't* forget him. . . . I've already fixed up a date with him, too.
. . . The point is that only we Americans can fix up
Europe. Maybe, after some kind of understanding with
Mother Russia, we'll be able to make some arrange-
ment even about the Ukraine and possibly even Armenia; we have lots of "Ukrainians" and "Armenians"

in America who are all up in the air about their old countries. . . .

And in the third and most important place, I'm talking with you, John—really *to* you, for the time being—because *you* are the guy who's really been running Europe, and running it into the ground! Oh, no, keep your shirt on, John; you know damn well that's true! Your balance of power! Balance, my Aunt Emma! Balance—when every ten years or so Europe gets all out of kilter, and the first thing I know I got to tear our boys away from their jobs, our American jobs, and from their homes and put them in the army; and tax our people till I blush to think of it, and take away the fruits of our progress. . . . Here I go sounding off like a senator in Washington for the benefit of the Folks back in Montana or Alabama, but it's true just the same. . . . I tell you, John Bull, I've just had enough of it! To hell with your balance of power—your divide-and-rule system! We're all sick and tired of it.

I'm not saying, John, that my system is perfect; God, it's lousy in more ways and places than you know; but it has worked for forty-eight separate and *united* states—and for three-quarters of a century there has been no conflict between one state and another, but complete harmony and unity. Wisconsin has no state navy, nor Michigan, nor even the coastal states. Each state has an army, but it's called *national* guard—see what I mean?

John: Yes, Sam; go on. I don't agree wholly . . . but I am most interested in your point of view and your ideas and institutions.

Sam: I'm sorry, John, if I got a little hot just now. I really shouldn't be sailing into you at this time when you have your hands full. But this idea we're developing is important to us.

I don't mean that we'll not consult with you; we will right along. Besides, you and I will be working together on other things—on the rest of the world, for instance. We'll have to, and it'll be a big job. And, as I say, we'll want to consult with Mother Russia, too; maybe just as much as with you. She'll be important; also I'm really fond of her, as I am of you. One thing I want her to understand, and her boy Ivan, is that we ought to get away from names like "Communism" and "Fascism." They label people, pigeonhole nations and persons. To hell with labels! They start causes which are just a lot of words. They start camps, and cliques and factions which are quite irrelevant to the working out of the human problem before us. They start terror, which leads only to more terror, to Moscow Trials. Democracy is not a label, but a way of life born of experience and grown into by a lot of people. Democracy was not invented by a bunch of cunning men who get together in a dive somewhere and conspire to foist it on the world. . . . All invented social schemes are fakes, and it is time the world faced that fact and quit pouring out its blood to refute it. . . . I'm going to talk to Mother Russia and her Ivan about this. Democracy has a right to talk because nobody invented it except everybody; nobody imposed it on anybody; it just got started and grew to be what it is—an imperfect, blundering but the most satisfactory and dignified way of life known to human experience.

We just got to get to work and fix up this world; no tags, no labels. Hell's bells, John, we're just a lot of people. . . . Trouble with Europe is that she's a great giant which is being suffocated, constricted to death by being kept in the binding nationalistic garments of civilization's childhood. And about all she needs, I think, is to have those didies and safety-pins removed and get used to moving and acting in a free, adult manner.

Anyhow, we in America, some of us, want to take care of Europe for a while, until she can get down to attending to her business as a civilization.

John: I say, Sam; I don't object, but what do you mean?

Sam: I'm sorry, John, I'm so dumb . . . and jumping all over the lot. But this is a new idea with us in America. Some of us are just doping it out; it's a little rough yet; details are still to be worked out; but it clicks. (I'll talk slow and try not to get excited, and make sense.)

In a nutshell it's this: that we Americans, we ex-Europeans, return to the Old World as its children, and grandchildren and great-great-great-grandchildren who have grown up in the New World and have made something of it, and who have learned a thing or two in the course of our Experience. We want to share with Europe, to learn from our Mother Countries things we have forgotten, and to help the Old World get itself on an even keel. It'll be a kind of tremendous exchange of experience, ideas, abilities and values.

You see, John, the old countries will need *somebody's* help. And we think we can help them better than you or anybody else; also better than you and us together. To do what we have in mind is going to be quite a job; it'll cost us a lot of money. And we won't do it out of philanthropy or anything snooty like that. We know it'll be the best thing in the world for *us*. It'll help straighten out the kinks and quirks in our American innards which come from the "old country," from the fact that we're ex-Europeans, escaped Poles and Croatians and Czechs and Scandinavians and Englishmen. And we'll visit you, John, on your great little island when we get lonely for the Anglo-Saxon part of our heritage. That'll help us too; broaden us—mebbe.

But most of all, I reckon, we want to do this job in the Old World because we're a little sore; fact is, we're good and sore. Our whole life is dislocated . . . and, damn it, John, we just can't afford these crises. We haven't even got started doing what we want to do in America. Build her up, make her beautiful. We want to be "just plain Americans," and we can't be till Europe is straightened out.

You and the French had a chance to fix her up. No go. . . . So now I think *we*'ll want to try; we ex-Europeans, her grown-up children. We want to help Old Europe heal her wounds and turn herself into a great federation—the United States of Europe consisting of many states or subfederations, some of which will consist of several autonomous units, all as free as possible.

I don't care how many units there will be; perhaps the more, the better. I like what Thomas Hobbes said once: "Freedom is political power divided into small fragments."

As I say, John, we're worried, we Americans.

Your young man Anthony Eden said a mouthful: Europe *is* going to be in a fix after we finish Hitler. We in America have relatives in every country . . . and we don't want the wrong guys to get the upper hand after the war: which is just what's going to happen, like it did in 1918 and '19, unless we start doing something about it right now.

That's our American idea and the more I think of it the better I like it. We want to see the decent people and healthy ways get a break. We want to supervise the disarmament of Germany and Italy. We think the way Germany and Italy will be handled, and by *whom*, is especially important. You British would be the wrong people for that. Joe Stalin would be just as bad.

I'm part German, you know, and I have some ideas about Germany and the German people. . . . True, Hitler came to power in Germany; a lot of Germans followed his incredible Nazi rubbish. But what does that mean? Among other things, that they are a dynamic, ambitious, impatient, flexible crowd. It's tragic that such a people fell for Hitler; but, to me, it's also evidence that they could and would go for intelligent, real democratic ways *if* they were given the opportunity, *if* democracy could be started in all of Europe, *if* it became a vital and dramatic thing, and *if* it fed and sheltered them. Germans prefer to be free. Lots of them were lured to America by that greatest of glamor gals, Liberty. . . .

But to get back to Europe as a whole.

We have some ideas about a European army if one is necessary; I hope not. Maybe only a small one for a while. Also we want to help create a European police system, a continental currency system, and a continental policy of relations with the rest of the world . . . which meantime should begin to become a Federation too. This'll take time, John, and you'll have a hand in it, of course. Maybe we should think of Union Now—but not too fast, and *definitely not as something exclusive* in which just you and I will be top dogs. To tell you the truth, Union Now With Britain I don't like at all. It's a "superior" idea. It leaves out China and a lot of other things I'm fond of. . . .

But I'm telling you what we'll do in Europe. Well, we mean to help establish a continental control of war materials, their production and distribution. And a continental traffic control. We'll help fix up a continental network of highways, railroads and airlines. Then we'll abolish passports gradually—and we'll zip and zoom from one country to another visiting relatives and just touring around, to see what they've got that we haven't and what we've got that they haven't. And all those people that Hitler booted around can stay where they are or go wherever they like, just as they please. It'll be up to them.

In other words, John, we want to set up a European

Nation of Nations with widespread equalized welfare and opportunity, and the principles and practices of freedom and democracy, law and order. We want to see the individual become important in Europe. We want to see him cease being a worm and help him become free.

We want to go way beyond those Eight Principles. *We want a European revolution;* a democratic revolution; the American Revolution (you'll pardon my mentioning it) extended to Europe, and no maybe about it.

This is a big order, I know, John, but some of us think we—and only we—can fill it. Remember, we started a great Republic in practically nothing flat, and our "German element" had a great hand in the job. They helped to strengthen our original Anglo-Saxon liberal ideas. . . . We're the only people in the world who rejected the idea of inequality.

As yet, we're not thinking of the headaches ahead. We don't want to. You can know too damn much about a job before you get into it; then you ball it up, or it looks too big and you back away from it. We Americans always go in half-cocked. We get into things which are impossible, and do 'em. . . .

Some of the governments in exile will object at first, and that'll be too bad; but what can you do? In a thing like this you're bound to step on some toes. But eventually, I think—I hope—most of the governments in exile will come in on it. It'll take them out of the vacuum and haze in which they now find themselves.

We have a few ideas about how to proceed in the post-Hitler Europe. Some are specific, and they'll work.

About most things we don't want to be too specific. We'll improvise and improve as we go along. The people in the old countries will teach us a thing or two at every step. We'll learn from them. And we'll help them. It's going to be a great combination.

But I won't give you the details now; they are our concern. I want to say that this is a *human* program, not power politics, not aggrandizement. I mean this. The folks in Europe have never seen most of us before, but we won't be strangers; not conquerors or invaders, or intruders—but visitors. We are their nephews and second cousins. We'll send the son of Alois Czulik to Slovakia. Alois emigrated from the village of Colnice in 1893, then worked all his life in Gary, Indiana, and Homestead, Pee-ay.

We'll take over an army mostly made up of the American-born sons of immigrants. Some of the boys will be immigrants who came over during the '30s as refugees; some who came earlier as children—but all Americans. And when they get over there they will visit the town of Grosuplje, in Slovenia, or the neighborhood in the city of Leipzig, where they or their folks were born.

That's the kind of army we'll send over. And who'll command it? Lieutenant General Walter Krueger, now head of an army corps with headquarters in Houston, Texas. He was born in Germany; just a "goddamn Hun"—except that he's a swell American and one of the best general officers we have. And as quartermaster officers, whom are we going to send over? Why, General Joseph E. Barzynski, son of a Polish immigrant born in St. Paul, Nebraska; and Colonel Emil Antonovich, a native of San Francisco born of immigrants from a little town on the eastern coast of the Adriatic, in Dalmatia. We'll send a whole batch of officers like that, thousands of them, in charge of companies, battalions and regiments, brigades and divisions, serving under General Krueger. One of the brigades or divisions will be commanded by General Davis, a Negro American.

In fact, John, we'll send over an officer, who's only a major now but whom we can make a general (why not?)—a man who is an old-time Virginian, but not an Anglo-Saxon American as you may think, John. His name is Mazzei, and he's a descendant of Philip Mazzei, the Wop who was a friend of Thomas Jefferson.

John: I say, Sam ——!

Sam: Please, John, wait; just let me talk now I'm going good. It's a long story, the story of this idea; it goes way back; it's coming to a climax now; just be patient with me, John.

John: Very well, Sam; I am *most* interested.

Sam: Thank you, John; that helps. . . . You see we won't come to Europe like Superman in one of our comic strips, nor like the supermen in your H. G. Wells' story, *The Shape of Things to Come.* We won't come with blueprints From Above; not as saviors or liberators— that's old stuff, John! We'll just walk in on them—'hi-ya, folks!' ——

We're naïve, we Americans, and often we get taken in, and we don't know what we are apt to stumble into; in this case, though, we know we'll have headaches, lots of them, right off the bat and all the way through. We know, for instance, that the higher-ups even in dumps like Slovenia or Albania won't like us. We're likely to interfere with their interests because we intend to mix with the common people whom, Lincoln said, God made in such big numbers because he must've liked them. The higher-ups will just have to get off their high perch and come on down on common ground, or we'll say: go chase yourself, Baron Schusivitz-Bartolemovsky zu Berghoff! And if they start any monkey business, we'll chase *them* as far as it'll take us to catch them. Some folks just can't be handled in any other way, I'm sorry to say.

We'll help Europe develop an economic system that'll work, and we won't care what anybody calls it. The chances are it'll be something to the left of what we have in America—a mixture of private property, controlled industry, public works, socialism and communism. We'll encourage co-operatives, like those in Sweden and Finland; or *zadrugé*, as they call them in Croatia. We'll be for a great continental labor movement; for collective bargaining, which isn't always pleasant, but is sound.

We'll favor diversity in most things if it can be organized into a working unity. In government, for instance. If France wants a President, let her have him. If the Dutch want Wilhelmina, fine. Serbia and Croatia will probably be parts of a South Slavic or a Balkan subfederation of the European Federation; and I suppose the head of the subfederation will be a president; but if the Serbs want their boy-king to head their country while the Croats want a president, we'll see that they both get what they want. The people will decide through the secret ballot.

We'll be tactful and considerate, but firm. We'll be in earnest. But we expect to have a lot of fun in Europe too.

One purpose of the Army will be just to make sure nothing goes wrong and to give the common people a sense of security and hope before things have a chance to turn for the better Over There. None of this revenge stuff! We'll see the new leadership has a chance to come and take over and get all the countries back to normal.

Now, let me make this clear, John, clear as daylight: we the people of the United States don't want a damn thing out of this. Materially we don't want anything from Europe. We'll take over food, as much as we can load on the ships without sinking them, and as fast as possible, to feed everybody; and we'll only hope to get paid for some of it eventually. We'll bring doctors and nurses if necessary; and also professors and engineers to take the place of those Hitler is killing. Fact is, we're the only country that'll be able to deliver the goods when the war ends.

John: I say, this is extraordinary, Sam. Frankly I don't know what to think of it.

Sam: That's all right, John; I'm not asking you yet. I'm just asking you to think about it. We'll discuss it back and forth—now, right here, as long as you like, and after I talk with Mother Russia and His Holiness. Besides, as I said, the whole thing is still only an idea. Nothing may come of it. Remember, John, I'm only

Uncle Sam, an old duffer with whiskers. But the idea is
in the air, and quite a few of us Americans are for it;
and maybe one of these days it'll kind o' sneak up on us
and we'll go hog-wild over it.

It isn't nice at all, John, to put you on the spot like
this—but when I ask you what you think of it, please
say "All right, Sam." This idea looks like the only way
to *really* win this war; perhaps *sooner than you think*.
And I don't care if for a moment you think me crazy.

Think about it, John; and please don't say "No." It
may not be easy to assent. But imagine what we'll do
on the day the war ends. Unless we start doing something about it *right now*, the first crack out of the box
will be the scheme that the United States and Britain
co-operate in taking over Europe. Clearly, though, this
scheme carries the seeds of its own destruction. In the
first place, Britain—feeling purified and revitalized by
her heroic stand—will insist upon a leading hand in re-
ordering the Continent, partly out of self-defense
against a possible future *blitz*. *But* against this obvious
and natural desire will be the bitter fact that Europe
will fear, distrust, and resent any guidance or domination from England—certainly the Germans and Italians
will! Humiliation will fester in them and break out
again some day in some violent fashion. On the other
hand, I feel the Germans will welcome us Americans on
the guarantee that Britain will have no active hand in
what needs to be done. This is going to be a bitter pill
to swallow, perhaps, *but . . . but* the price of stabilization
and peace must be the swallowing of hatreds and vengeance and prides. Fact is that a British-American domi-

nance or guidance of this sort, and it's apt to be mostly dominance, will be very dangerous for the world's future. It'll inspire the formation of defensive counter-unions, such as pan-Orientalism, pan-Slavism, *et cetera*; one collective against another, until the next war would be, literally, a racial war or worse.

Besides, you and we together could only "police" Europe; by ourselves we can ignite a democratic revolution in Europe. Wilson could have done it easily in 1919, had he not been hamstrung by the other three of the Big Four.

And, I tell you, that's what we are interested in— revolution for freedom and equality and human understanding. That's what we Americans want, whether at the moment we are for this idea or not. Some of my nephews and nieces are suspicious of you, John—of some of your big shots. Churchill and Bevin and Morrison are O. K., we think; but how about the rest? Also most of our German and Italian Americans and quite a few of our Dutch and Scandinavian and Finnish Americans, as well as some of our people of other continental strains are rallying around the America First Committee or supporting the isolationist senators. And our thirteen million Negroes don't think much of the British record as regards the colored people. Lots of us are asking: How about India?—and questions like that, not forgetting that our own record as regards the colored folks is nothing to be proud of. . . .

All of which really means that if the scheme for a British-American collaboration in "policing" Europe is suddenly put before us when the war ends, our various complexes will tie us into a dozen knots, and mark my word: the upshot of it will be that we'll have nothing to do with it. Then where'll you be? Where'll we be? . . .

These are facts, John, told to you by your friend. We're interested in the creation of a new world *right* after Hitler and his Nazis are finished. And how can we all get that idea so we'll believe it?—for remember we're a lot of skeptics who have been debunked. We will have faith again only if we start creating a new world *right now* as part of our war effort.

John, we're blowing up the accumulations of generations. We can't afford to do this indefinitely. We must find a plan to end the war *soon*.

I'm all for using "naked force" on Hitler, all we can give 'im; but that's not the only kind of force. I am also for a moral and spiritual *blitz*. Can you imagine what will happen in Europe, particularly in Germany, when the people there hear of our idea? Hitler will be on the skids.

We've got to end the war soon; it mustn't last till '44.

If we only pay attention to the military and production problems, by '44 we'll exhaust ourselves not only financially—I'm part Yankee, you know, and that's important to me—but morally and spiritually: and then, where'll we be? Even now morale in our army camps isn't too high, and you can't blame the boys. Most of them are sons of immigrants who escaped Europe in order to get away from war. That impulse is still in them. Naturally! They're damn good soldier material, but they're also Americans; they've got to know what this war is about. And, by God, John, they just don't yet. Until the middle of August, when your Churchill and our F.D.R. put out their Eight Principles, the war on our side was "to beat Hitler." All right; but what else? And the Eight Principles, when you look them over closely for a plan of action, aren't much better.

We're an action-people, John. Words don't mean much to us. We must get busy on a thing before it registers and kicks up enthusiasm in us. We're a do-people.

John: I say, Sam; I think I am beginning to get the drift, to use the excellent expression you taught me earlier in our—er—conversation. At the moment I see no objection to your 'taking charge of Europe' after the war. Nor do I see why Britain should 'interfere'. It is probable that the United States will be the leading power after the war, or perhaps earlier. But, Samuel, I should very much like to hear how you intend to proceed. . . . Tell me anything! . . . How will your European Nation of Nations differ from the old League of Nations?

Sam: Profoundly, John. If our idea is any good, and if we hit on the right approach to it, it will click with the average person: with Johann Schmidt and Ivan Kovach. He will be fired with hope and enthusiasm over an attainable future. I think we have the approach.

The League of Nations, as I see it, never took with the masses. It couldn't. It didn't have what it takes. It was cooked up in a hurry by the Big Boys, then superimposed on the European peoples. It was only a gimmick, a contrivance; and, never comprehending it simply and deeply, that is, enthusiastically, the people were only vaguely "for" it. They never got *involved* in it. The people have passion, all right, but the League was no avenue through which they could pour it. It was not their idea.

The League never had any future. It was devised to control the conflicts of *the world as it was.* So it was bound to fold up, for by the 1930s the people were not interested in the world as it was. They were sick of it. Their impulse was for a new order. Hitler knew this; he came from below, from the masses; he had that advantage— the tragedy is that he's a bully, a ruffian and a madman who is also a genius interested in a gigantic subversion of values.

But our idea will appeal to people in both America and Europe. It will *involve* everybody. It will evoke and release passion. Let there be passion, John! Let's set it free. Let's keep it from turning back upon itself in frustration. We need it. Or the world will die.

Do you see what I mean, John?

John: I think I do, Sam.

Sam: Our idea is important to you too, John. It'll interest your Labor leaders who are going around saying, "You can't make a revolution and fight a war at the same time." Doggone it, John, making a revolution everywhere is the best way of fighting Hitler.

[*John Bull nods.*]

Sam: Of course the idea is just chuckful of dangers. It can be queered in more ways than one. We can ruin it in America before it gets a chance to show what it can do in Europe. The wrong people can get at the head of it: the pious snobs and zealots, the snooty good-doers who'll want to "save" Europe and won't see that the Passage Back is necessary for our own sake as well as Europe's and the world's; and that it is, besides, our unavoidable duty to history.

Also the idea may be seized by the big-business boys who'll play up to the idealism of our John Smiths but secretly pooh-pooh it and turn the scheme into a trick for commercial expansionism. We'll have to watch 'em.

But, with a little luck, John, we'll get at it intelligently—humbly.

[*Uncle Sam and John Bull talk on . . . . for days . . . for weeks . . .*]

John Smith, Sr.
talking to his son John Smith, Jr.
in the 1950s.

The Passage Back idea popped up all over the country. All of a sudden. It hit me sometime in August '41. Just like that ——

Then Uncle Sam talked it over with John Bull; that must of been quite a talk ——

Then Sam went and talked to Mother Russia and Ivan Ivanovitch. He told them people in America don't like labels, not much, specially labels like "Communism" and "Fascism." Fact is, he told 'em we don't even like "Americanism"—we invented it to have a tag because everybody else had one. And when Uncle Sam told this to Mother Russia and her boy Ivan they got it in a flash.

Then Sam went to the Vatican and talked with the Pope; which must of been interesting too.

Well, anyhow, the Passage Back idea got going . . . F. D. R. got interested in it . . . he sent the so-called Formula to Congress; and, Johnny, was that a debate! One of the goofiest, most wonderful debates you ever heard of. The Lend-Lease debate was nothing compared

to this. Both the isolationists and interventionists were
at the same time for and against the Formula. The
interventionists were for it because it certainly was
intervention and against it because the isolationists liked
it, and the isolationists liked it because its aim was
really isolation in the long run. After all, we Americans
want to live in peace and not be interrupted and dislocated by wars. But at the same time the isolationists
were against it because it was intervention.

The debate showed up the whole mess in America.
All kinds of side issues developed. The alien-baiters, for
instance, got behind the Formula because they thought
that's how they'd clear the country of all the goddamn
"foreigners." . . .

There was lots of fun too.

For one thing, the Indians "invaded" Washington
carrying signs like: "WHY DON'T YOU *ALL* GO
BACK, YOU DERN FURRINERS? LET THE BUF-
FALO GRAZE AGAIN!"

The Irish in Boston held a mass meeting demanding
a Passage Back Also to England.

The funniest were some "Americanized" foreigners
who tried to be two-hundred-per-cent Americans by
yelling their heads off that the whole scheme was un-
American, unconstitutional, and contrary to the isolationist tradition established by the Father of Our
Country.

Another thing that tickled me was the way the governments in exile reacted. Lots of people were afraid
the idea would hurt their feelings. Of course it did hurt
the feelings of some of them. To others it came as a

relief, because before they didn't know what the answer was to anything connected with the future of their old countries. And it wasn't long before several governments came out in full support of the idea; some because they felt the people back home were for it; others because that was one safe way to return home when the war ended. A few of the governments held out and broke up arguing as to what they should do.

Finally, the Senate ratified the Formula, which F. D. R. wrote; but it was really our idea—mine (if you'll let me mention myself first), and Harold Abramson's and Bill Switalski's, and John Suchy's, and Jim Kirby's, and Barbara Lucas', and Charlie Kikuchi's (a *nisei* out in California), and Steve Yastrofsky's, and Toni Libonati's, and Lee Jorgensen's, and Mary Pulak's, and George Pyle's, and Ben West's, and Sam Roth's . . . and we put it over.

Not that F. D. R. wasn't for it; he was; he made his best fireside talk on it. And Henry Wallace was for it, and Harry Hopkins; all the important people . . . but it was really us that got it moving. We certainly did. I told you before that I was in the great and historic March to Washington. Boy, was that something!

When we came to the Capitol, there on the steps were mountains of telegrams tied up in bundles. There was no room for them inside. Western Union and Postal Telegraph boys sat on the bundles, chewing gum. And as we passed by the White House, there on the lawn were more bundles of telegrams, bales of 'em, piled up high as the trees. There wasn't any more room inside the White House either. Everybody was wiring, even after we all knew the Formula would be approved.

The Bill was passed that week. . . .

I got a little scared when F. D. R. started the Office of European Reconstruction and everybody got to calling it OER, like WPA and AAA and so on. "What the hell is this?" I thought. Another one of those outfits I think of every time I eat soup with all those letters floating around that are dough and ought to be noodles?

But Roosevelt had to start the OER; it was right in the Bill that Congress passed when it ratified the Formula.

I was afraid the idea would go all haywire, and maybe it almost did, but the way it looks now it's turning out pretty well.

Of course guys like me are dumb in a way; we get hunches and notions, but we don't realize that putting them over is a practical matter which has got to be worked out. You got to have an office, lots of offices; lots of people able to do all kinds of things; typewriters, clerks, files, books, stationery, stamping machines, inkwells, water coolers, wastepaper baskets—all to get an idea going. Hell, we may as well put up with it. We got to have a government, even if it is a nuisance.

F. D. R. was all right, though. He made Wendell Willkie head commissioner of the OER, and appointed four others like it said in the Bill—Felix Frankfurter, Ferdinand Pecora, Wilbur Thomas of the Carl Schurz Foundation, and William Donovan.*

* These and other names in this chapter are used without permission of their owners. As I say in the Author's Note at the beginning of the book, the idea was not discussed with anyone in the public eye.—L. A.

You know all about that, Johnny; now it's all written up in books. . . .

Funny how a guy's opinion changes. I had no use for Willkie in 1940; now, when F. D. R. appointed him, I thought he was just the man for this new job . . . and a lot of us began to root for him to be made chief of the American Provisional Government in Germany.

These provisional governments—now, that was a good idea, whoever thought of it first; I didn't, I know. In fact for a while it struck me kind o' funny to have these American Provisional Governments in every country Over There. I thought we were going too far, and it looked like I was right.

Talk about a mess!

Willkie and the rest of the commissioners and all their experts, consultants, secretaries, members of governments in exile who came in on the idea, and what-have-yous—hundreds of 'em—were running around like a lot of chickens with their heads cut off.

Passage Back—hell! It was more like "I'm Going Crazy, Won't You Come Along?"

But—I still don't know how—things began to happen. The Provisional American Governments *were* formed one after another, twenty-odd of 'em, mostly of people who were immigrants or whose parents or grandparents were immigrants. But most of the governments included one or two old-stock or mixed-strain Americans who happened to like certain countries, used to travel and were well-known there, and wanted to help out.

For a while there was a big argument about these governments. Some of us thought they ought to be called *Temporary* American Governments, so as to make what we had in mind clear as a bell to Europe. But we lost out because it's hard to change something once it's been printed. As it turned out, it made no difference anyhow. The people of Europe got it all right that these governments were temporary. Their chief job was to work themselves out of office—and back to the U. S. A.

Jeez, but it was interesting to read the papers and listen in on the radio those days.

Something was going on!

Willkie, who tried to be President of the United States, got made chief of the German government! And M. S. Szymczak became head of the Polish government, "Big Bill" Knudsen of the Danish, Pecora of the Italian, Spyros Skouras of the Greek, Tom Amlie of the Norwegian . . . and so on; it's all in the books now.

Then these guys went ahead and organized their cabinets just like real governments—while Hitler still had their countries! They were put on salaries (pretty soft for some of 'em!) and were called ministers and prime ministers; and each government was given a budget for expenses; then they began to bone up on the problems of their countries three or four thousand miles away!

If two countries had some kind of argument, like over their borders, their American Provisional Governments got together and ironed things out—*provisionally*, to be finally O.K.'d or rejected by the people in Europe.

It was funny as hell; papers pulled a lot of wisecracks

about the A.P.G.'s; and I can still laugh as I think back; but it was all right. Names making the headlines, besides those I mentioned, were like Stoyan Pribichevich, Max Ascoli, Sigurd Arnesen, Victor Ridder, Janko Rogelj, Lester Roth, Frank Aaltonen, Fiorello La Guardia . . . and so on.

The governments got in touch with the immigrants from the country they intended to govern; and this was something too! All the goddamn "foreigners" became more "foreign" and more American at the same time. Even Westbrook Pegler saw this, and he came out for the Passage Back idea too.

Talk about unity. We used to talk about it; now we had it.

The German and Italian Americans came in with a rush. You never saw anybody so down on Hitler and Musso. They became the advance guard of the American Fifth Column Against the Axis, and were joined by the German and Italian elements in Latin America.

Jeez, it was like that festival in St. Paul everybody talked about for a while. The A.P.G.'s, with their ministers, and the "foreign" groups were mixed up in a kind of play, like a crazy movie or something; but it was real at the same time.

It was real, all right, all right.

Felix Frankfurter got the most important job next to Willkie's. He was put in charge of what got to be called the Gentile-Jewish Psychosis in Europe. At first hardly anybody knew what it meant; then the meaning dawned on us . . . and, boy, anti-Semitism began to disappear in this country like snow when the sun gets warm.

But "Wild Bill" Donovan's department interested me most.

With General Krueger (he was made a full general right away), Donovan got down to organizing the units which were to be sent Over There. It was decided that the Headquarters of the American Expedition to Aid Europe was to be in Berlin; and the largest body of troops was to go to Germany.

I forget now if it was three or four divisions; but half of the officers and men were either German immigrants or sons and grandsons of German immigrants. The other half were Americans of all descents, including Negroes, Indians and Chinese and Japanese Americans. Two of the generals under Krueger were Jews; another was a Negro.

Every other unit was organized on the same principle. That is, the division sent to Italy was in command of Major General Mazzei, who was promoted not because he was a great general (although maybe he was), but because his name was Mazzei, which had "propaganda value." Half the men and officers under him were Italian Americans—Wops from Harlem and Philadelphia and California.

The two regiments for Poland—the same.

The battalion for Slovenia—the same. I think it was in command of a Major Podgornik, or some such name.

The regiment for Bohemia—the same. A colonel named Vlchek commanded it.

Then the Educational Division of the OER fixed up a book for the military unit of each country, and there black on white were the names of all the officers and soldiers in alphabetical order, and the facts (in European languages) about their background—like where they were born, the village or town their people came from, their religion . . . and so on.

The "German" book was thicker than three New York City telephone directories bound together.

I read that a copy of the "Italian" book was sold the other day for $175. All those books now are what's called "collectors' items."

Of course all this was getting lots of attention in Europe. Hitler couldn't prevent it. He ordered Goebbels to discredit the idea, but Goebbels couldn't. Every lie he put out boomeranged. He proved that, as that Spanish writer Ortega said, "the lie is but a parasite on the beautiful body of truth."

Europe went nuts over the idea. There were riots in Germany. You know all about them. . . .

In fact it looked for a while as if something would have to be done to postpone Hitler's collapse so we'd have time to get ready.

But we got ready in time all right.

Then we just shipped the whole scheme over: the governments . . . the Frankfurter Group of Jews and Gentiles who were in charge of the Gentile-Jewish Psychosis in Europe . . . the Army . . . the books about the army . . . also other books in various languages explaining the whole thing . . . doctors, teachers . . .

and medicine and food. We used planes, merchant vessels and battleships. One day over seven thousand American planes were in the air heading for Europe, while below them sailed about a thousand ships in the same direction.

Nothing like it—ever. A *blitz* for life—not death.

Willkie and Krueger were a terrific hit in Germany; all over Europe. We couldn't find a French American to head France, so we sent ex-Ambassador Bullitt for a while. That happened in a few other countries too.

Well, Europe—the plain people of the different countries—realized what America was. And they helped us to realize it.

The American soldiers just traveled all over and behaved well. Of course they were instructed what this was all about, and knew behavior was important.

Talk about propaganda for democracy and for unity in diversity! It was nothing but. Everybody talked about how in America Jews and Germans and Poles and what-have-you's got along pretty well in normal times and not so bad even when things were abnormal.

The peoples of Europe got the hint. Couldn't help it. The whole thing was as clear as that St. Paul festival I mentioned.

All Europe took up baseball, while lots of our boys learned to play chess and things like that.

We were the International party that Russell Davenport wrote about in *Fortune* magazine in '41.

Our army was an international army to begin with.

It was made up of Polaks, Wops, Kikes, Hunkies, and
so on. So it began to recruit men in Europe for the
European army. Then our boys began to come back.
But quite a few stayed there. Married and became Europeans. Why not? Some married and brought their
wives home.

I'm telling you things you've read about, but I like
to talk about 'em. It was the greatest thing that ever
happened. It shortened the war by at least a year,
maybe two; and somebody figured it out that the
U. S. A. alone saved between thirty and forty billion
dollars.

There were headaches of course. Things happened
that upset everybody: like the time when that crazy Nazi
shot at Willkie but missed him. Two other heads of the
American Provisional Governments were assassinated.
In one of the American Army barracks a bomb exploded
and killed three men. . . . Things like that.

But in no time, almost, Europe was remade. All the
things Uncle Sam mentioned to John Bull were put into
effect.

In some of the countries the American Provisional
Governments turned the power over to fine men and
women they found there four, five or six months after
we got Over There. The native leaders appeared pretty
fast; some swell ones; and they went before the people of
their countries and were elected. In Norway, Denmark,
Holland and Finland, the A.P.G.'s had very little to do.
After the first two or three weeks they were nothing
more than a sort of advisors and the connecting link

between those countries and the A.P.G.'s central office in Vienna, where a lot of Americans and Europeans were working out the whole continental setup.

Willkie, as you know, was the head of the German government for four years. Then there was a movement to elect him President of the United States of Continental Europe. But he said nothing doing. "I'm an Amur-r-rican!" he said. And he came home.

It's all in the books now, but it was us—the people of the United States of America—who hit on the idea.

Now we can be just plain Americans while we're citizens of the world.

The End

THE PROJECT

The Second of the Series

Two-Way Passage is the second of a group of independent books which I hope will result from the "Plymouth Rock and Ellis Island" project. The project is outlined and explained in the main body of the volume and also in the ensuing "broadside."

The urgency of the problem caused me to write this book in a little over three weeks. But that was made possible in great part by the fact that during the previous two or three years thousands of people all over the country have written and talked to me about the various phases of the subject. It is impossible to list them. I am greatly indebted.

The *Two-Way Passage* idea clicked in my mind suddenly, then I dropped everything else to write the book. But again I could not have done it so quickly, had it not been for the help of my friend Ross B. Wills, who came East from California on the shortest notice; my assistant Isabel Mangold; and my wife Stella.

Also, without the Carnegie grant-in-aid I could not have begun my project and brought it thus far. To Frederick Keppel, president of the Corporation, and Charles Dollard, his assistant in charge of personal grants, I wish to express my deepest appreciation for their interest and helpfulness.

The script of *Two-Way Passage* was delivered to my publishers in mid-August. Some material was added in proofs, read in September.

315

Unusual circumstances prompt this *questionnaire* broadside. I have tried other, more familiar ways to get at what I want and found them unsatisfactory. . . .

In the part entitled "Plymouth Rock and Ellis Island" of my book, *My America*, published in May, 1938, I try to point out the following facts and ideas:

(1) That, in point of the composition of the population of the United States, Ellis Island is rapidly becoming as important as Plymouth Rock and Jamestown.

(2) That the United States today is—racially, socially, culturally, religiously, spiritually: in short, humanly—an extension not alone of the British Isles, The Netherlands, France, Germany, Ireland and Africa, as it was at the beginning, but of all Europe, of the West Indies and Mexico, and of parts of Asia.

(3) That present-day United States, with its great industries, sky-scrapers, endless railways and power lines, is as much the result of the labor and genius of immigrants who have come over in the last sixty or seventy years as of old-stock Americans, who are mostly, or regard themselves to be, of the Anglo-Saxon strain.

(4) That in the upbuilding of the country in the last century more immigrants from various European countries have perished in industrial accidents than early American colonists were killed in subduing the wilderness and in the War for Independence; and that this fact—which is an important part of the American background of tens of millions of our citizens

—should be realized and appreciated by the country as a whole.

(5) That the United States is rapidly ceasing to be preponderantly Anglo-Saxon, for our population now includes tens of millions of non-Anglo-Saxons; and that, therefore a new conception of America (along the lines dimly suggested above) is necessary.

(6) That the presence in the United States of this vast new-immigrant element is an unprecedented opportunity for creating on this continent an extraordinarily rich culture and civilization, at the same time that it immensely complicates American social, economic, political, cultural, and spiritual forces and problems; that inherent in our present population are certain tensions dangerous to America, to her liberty and unity, democracy and trend to equality, as well as to the various old-stock and new-immigrant groups as such; that alien-baiting, anti-Semitism and kindred attitudes and ideas are spreading . . . and, lest these dangers to America and to the various groups increase and intensify, all of us—new and old-stock Americans—must begin to become intelligently, actively, *critically* interested in the whole situation, now generally wrapped in darkness and shot through with fear and sentimentality.

My subject is scattered the country over; its most important facts and phases are hidden in the least likely places . . . and my project will continue to strain all my resources. I need and seek all the help I can get, and this prospectus is addressed to anybody in the United States who happens to read it.

Please read and study *all* the questions, then write me a letter—one page or fifty pages—answering in your own way as many of them as you can or wish to answer. Feel free to write me about anything else connected with the subject.

I ask for utter candor. If you wish, mark your letter "confidential"; I shall so respect it. If nothing else, tell me if you approve of this project; tell me especially if you disapprove of it, giving your reasons.

Please do not assume that someone else will write to me, or that I already know, the facts and ideas which occur to you as you read the questionnaire.

I am seeking information, I want to be instructed. I have certain ideas, but my mind is fluid; the ideas I have are open to revision. The fixed factors in my viewpoint are concern for the United States, its culture, its traditional democracy, the future development of human beings here, and the conviction that the successive waves of immigration into this country contain a great promise for the future which, if we do not work for it, will turn into a great danger, especially now in connection with the new world war.

Please let me hear from you as soon as convenient. If you cannot write to me at once or in the immediate future, put this questionnaire where it may arrest your attention later. My present tentative plan is to continue the survey part of my project till the end of 1941. This may possibly be extended into 1942. . . . If you write to me about something that especially interests me, I shall try to come to your city or town and study it further.

I am distributing hundreds of thousands of copies of this broadside (to be revised from time to time). I hope to get some of them posted on the bulletin boards of clubs and organizations and social and educational institutions, and to receive their aid in distributing them. I shall be grateful for addresses to which one or more copies should be sent. If you yourself want more copies, please let me know, stating the number desired. No charge.

Social science departments of several colleges and high

schools have found the broadside useful as an aid in studying immigration and population problems.

Questions for Immigrants and Their American-Born Descendants

What is the history of your racial or national group in the United States? In your community, or where you lived in the past? Is there any written material? Where and how could I obtain it?

When, why and whence did people of your stock first come to America? When and why did they first come where you now live? What did the majority do at first? What do they engage in now? What did they have to go through to gain a foothold? (I think the stories of the earliest immigrants of the various new-immigrant groups are quite as interesting and significant as those of the earliest Anglo-Saxon or Dutch colonists. The wilderness of American city slums or mining towns of sixty or seventy years ago was perhaps worse than that of the virgin region of New England with its Indians in the seventeenth century.)

Which towns in America were started by your people? When, how, and why? Are these towns still inhabited mostly by your people? Who could tell me the stories of these towns?

How does America look now to people of your racial or national stock? How did the Depression affect them? How does the present war affect them? What are they thinking, saying? Are the oldtimers glad to be here or sorry they ever came over? Why? Are some of them planning or dreaming to "go back to the old country to die"? Are most of your immigrants naturalized? If not, why not?

Do they mingle with people of other new-immigrant backgrounds? With old-stock Americans? To what extent? Are they going into local, state, national politics: to what extent?

Are they encountering prejudice or discrimination because they are "foreigners"? How do they cope with it? Does this prejudice include the immigrants' American-born children? What are they doing about it? Are there any organized efforts in your community to cope with open and hidden intolerance?

What are some of the other problems facing your people in your city or town today? In America at large?

Do many change their names: why and how?

Do members of your group tend to be prejudiced against other groups? If so, against which groups? And why? How does their prejudice manifest itself?

All immigrant groups have contributed vastly to the upbuilding of America. Who were or are some of the outstanding people of your national group in the United States? In professions? Sports? The arts? Industry and business? Education and religion? In special fields? In the labor movement? In politics? Are their life stories interesting, dramatic, illustrative of the life of your people in America as a whole? I am especially eager to hear of immigrants or second-generation workers who are not widely known but who have invented "gadgets," and new production methods which are now a part of American industrial operations, or have made other important but not generally recognized social, economic and cultural contributions.

I should like to hear of old couples of your race or nationality who have been in America a long time and whose children, grandchildren, and possibly great-grandchildren are by now scattered all over America, performing various functions, facing different problems, living interesting or average American lives. What are their names, where do they live? Who knows the life stories of specific families?

To what extent are your "national" or "racial" colonies in the various cities breaking up? How are they breaking up? What does that mean in terms of living to the old immigrants and their American-born children? Is it good these colonies are breaking up? Why or why not?

What are some of the characteristics, good and bad, of your people in America? Which characteristics are being destroyed or strengthened by American forces? Which would benefit America if they were preserved and developed here? What have your people brought over in them that, if it became part of American life in general, would add to the color and tone of the culture of the United States and would enhance American democracy and devotion to liberty? Your people brought to America certain cultural gifts and talents. Which of them were destroyed, perverted, or damaged by conditions in this country? Which were enhanced? Which have any value for the future of America? Why? What can be done to restore those that were damaged?

What role does organized religion play among your people? In your own life?

How has the Depression affected your people? Their attitude toward the United States? How has it affected you personally, and your attitude?

How do you, personally, swing politically—say, in reference to the New Deal? To the current "Defense" problem and our foreign policy? Are you typical of your group?

Who, to your mind, are the great men and women of America?

How important in Al Smith's defeat in 1928 were the facts that he is a Catholic and the son of immigrants? Did you consider the anti-third-term tradition in the 1940 election? Did the fact that Wendell Willkie is a son of German immigrants affect his campaign?

Immigrants' children and grandchildren interest me. My observation is that many of these New Americans, as I call them, are oppressed by feelings of inferiority in relation to old-stock Americans, to America as a whole. Is that your observation too? How do those feelings of inferiority manifest themselves? Are American-born children uneasy or unhappy because their names are "foreign"? Are some of them ashamed of their "foreign" parents? Do many leave home? Why? What happens in such cases? How do they overcome their feelings of inferiority?

Are people of your strain marrying persons of other backgrounds? Are such unions successful? What are the problems of children born to such couples? I'd like to get case histories.

Do critical developments in the Old World and the backwash they send here tend to enhance the consciousness of your people in America of their old-country beginnings and backgrounds? Do they affect their American-born children? How?

Has the Second World War affected your people? In relation to the "old country"? To America? How do you imagine the world after it is over? Are you worried?

What do you, personally, think of your people as a part of the forming American nation? Of other new-immigrant groups with which you are familiar? What proportion of Italians and Germans here are pro-Fascist or pro-Nazi? I shall welcome answers to this question particularly from those of Italian and German origin. What are their special problems in this period of crisis, our foreign policy being what it is?

How do your people speak among themselves of old-stock

Americans—bitterly, enviously, with admiration or respect, or how?

Your opinion of the old-stock Americans you know well? Of the old-stock Americans generally as the dominant group in the United States? Do you feel that old-stock Americans are "dying out," "slipping," that is, not reproducing themselves as numerously as the new-immigrant groups; and that, as a writer hints in the November, 1938 *Harpers*, the future in America "belongs to the Bohunks," meaning people of new-immigrant stock? If so, are the latter fit, or becoming fit, to run the country as well as, or better than, it is being run now? Will they be disposed and able to continue America on the basis of the principles and ideas which motivated the Founding Fathers?

Questions for Old-Stock Americans

What do you think or feel about all "these foreigners" being here? By and large, are they an asset to your town or city: to the country at large? Or ought they to be "sent back where they came from"? In either case, why do you think so? When you speak or think of the "foreigners" in your town, do you mean—consciously or unconsciously—to include the immigrants' American-born children, or their grandchildren, if their names are something like Stankovich, Zlamal, Zamblaoskas, or Mioduszewski? Do their names make them so very "different" from you? Would you like to have them change their "foreign" names? Or is there something else? Are you, as an old-stock American, occasionally uneasy—deeply or just a little—as you glance about and see "for-

eigners" making their way into American life? If so, why?
What is your reaction to these facts—that La Guardia is
Mayor of New York; that Lehman is Governor of the State of
New York; that Knudsen and Hillman, immigrants from Denmark and Russia, are in charge of "Defense"? I know old-
stock Americans who confess they feel like aliens in their own
country. What with all "these foreigners" around, this is no
longer their kind of America! What is there to be done about
that?

If you are an employer, a factory superintendent, an office
manager, or a foreman, will you give me your opinion of the
new-immigrant groups represented in your shop, mine, or
office?

What were some of your thoughts as you read my questions addressed to the immigrants and their American-born
children?

I hope to hear from many social workers, teachers, li-
brarians and other people, whether of old- or recent-immigrant stock, whose work touches on this problem.

General Questions

Calvin Coolidge once said: "Whether one traces his Americanism back three centuries to the Mayflower, or three years
to the steerage, is not half so important as whether his Americanism of today is real and genuine. No matter on what
various crafts we came here, we are all now in the same boat."
More recently Franklin D. Roosevelt said that "we are all
immigrants here." Do you agree? Please give the reasons
for your agreement or disagreement.

I want to hear from Americans who are of many backgrounds—say, English, German, Czech, Jewish, and Armenian; or any other combination.

President William Green of the American Federation of Labor once said: "Our republican institutions are the outgrowth of ten centuries of the same people in England and America. They can only be preserved if the country contains at all times a great preponderance of those of British descent." In view of the fact that those of British descent are no longer in "great preponderance" and their number is not increasing in proportion to those of non-British descent, do you think that our republican institutions are doomed because of this change in our population? Personally, I don't think so, but your thoughts may be different on this point. I believe because of this there are serious dangers ahead for America, for her entire culture and setup, but we can act to avoid catastrophe. If you share this thought with me, *what* can and should we do? Adult education? What kind?

What about the Negro? . . . I hope to hear from many colored people: what is your opinion of, and attitude toward, the "foreigners" of various nationalities? The "foreigners'" attitude to you. (I have a special *questionnaire* on the Negro-white problem, which I will send on request.)

And what about "Americanization"? . . . As I see it, the old "Americanization" idea, often fear-motivated, was aimed at purging the immigrant of his old-country background (of which the "Americanizers" had no clear notion except that it was bad because "foreign") and at turning him neatly into an imitation Anglo-Saxon American, endowing him in a few night school lessons with the background of America from the Colonial days on. Assimilation was supposed to work one way: from the immigrant's natural old-country background to Americanism as conceived by patriotic old-stock

Americans. Millions of aliens were naturalized and learned some English, which gave the "Americanizers" the illusion that their idea was headed toward success; actually, the average immigrant remained a good deal of the national he was in the old country. Implicit in the old "Americanization" idea, which scorned his natural background, was an insult to him, and he resented it. Also he was a little scared. In many cases, as he inevitably and silently compared his adopted country with his native land, he became more conscious of his old-country background than he was before he came over, and he frequently followed his natural inclination as a foreigner and drew aside, away from the main streams of American life, into his semi-defensive "national colony" or "foreign section," where, to a great extent, he is to this day, and where his children were born.

The result is that many American-born sons and daughters of immigrants, when they say "we," mean their group in the "foreign section" and the "old country." In their own minds and feelings, they are imperfectly identified with America.

To my mind, what is now needed is a new consciousness of America, of ourselves as a people made up of over fifty races and nationalities. What is needed is a new Americanization idea which will recognize and *accept*, not merely tolerate, the various national and racial groups as such; which will see the desirability of diversity in our population; which will take a firm stand against alien-baiting and insist that immigrant citizens and their American-born children belong here as much as old-stock Americans—this is their America as much as anybody's; which will help all citizens to identify themselves with the United States; and which will, thus, work toward national unity—against fear in our national life—toward gradual assimilation or cultural fusion that will operate naturally, not one way, but in many directions. By that I

mean that Anglo-Saxons will have to become partly assimilated or fused into the various new-immigrant groups just as
the latter will have to become partly assimilated into the
Anglo-Saxon group and into one another.

Am I right or wrong about this? How can desirable inter-
penetration be encouraged, helped? I feel that every American,
old or new stock, ought to have a thought on this matter.
What is yours? It may be important. Please let me have it.

As I say, I began this project in 1938; now, with the
United States suddenly caught in a complex emergency, the
problems I am trying to examine are all the more urgent and
important. Our national unity and future hinge on them. I
have elaborated on this point in a pamphlet, "This Crisis Is
an Opportunity," which you may have free on request.

Again: I need and ask your help.

Louis Adamic
Milford, New Jersey.

P.S.: *I am most eager for your comments on* Two-Way
Passage.

Note on the St. Paul Festival of Nations

Requests for specific information about the technique and methods used in the St. Paul Festival of Nations may be addressed to Mrs. Alice L. Sickels, Director, International Institute, 123 Fifth Street, St. Paul, Minnesota.

The Festival will be held again late in April 1942.